Waiting 'round the Bend

A Life in Australia's Foreign Service

FOURTH EDITION

Howard Debenham

First published in 2017 by Barrallier Books Pty Ltd,
trading as Echo Books.

This edition 2024 by Echo Books

Echo Books is an imprint of Superscript Publishing Pty Ltd
ABN 76 644 812 395

Registered Office: PO Box 669, Woodend, Victoria, 3442

National Library of Australia Cataloguing-in-Publication entry:

Author: Debenham, Howard, author.

Title: Waiting 'round the bend : A life in Australia's foreign service/
Howard Debenham.

Edition: 4th Edition.

ISBN: 978-1-922603-34-0 (hardback)
ISBN: 978-1-922603-37-1 (paperback)
ISBN: 978-0-6481107-2-9 (e-book)

A catalogue record for this book is available from the National Library of Australia

Painting by Ken Strong for the book title – *Waiting 'round the Bend.*
Sketches by Ken Strong.

www.echobooks.com.au

Contents

Waiting 'round the bend –
maybe a dream,
sometimes a friend,
always an adventure.

Prologue

My childhood and youth, though springing from a fairly rich, if typical, tapestry of life in early Anglo-Australia, was in most ways unremarkable and not pointed in any particular direction other than chance and survival.

I entered the Australian Foreign Service by one of those chances, stayed for what became a continuously unfolding adventure and, along the way, came to understand something of the world and the people in it.

In these recollections, I have tried to paint pictures of the paths travelled by one young Australian into a career of this kind and then to show as much about how he lived it as to offer political or other commentary. Wherever I could, I have tried to provide digestible historical settings.

I hope that they will provide some insight into the enjoyment, the inspiration and the challenges which many of our Foreign Service people live out. More so in this case by those who participated in walking our Foreign Service out of its infancy in the colonial master-class era into one of instant information, the resurfacing of ancient cultures and the entirely just stirring of disempowered underclasses in the world community.

Little of this journey would have been as fulfilling without my great companion of most of those years and all of those since – my wife, Joosik. We were two drifters of a similar kind really – off to see the world. And we did.

Howard Debenham

Family

Gone

There was nothing unusual about her napping in the morning. Still a little weak after her most recent return from hospital, she was not that comfortable sleeping on their mattress in the living room, sandwiched as it was between the long chintzy silvery-threaded, though goldy-coloured, couch and the large ever so fashionable blonde-wood radiogram and mirrored cocktail cabinet, while my father took his time painting their bedroom. Why he chose to paint it while she was sick completely escaped me, but that's the way he was.

She was heartbroken to have discovered that he had been doing more than just buying for their two fashion stores, one in Queanbeyan and the other in Canberra, on recent trips to Sydney. A discovery that had involved a private detective and a harrowing trip of her own to Sydney while he *was*, as it turned out, running around. It knocked the stuffing out of her and put her back into hospital. He didn't know we knew and we didn't know whether she had yet confronted him with it. She hadn't told anyone else and couldn't.

We were holding our breaths and wondering why she had, only a day or two before, given us thirty pounds ($60) to share between us. At $20 each, this amounted to more than a week's pay for an adult in those days. We were not to say anything to him about it and she didn't tell us why she had chosen this moment to do such an odd thing. She would presumably do so soon enough, but until then we put it under a corner of the lino just inside the door to my elder sister, Barbara's, room.

At sixteen, on my first day off after some early starts and long days of laboring with some mates for a building contractor during the first week of the May school holidays of my final year of High School, I was sleeping-in when my father and Barbara left for the shop down in the main street of Queanbeyan at about 8.45. Not quite awake, not quite under.

Soon after, she called my name, softly and, so it seemed, without urgency. Just a little longer, I thought. But hunger soon got the better of me and I went to get my corn flakes from the kitchen, next to the lounge room. Fumbling around. Sleepily. Good old cornflakes with a drizzle of honey. Health food of a nation.

That she was a little ill wasn't such a bad thing for me, because she had never been able to take a break from the shops during school holidays and I would now have her at home all to myself for my last week or until she was well enough to go back to the shop.

The door from his garishly painted kitchen (surely only an Englishman could choose red and yellow) to the living room was open and, gingerly balancing my brimming bowl across the room to the couch at the foot of the mattress, a glance revealed that she was slumbering peacefully. On her left side towards me, head rolled down a little, chin tucked in. Comfy-cozy.

With the bowl on my knees and the bright morning out there on Erin Street slatting through the pale green venetians behind me, I was careful not to disturb her by clinking the spoon on the bowl or crunching too loudly. We would be chatting soon enough. Me about maybe getting some study done, she, in her warm and reassuring way, glad to have me there.

Quietly munching away, getting down below the brim, cobwebs clearing, I looked again, anticipating her pleasure at waking to find me there.

I could see her face a little more fully from where I was sitting. Not the usual glow? Somehow, even when she was ill, she glowed. Or at least to me she did.

Something didn't seem right. She hadn't moved and now her head seemed to be so heavy on the pillow. A few more crunchy mouthfuls, though even more cautiously and a little less savoring.

Nothing changed.

I put my bowl aside and knelt on the floor beside her. Her eyes were, oddly, so slightly open and she was so still, so pale.

Perhaps it was the medicine.

I waited, wondering if she would be startled to wake and find me so close.

I put my hand gently on her shoulder. Nothing. I squeezed a little. Still nothing.

OK … softly take her wrist and feel for her pulse. That will do it.

Hello silly, what are you doing? she would say.

But she was cool, so cool. I couldn't find a pulse and I just knew she wasn't breathing. I swayed back on my haunches, stomach knotting.

Gently brushing her eyes closed with my fingertips. Slumped there on the floor beside her. Disbelieving. Not wanting to move. Surely the spell would break.

Numbly, I fumbled for the phone behind me on the little table near the front door and gave the operator the three digit number of the shop.

He answered in his usual brisk manner. 'Mum won't wake up' I managed. A tight little gasp and he hung up. Not a word. He was on his way. I turned back to her side and gathered her cool hands in mine. Silently pleading.

Minutes later, he pulled into the driveway in his flashy little sky-blue Ford Zephyr sports convertible, brushing me aside as I went to meet him at the kitchen door.

Doctor Roach arrived soon after and Barbara came later. Ashen-faced, frightened. As mother and daughter they had been especially close. He had left the shop without telling her. I didn't know who had. We weren't religious, but had a priest materialized?

I was in a fog. Was this really happening?

Yes, it was.

On 19 May 1960, she was dead. At only 36, this, gentle, loving person who had never uttered an angry or unkind word to her children, or anyone else to my knowledge, had gone. Gone suddenly and without warning. Gone alone. Gone forever without a chance to say goodbye – to anyone. Though I knew with an enduring sadness which could not be shared that she had tried.

The good doctor blankly assumed that our father had prepared us.

o O o

Dennis, 19 and working in Sydney, drove up that evening in his lumbering old dark green Morris Oxford with the kind of column stick shift and other oddities that only the English could love and the Indians deify. What an awful drive it must have been. Five hours at best. Alone with his thoughts and his memories and his disbelief. How good it was to see him walk through the door. Our big brother. Shaken, but with some of the grit and the composure we needed. We siblings did our best to comfort each other.

My father was so possessed with broadcasting his own grief that no one else's mattered. Earlier, in the morning, I had gone to him as he lay flat on his back up on the back lawn among the fruit trees, sobbing. But he had dismissed me with a sharp gesture and I didn't try again.

His grief, such as it was, came first. I was, perhaps not so oddly, more or less unmoved by this. What, after all, was I to expect from a man who had never offered a hand or a hug or, for that matter, wisdom or encouragement.

o O o

Relatives came and went. Some stayed longer than others. Most had little to say. So hard to talk when everyone is in shock. Comfort was very thin on the ground.

It was hard to think at the church. As far as the hymns were concerned, a kind of eventide had certainly fast fallen, but the Lord was just as certainly not abiding with us. How I despised the assurance of this having been a part of God's Plan. Damn the heartless plan and damn the only-the-good-die-young nonsense! The dirges may have helped others, but they did nothing for me. I sat there in the kind of numb state that only truly heart-rending shock can induce.

We three siblings went to her funeral on the back seat of someone's car just behind the hearse with little to say to each other. Each of us still struggling with our loss. Each of us having loved her so completely. Each of us with their champion gone.

There were too many people there for my liking. Crowded around all in black. Too many aunts and uncles and cousins and assorted townsfolk for any chance at a quiet goodbye. In its stoic Anglo way, not much of a warm family anyway. With the exception of her sister and best friend, Vi, and Vi's family, not one that had done much reaching out when it mattered – when she was alive.

It wasn't in any case a time to be smothered by a clan which, with fair uniformity, had disliked my father with such mute intensity, probably at first for sweeping my mother off her feet when she wasn't much more than a child, but then for his superior manner and his modest success, that some had come to be not that bothered about her either.

Some of it rubbing off on me – or so I thought – for the belief that I had somehow been his favorite. A belief which did not explain why I had been the one who, not that long ago, had missed a few days of school until the split lip from a drunken punch and assorted bumps on my head looked a little better. The intensity of her quiet fury over this had been my only consolation.

So I found myself standing near the cars back in the tree line, looking on from a distance over the green expanse of the perfectly indifferent cemetery with the little knot of people shuffling around the dark hole in the ground and the obscenely big mound of uncaring, cold, Canberra clay alongside it – soon to be covering her.

Uncomprehending. Confused. Not yet able imagine life without her.

Tough old 'Gunner' Robinson and his kindly wife, our next door neighbors, came over and put out a comforting hand.

We rode back in the same car, three abreast again, not much to say, glimpsing our father slumped for all to see against the cemetery wall near the main gate. On display.

o O o

For a time that Thursday night, finding myself at home alone with him, I was struck with a desperate realization that I could not bear to remain in a house which would never again glow with her love or approve of her restraining hand on him.

Dennis and Barbara had known how to stand up to him, but I had long been deeply apprehensive. There was an unstable side to him. One which had developed a more alcoholic and more physical character since Dennis had made a stand and my father, with his local pull, had promptly arranged for him and his Woolworth's management traineeship to be transferred to Sydney.

I had to escape and boarding at Grammar was the only way I could think of doing it. I should have known that this would be much less difficult to achieve than I had imagined – finding myself unpacking into an eight bed dormitory there three days later.

Dennis and Barbara joined forces to help keep our father's businesses afloat when he just disappeared for a few weeks, but soon after his unaccountably angry return they retreated from the Queanbeyan store one morning with Dennis being obliged to physically stand up to him. Dennis promptly returned to Sydney and after a testing day or two at home alone with him, Barbara moved in with an Aunt.

o O o

Within six months he married again. How could he? Who was she?

Well she was, unsurprisingly, from Sydney. But they divorced within a year.

June was her name and she was barely seven years older than me. I was boarding at Grammar and, at his teary insistence, I went to Sydney by myself on the train for the wedding. Was it really left to me to tell Dennis and Barbara? He was such a coward.

I was to entertain myself or stay out of the way in the city until later in the afternoon when someone would pick me up somewhere and take me to the church. So, needing more of a distraction than strolling around the unfamiliar streets would offer, I took in Alfred Hitchcock's latest thriller, *Psycho*, in a George Street theatre. At that time of the day, the theatre was almost empty except for the two women a few rows behind who scared the hell out of me when they screamed louder than the gorgeous Janet Leigh as Tony Perkins yanked that cheap plastic shower curtain back and set to with his big carving knife.

The wedding was performed at a pretty enough little sandstone church somewhere in the inner city. Me the complete misfit. Feeling betrayed. Feeling like a fool. Having to wear my bloody Grammar School uniform as I didn't have anything else. Hell, I was practically a man … wasn't I? (Yes but, more so, perilously young.)

I couldn't wait to get back on the train to Canberra.

In the middle of the night, half way up deserted Flinders Way on the long walk from the Railway Station at Kingston back to Grammar, I saw a very bright satellite moving in a slow arc high in the black sky. Larger and slower than the usual ones which, since the first Russian 'Sputnik' a few years before, could be seen whizzing around in ever increasing numbers. No such thing as stationary orbits in those days and me completely clueless about what this meant, let alone about the likes of the father of geostationary satellite communications, Arthur C Clarke, with whom I would become friendly years later in his refuge in Sri Lanka. It nudged me a bit off my own puny little trajectory of morbid introspection.

o O o

Six months of boarding at Grammar, unadorned as it was by contact of almost any kind with family, provided me with a refuge and time to get a grip. How well it suited me, but how short-lived it was.

Roots

Mine was in fact an unremarkable childhood. Comparatively typical for a white Anglo-Celt Australian in a typical Australian country town with a typical main street running from the usual willow-lined muddy river to the essential dry and dusty showground.

My brother Dennis was born in 1940 to a young couple who were no doubt head-over-heels for each other. Never mind that they got to the altar a little late for the standards of those days. They copped it, but were sustained by their love which was so new, so special, so complete. And when Den came along, how smitten they were with him! Not surprisingly. They were a beautiful couple. She petite and demure and very much the wholesome country girl of the bobbysoxer, big-band, crooner era. He lean and handsome and, under the cocky veneer, with a vulnerability that only she could see.

Amy Clarice 'Clarrie' and Francis Drake 'Frank' to some, 'Mick' to others, Debenham.

Later, when she was pregnant with Barbara from one of his AWOL's from army training, he was shipped off with the 6th Division to North Africa and she was born in 1941 while he was one of so many who were risking everything somewhere over there.

With her two little babies, Clarice stayed with her mother and father out beyond Canberra in the little bush village of Tharwa on the banks of a picturesque stretch of the Murrumbidgee river between the wealthy wheat and wool Stations of Lanyon and Cuppacumbalong and beneath the lowering, oddly leaning, Mt Tennent.

Tennent – named however perversely for one of the district's more unremarkable and least durable bushrangers, John Tennant. (Who knows how the spelling difference came about.) Having decamped from his assignment as a convict to the owner of Canberry Station, Joshua Moore, Tennant, using the mountain (originally the Ngunnawal's Tharwa) as his refuge, had in the 1820s stuck up or otherwise caused grief to some of the more notable early settlers of the district, starting out with a veteran of Waterloo and overseer of Robert Campbell's Duntroon Station, James Ainslie. Both of whom had early Canberra suburbs named after them.

Anyway, cards and letters came so slowly from such frighteningly exotic places on the troop ship's route as Colombo, Port Said, Aden and Haifa, in what was then British mandated Palestine, where they had been disembarked to stretch their legs and try to stay out of trouble. But from there she knew they would be thrown into the maelstrom and she could do nothing but wait and hope, fear and foreboding in her heart.

People she knew were soon receiving the dreaded telegram or a visit from a priest about a loved one lost. But his cards and photos kept coming. In a trickle, but still coming.

She had a black Box Brownie camera and sent him pictures, lovingly notated, of the babies. He replied with photos of him smiling that beamingly broad smile. Here in his slouch hat with a mate, there in his heavy army coat in the snow outside Damascus, and somewhere else in a squad of gas-masked soldiers 'Guess which one?' somewhere in Palestine. She cherished each letter and photograph from him and the hope they gave her that he would make it back.

Then word came that they were on their way home. But, then again, that they would have to wait in Ceylon while Curtin argued with Churchill about whether they should go to Mountbatten's and Slim's

1941. Clarice and Frank – off to war.

Burma campaign or back to defend Australia against the all conquering Japanese.

Curtin prevailed and my father arrived in Melbourne on 7 August 1942. Within a week, he went AWOL for nine days to put in a completely unannounced appearance at Tharwa. Down that long seventeen miles of dusty road from Queanbeyan, hitching if he could, but probably walking most of it. Finally, over the Murrumbidgee on the fine old white painted timber bridge, up the narrow lane past the Wests and the Sheedys, through the front gate next to the old hawthorn tree and into her arms.

Of course he was punished when he returned to barracks, but the war was already over for him. Emaciated from unresolved illnesses, he went AWOL again from 10 September and did not return. He was, justly, discharged as medically unfit for service, especially in the tropics where his mates would be going into the mud and the slush and the slog and the hell of a different kind of warfare in deeply tropical New Guinea. I was born about nine months later, plumpest of the three of us at birth, happy and healthy.

o O o

His had been a forlorn kind of childhood, not uncommon in the England of those days.

His mother, Muriel, was born on 24 March, 1891 at Harlington Road, Southend in the County of Essex, to Alfred and Emily Milner. Alfred was, by profession, a solicitor's clerk and a respected member of the community. An auspicious kind of beginning for Muriel in the straight-laced England of those days. But when she was old enough, she left home and the support of her parents for the siren call of the stage. Her parents were aghast. The daughters of genteel folk were not to aspire to what was, at that time, regarded as a loose and frivolous lifestyle. But she could not be dissuaded and her father promptly disowned her.

In due course she had four children to two men, marrying neither, but refusing to play the part of a fallen lady.

When he found out that she was pregnant, the father of the first born, Dennis, joined the army and disappeared.

Continuing her life on the stage, Muriel was pursued from town to town by Francis Drake Pearce, a married man, and the relationship produced three children – my father, Francis Drake, Jack Alfred and Muriel Elizabeth. Milners all. The lean years of the Great War and its aftermath tipped her already precarious existence from just coping to damned tough. A spirit of single-minded independence was just not going to be enough to pull a girl through.

In 1923, her father, by now occupying the prestigious office of Poor Law Officer at Worcester, perhaps both relenting his disowning of Muriel and fearing publicity of what the times would have regarded as his daughter's disgrace, went searching and found her close to being on her last legs. Poor she indeed was, and in need of the kind of help that a Poor Law Officer such as her father was equipped to deal with. But probably more in need of a bit of fatherly kindness and understanding.

Muriel Milner as a Principal, Ilona, in Gipsy Love *at the Grand Opera House, Belfast which opened on 14th September 1925 – the year after she had put her children into Dr Barnardo's Homes. The music for this operetta was written by Franz Lehar, who was celebrated for other significant works such as* The Merry Widow. *And the script was by Adrian Ross who had established himself through associations with up-market outlets such as the Gaiety Theatre in Westminister, London.*

Muriel, third from the left, with the cast of Gipsy Love.

She had put the children into the care of a Mrs Bancroft at Retford, Nottinghamshire, but Pearce, who for a while had been paying Mrs Bancroft for their shelter and sustenance, had disappeared.

Muriel's father rooted him out and he agreed to resume support. But it wasn't long before his business went bad and he no longer had the means to continue doing so. In due course, he took off for a new life in Canada.

o O o

For Muriel, life and earnings on the stage or anywhere else did not improve. Despairing of even coming close to making ends meet, and with the children now underfed and sickly, her choices for herself and for them became even starker.

On 18 November 1924, with winter closing in, she placed Dennis, aged eight, and Francis, aged six, with Dr Barnardo's Home at Boys Garden City, Woodford Bridge, Essex. She found a foster home for their sister, Betty, and her father took the youngest, Jack. With everything more or less neatly packaged as far as her father was concerned, father and daughter resumed their distance from each other. Dennis and Francis would not see Jack and Betty for a long long time and contact with their mother would almost disappear.

Francis was taken in just in time. A few months shy of seven, Barnardos initial medical examination revealed that he had already had measles, scarlet fever and whooping cough. His gums were septic, he had bronchitis and his nose was running. And there was more. He had swollen glands, his tonsils and adenoids were suspect and his hands were blue. He weighed 38 pounds or just over 17 kilograms. Lean he was and lean he stayed for most of his life.

1924. Francis and Dennis upon admittance to Dr Barnardo's Home, Boys Garden City, Woodford Bridge, Essex, England.

MILNER Francis Drake

Born .	02 . 02 . 1918	
Adm .	18 . 11 . 1924	
	19 . 11 . 1924	BOYS GARDEN CITY .
	01 . 02 . 1926	FELIXSTOWE .
	11 . 03 . 1926	BOYS GARDEN CITY.
	10 . 12 . 1928	FELIXSTOWE .
	04 . 01 . 1929	BOYS GARDEN CITY.
	09 . 10 . 1929	FELIXSTOWE .
	27 . 11 . 1929	BOYS GARDEN CITY .
	06 . 06 . 1930	TO NEW SOUTH WALES.

Aust. Party Book 16 Pg 34 .
BROTHER:- Dennis Milner; adm . 18 . 11 . 24 .

Extract from Dr Barnardo's movement register.

For a time, Muriel's stage career went through a substantial resurgence. Unencumbered by her four children and possibly hoping to earn her way towards a future with them, she enjoyed some years of success until the Great Depression and World War II put a deep and prolonged dampener on paying theatre.

o O o

From all accounts, including my father's, Barnardos were stern, but not without kindness. The boys were properly fed, clothed and housed, and provided with the rudiments of an education. While Barnardos had programs for fostering children out, the children were, curiously, never allowed to stay beyond agreed periods, regardless of a substantial incidence of impassioned attempts at adoption by their fosterers. The reason being that it was very much a part of British policy in those days, and the funding support which the government provided for institutions of the Barnardos kind, that these children were needed to help keep up British stock throughout the Empire – in the colonies. As it happened, neither Dennis nor Francis were ever fostered out. Barnardos didn't like to separate siblings and it was not in any case easy to find homes that would take two.

In 1931, at twelve, and with Dennis already gone, probably to an apprenticeship of sorts somewhere in London, Francis and many others were shipped off without much ceremony to a Barnardos farm school on the outskirts of Picton, a little country town a hundred kilometres or so south west of Sydney. Gone to an Australia which he at first believed to be somewhere in the warmer south of England, where he thought those lovely Australian apples which they saw advertised on the side of London's big red double-decker buses were grown.

They spent a month or so at sea on the SS *Balranald* and then, upon arrival in Sydney on 21 July 1930, were soon bundled onto the back of a truck bound for a bouncy ride out to the school. Even though he and the others may well have been sustained for the moment by the adventure of it all, everything and everyone they had ever known were now on the other side of the world and would most likely never be seen or even heard of by them again.

A day or two out of London, he pencilled the following forlorn letter to his mother.

> My Dear Mum
> I hope you received my last letter. I have written to Grandpa and ma and Jack – to night I shall be writing to Dennis when I get in my berth. I have two or three friends with me. I am head boy of a cabin. I bought six penney worth of stamps and put them on the envelopes. I think it a wonder I have not been sea-sick or something of that sort. Well I hope to get on in my new land and I will try and get you a photo of the liner we are on. Our next stop will be at Malta. I have not much time to write to you as I have two or three duties to perform on top deck. Goodbye till I write next. I hope you are happy and healthy. Please write as soon as possible. With the best of love from your loving son.
> Francis xxxxxxxxx

At Picton, they were taught the hard side of farming. Jackaroos of a kind, but more so laborers. Up at the crack of dawn to milk the cows, muck out the barns and the pens, deal with a range of farm animals and equipment, help dig post holes and put up fences. But with some instruction in the three R's tossed in.

Corporal punishment there certainly was, but nothing worse and nothing particularly vicious by the standards of those times. He knew of and was able to learn very little about family life, love and protection. He knew nothing of his father and little of his mother.

In 1933, when he was fifteen, Barnardos placed all the boys of his age on farms all over New South Wales, Victoria and Queensland. Barnardos paid their bus and rail fares and did their best to monitor their meager pay and conditions. No more meager though, and no more exploited than other youngsters from other backgrounds starting out in this kind of work.

If things didn't work out at this or that place, Barnardos found another for them and arranged their transport to and from. Whenever they were in Sydney between jobs, Barnardos put them up. And the Barnardos guide for thriftiness included keeping a portion of their pay as savings in carefully named and managed bank accounts. No monkey business. All to be made available to them at an appropriate time.

Francis now learned about a new kind of loneliness. Miles and miles from anywhere, out in the vastness of rural Australia, a few grown farmhands replaced the companionship of the other boys at Picton. The rude huts, usually at some remove from the homesteads and providing the most rudimentary of facilities, replaced the familiar dorm. Few bothered about his needs for companionship and none drew him to the family hearth.

He was liked enough at some places; disliked, though not overly, at others. Some found him bright and industrious, others lazy and combative. Surly? Goodness, why so?

He roamed from place to place – usually with Barnardos help, sometimes of his own volition.

Horses were alright when you could get the use of one, but he took the boss's car for a spin one day without bothering to get his permission and was promptly reported to the police for his trouble. They were already out looking for him when he blithely drove up and the boss, who had assumed that he had decamped, gave him a good telling off, but forgave him.

Barnardos had maintained some contact with his mother in England and he started writing to her. Also with Barnardo's help, he was writing to his brother and childhood protector, Dennis, who was finding his way in London. He had neither returned to Barnardos nor been shipped out to one of the colonies. But the responses to his letters were few and far between. He passed the nights reading, by flickering candle or pungent kerosene lamp, anything he could get his hands on. Later on, we were to see the benefit of this for him in his ability with public speaking, a sustained interest in both reading and composing poetry (of a distinctly Australian kind), and a remarkable ability with all kinds of crosswords. His roles in the town affairs of Queanbeyan included a period as President of the Chamber of Commerce.

o O o

Francis (whose family name to this time had remained that of his mother – Milner) walked into Canberra from somewhere out west when he was nineteen. He camped, initially, under the old timber bridge on Commonwealth Avenue, which at that time was the only bridge over the muddy, willow-lined, Molonglo River.

He soon linked up with another Barnardos boy, Bill Debenham, and found some laboring jobs, including at a dairy over near today's Fyshwick. He and Bill knocked around enough together that Francis was assumed to be a Debenham. He would give more fanciful reasons for adopting the name, including having been sponsored at Barnardos in London by the famous Oxford Street department store, Debenham's, but his connection with Bill was the most likely one.

For the first time since leaving London he was in a town of a reasonable size getting steady enough work and mingling with others. He knew he would never go back to work in the bush – though in later years he came to love it and to occasionally seek a kind of refuge in it.

Young men and women met by going to this or that Saturday night dance at one community hall or another around Canberra and it was most likely at such a venue that he and Clarice, my mother, met.

o O o

Born in 1924, Amy Clarice Kirchner was the fourth child of Robert and Mona Kirchner. Six more had followed her. Reuben was the eldest and Roger, born in 1939 and only six months older than my brother Dennis, was the youngest.

o O o

'Bob' Kirchner was born at Tidbinbilla in 1894. He was the fourth of Karl and Nellie Kirchner's thirteen children. His grandfather, Friedrich Kirchner, and grandmother, Hanne Pokrandt (Friedrich's second wife), were born in Prussia. Friedrich and Hanne arrived in Australia in 1847. They got off their ship, the *Heloise*, in Adelaide where a German community and its wine-making industry was in the making.

Life wasn't all that easy and Bob, like many other youngsters out farming with their families on small holdings in the bush at that time, grew into a young man knowing more about hard physical work and the company of men than book learning and home comforts. From a young age, he became skilled in the ways of the bush and men and how to survive both, though this did not get off to a good start. *The Queanbeyan Age* reported on 1 September 1903 that:

> A little boy, about 9 years of age and a son of Mr Kirchner of Tidbinbilla, was admitted to the local hospital yesterday, suffering from severe burns received the previous night while lying near a log fire. It transpires that the little child was in company with some of his relatives camped some distance from home, and having gone to sleep by the fire his clothes became ignited. The poor little patient is severely burnt about the arms and body and is not expected to recover.

But recover he did through fifteen challenging months of hospitalization in Sydney.

Bob didn't have much use for either alcohol or religion – though he did make a point of singing grace at both Christmas and Easter Sunday lunch. Deep voiced and plain speaking to a fault, he never had an ounce of flesh to spare on his hard, bony frame. He didn't have much of a waist to hang his trousers on, so broad, well worn, braces were always the go.

o O o

Mona Tyrie, of English, Scottish and Irish descent, born in 1898, was in the line of a first fleeter, the convict Thomas Akers, or Acres – my mother's great, great, great, great grandfather. Add another one for me.

Akers was born in Devon, England in 1758. A shoemaker by trade, he was sentenced, in 1785, to be hung for having held up and robbed

Mr John Squance of ten shillings on the Kings Highway. After a little more than two years on the prison hulk *Dunkirk* on the Thames River, Thomas's sentence was commuted to seven years on condition of transportation to the colonies.

Sent to Botany Bay on the *Charlotte*, he was in due course freed and received a land grant of twenty acres at Mulgrave Place on the Hawkesbury River, eventually moving on to a new land holding at Campbelltown with his wife to be, Ann Guy. They had five children. Thomas died in 1824 and, though a Catholic, was buried at Saint Peter's Anglican Church, Campbelltown. Ann died in 1831.

A public school in Ambarvale is named after Thomas Akers (now Acres) and is built on what was his Campbelltown property.

Their daughter, Mary Ann, married Dudley Hartigan and in turn their daughter, Eliza, married Thomas Tyrie in 1802. From there, the Tyrie name survived through the male line to Mona Tyrie, my mother's mother.

o O o

Like many others out in the bush at that time, the Tyries eked a living out of land holdings in the Tinderry Mountains, southwest of what was to become Canberra. Apart from Shanks's pony (walking), horse or horse and cart were the best available means of transport in those days, making the closest towns a challenging ride along dusty rutted tracks, but a rare treat nonetheless. Nothing to complain about. That's the way it was and few probably felt the worse for it. Many preferred it.

The country was rugged and remote enough to provide opportunity and refuge for the bushranger class. Few were of the desperate, murderous, kind. Most were probably simple enough folk who had their reasons for keeping their distance from the law. Mona once told me that if these kind of bushmen took a sheep or a cow for their tucker, they sometimes left the skin draped over a fence for recovery by the farmer.

But there were indeed some rogues, and worse.

It seems that Mona's grandfather (my great, great grandfather), Andrew Tyrie, was one of the ringleaders of what was known in the mid-1800s as the Jingerra Mob and that they had had a loose connection with the notoriously marauding Clarke-Connell family of bushrangers and murderers. Not that they were ever implicated in any of the bad stuff of the Clarke-Connells.

According to Dennis Chamberlaine's *Tyrie Family History:*

> The Jingerra Mob was named after the mountain range east of the Tinderries where many members of the mob lived. The mob took its origins from the tightly knit community of poor back-country people who made much of their livelihood from cattle-duffing and who helped one another evade the clutches of the law.

During the mid-1800s, Chamberlaine continues:

> … the mob preyed on the cattle and horses of other settlers on the richer properties, driving the stolen stock into the secluded areas of the mountains and cutting out the identifying brands. One such area of the Tinderries was a spot known as the Beefcask near the summit of Tinderry Peak where the rock formations had created a natural and well-hidden stockyard.

Then commonly known as a duffing yard.

How remarkably some of this coincides with Rolf Boldrewood's description of the focal point of his Captain Starlight's cattle-duffing capers in his best-selling *Robbery Under Arms* which, following its serialization in the *Sydney Mail*, was first published in 1888.

Boldrewood was the pen name of Thomas Alexander Browne who, like many novelists, was given to drawing some of his material from real life events. As Police Magistrate in Dubbo when he wrote the book, he had a trove of such material at his disposal and may well have come across the exploits of the Jingerra Mob. In his 1968 introduction to *The Australian Classics* publication of the book, A T Brissenden noted that:

> … several incidents are based on the exploits of Frank Gardiner, Ben Hall and the Clarkes of Braidwood during the 1860s

All of whom, and most particularly the Clarkes, operated within easy range of the Jingerra Mob.

Most striking is the similarity between Boldrewood's 'wild gullies and rock strewed hills of Broken Creek' – where Starlight and the Marstons had their duffing yard en route to Terrible Hollow behind Nulla Mountain – and the remote, naturally formed, Beefcask holding place for the cattle duffers of the Tinderries.

o O o

Mona met Robert at a woolshed dance at the homestead of the historic Cuppacumbalong sheep station (large farm or ranch). She had been looking after a sick sister at nearby Lanyon station and Robert was working up in the nearby Naas valley.

Woolshed dances, enthusiastically supported by the farmer-graziers who owned or shared them, remained common and very popular community venues around the Australian countryside and on the fringes of the cities and the big towns through the 1970s. One such popular venue in my youth was the Yarralumla Woolshed over near Government House where Johnny Horton's little country and rock ensemble, which included an uncle of mine, Bobby Kirchner, used to often do Saturday night BBQ and dance gigs.

o O o

Bob and Mona married and began their lives together in a tiny slab-board hut which had been, as was then common practice, hewn from the right kind of native gums in the surrounding bush. It was located in a picturesque setting, west of Canberra, on the banks of the sweeping Murrumbidgee river, just a few kilometers below Tharwa village where they would come to live out many of their years and raise their large family.

Over the ensuing years, Bob and Mona lived and worked and raised their large family as best they could around the district of their childhood. Bob became highly skilled in just about every trade needed to keep a farm running. When work wasn't available locally, such as during the Great Depression of the 1930s, he went to wherever he could find it, sometimes having to be away from home for months at a time, but always managing to keep enough food on the family table.

Out in a little bush village, more or less on her own, with the little cottage and a growing number of children to keep going, there must have been times when Mona could have readily identified with Henry Lawson's tales of such women and such times. She certainly had the temperament, the endurance and the strength to live up to Lawson's take on such iconic mothers of rural Australia.

o O o

So there it was. I was descended from the Anglo-Celt mixes of Europe's Middle-Ages, which had in the Australasian chapter of its diaspora incorporated, apart from a very sound complement of fine upstanding souls, highwaymen, convicts, bushrangers and cattle duffers. It was a pretty normal and pretty sturdy early Aussie brew really, but one which wouldn't be harmed by a little genetic infusion from, say, some Hermit Kingdom far, far away. But who was to know around which bend such a possibility could be waiting?

My Queanbeyan

When I was four, my father's mother, Muriel, who had lost everything during the German blitz of London, arrived and we all went down to Sydney to collect her off the ship. She moved in with us in our little flat above Koorey and Wade's fruit and vegetables shop in the main street of Queanbeyan, our father having somehow fitted an extra bed into the room which we three kids occupied.

In her fine English accent, she would read to us in the evenings in

Kindergarten 1948 at Queanbeyan Public School.
Howard, five years, front row fourth from right.

The year of being cute–Howard and Barbara, 1948.

such an absorbing way and tell us stories of far-away places. Sometimes she would sing in her sweet, well trained, soprano. Songs of Britain. Songs of Europe. Songs, wistfully, from her gypsyish life on the stage.

o O o

At the beginning of 1948, when I was four and a half, 'England' Nan was assigned to take me to the Queanbeyan Primary School for my first day of kindergarten. She handed me over to one of the teachers at the front gate and off I went. No fuss. I was a happy little kid.

Mrs Moore, wife of a chemist who had a shop down in the main street, was my first teacher. She could be stern, but she played piano, sang well and, with us all sitting around in a circle, taught us the usual songs. David Bates, Elizabeth Hill, Terry Snow, Deidre Miller, Dougie Alexander, Bruce Thornton, Jimmy Hall, Ellie Van Keulen, Mervyn Rose, Gordon Taylor and the others. Much to my discomfort, she soon singled me out to sit on her lap to help her get the singing started.

Before long, my father had entered Barbara and me in the annual town eisteddfod where we won the grand sum of ten shillings singing *Over in Killarney*. I would have been five and Barbara six.

No doubt at the further urging of Mrs Moore and others, I was entered next year to sing a favorite standard of the years of the Great Depression (then not so long ago) – *Hallelujah I'm a Bum.* My father gave me the word before going up to the backstage that if anyone asked me to sing tramp instead of bum, I was to politely decline. Sure enough, Mr Bradstock, the towering and angular, though kindly, Headmaster asked me to do just that. My father said that I was to sing bum sir, so I'm sorry, I have to sing bum. The first hesitant bum brought the house down and I pocketed first prize.

Although I thought I did a pretty good job of *Down in the Valley* the next year, I didn't get a prize. Seven was not as cute as six. Anyway, that was it as far as my father was concerned. There would be no more eisteddfods for Howard. It had all been his idea anyway and I did not mind foregoing more stage fright.

o O o

One night, Barbara and I hatched a plot to see the world. Not because we were unhappy, because we weren't. Didn't really know the meaning of it then, apart from as it concerned occasional spankings by my father with his leather slipper. But there was so much to see and we thought we should get on with it. Dennis wasn't going to be in such child's play.

We packed a yellowish cardboard suitcase and shoved it under Nan's bed. Very early the next morning, we slid the bag out from under her sleepily amused gaze, crept down the corridor past our parent's bedroom, reached up and ever so quietly opened the door, wrestled the suitcase down the steep stairs and headed off down the lane behind the flats and out into Surveyor Street opposite the leafy town park.

The bag wasn't that big, but we were small and it was taking the two of us to lug it along. We had barely got to the corner of Surveyor and Campbell when my father's big old green Ford, his first car, which his mother had helped him buy, lumbered out of the lane into the street and headed our way. We hid in line behind what seemed to be a big enough timber lamp post and held our breaths. He pulled up alongside and we got in. He was not amused.

There was a hushed, tense kind of discussion between my father and Nan about all of this after we got back. We were too young to have been able to make much of this, but he obviously had not seen the harmless humor in it that she had.

It wasn't long after that she found a job at the Superannuation Board in Canberra and moved into Mulwala House, a collection of fibro buildings which had not that long ago been relocated from the Riverina's town of Mulwala. Positioned on a rise above the Molonglo river on the northern approach to the old timber Commonwealth Avenue bridge and not that far from Civic Centre, it was part of a plan to accommodate Canberra's growing workforce. It served its purpose, but was always an eyesore and was the first of these structures to be demolished some years later.

Anyway, there wasn't much else around the Civic Centre of those days. Just the two very British, very colonial, colonnaded city blocks housing shops at ground level and flats above. Exactly the same kind of architecture which I was to find in Singapore and New Delhi's Connaught Place years later. Off in the near distance was the more substantial and still surviving double-brick Gorman House which Nan moved into a few years later. On the other, western, side of Civic Centre, beneath Black Mountain, construction of the Australian National University was getting underway.

o O o

When I was about six, we were playing cowboys with the son of the Postmaster who lived behind the post office over the fence next door. We all agreed – him, Dennis, my best mate and neighbor above the butcher shop, Phil Wade, and me – that the Postmaster's son would play the part of the one to be strung up by the goodies. There was plenty of rope around in those days, so we threw a good length over a sturdy branch of the big tree between our two places. Just like in the Saturday afternoon matinees at Freebody's Star Theatre down the other end of Monaro Street.

Perfect.

A good enough noose was fixed and then looped around his neck. True to the script, his hands were tied behind his back – tight enough so that the bad guy wouldn't be able to squirm out of it. Whether he played Defiant or Repentant didn't really matter. Dennis took up the slack. As it turned out, a little too much.

Suddenly the bad guy was on his tippy toes and there was enough of his weight on the rope for it to catch on the knarled branch. While we were giving him as much lift as we could and someone was trying to get at the tightening knot, Phil materialized in his mother's kitchen asking for a knife, but hesitating to say why. Hot on his heels, she shooed him down the stairs, following him over the fence and, aghast, to the rescue of the villain.

There would be no more hangings. Not then, not ever.

o O o

At around the same time, Dougie Sewell, a mate of mine from Queanbeyan Primary, used to come around and play with Phil and me down the long and dusty old lane behind the flats. We would find long sticks to use as pretend horses for our Tom Mix and Hopalong Cassidy roles. 'Borrowed' tomato stakes from behind one of the nearby shops were greatly prized as the palominos of these stick horses.

Goodies and Baddies were played out from favorite parts of the Saturday matinee movies. There was plenty of long grass to hide in and we were just big enough to be able to clamber over the high paling fences.

With the chase in full gallop one morning, Dougie hurled his horse over the fence and, with his pursuers gaining fast, six shooters blazing, he made it up to the sill of the window right above the bat-winged saloon door and launched himself towards his good old snorting, quivering bronco below.

But he didn't gallop off.

Because he had missed the saddle and got the jagged broken bottle.

Unknowing, Phil and I were on him in a flash. But, to our horror, Dougie rolled over and came up gaping – in two places. The first, a look of disbelief on his face, the second an awesome gash right across the outside of his left thigh – about half way up. Wide open.

At first, there was so little blood that, crouching as we quickly were beside him, we could see a scratch on the bone. Honest.

My parents were off at their little store in Crawford Street and Phil was already running down the lane yelling for his mother. 'Stay here Dougie!' I begged. But, clutching at his leg, he stumbled off after Phil and then I too was running and yelling.

As Phil's yells would have stirred the dead, Phyllis met us about half way down the lane. She tried to pinch the bleeding wound together and bind something she was carrying – most likely a tea towel – around it before sweeping him up into her arms and dashing down to the doctor's house at the bottom of the lane.

Dougie was saved, but I can't remember him ever being allowed to come and play with us down the lane, or for that matter anywhere else, again.

o O o

It was an interesting lane. Enormous trucks were parked there sometimes and quite often so too were coils of thick power cables on huge wooden

1949 – 'It was an interesting lane. Enormous trucks were parked there ...'
Phillip and Timmy Wade, Howard, sister Barbara, the Postmaster's son and brother Dennis

rollers. We could just manage to roll some of these around and one day we really got one going. Scooting around in front of it, I slipped, fell in its path and was transfixed by it lumbering down on me when Dennis suddenly whipped around and threw his shoulder against one of the rollers as I scampered free. What impressed the hell out of me though was that he had done this with a wincing grin on his face from having also brought his heavily bandaged forearms to bear.

Heavily bandaged?

Well, at that time, when he would have been 9, Barbara 7 and me still 6 (it was a busy year), our mother and father had to go to an early evening function of some kind after closing the shop and dinner would be late. They rushed in for a quick change, she put a leg of lamb and some dollops of dripping into a baking dish, slid it into the wood-fired Metters oven and off they went.

Dennis would take it out of the oven at the appointed time. Yes, we could play down the lane for a little while after dark. And, no, we wouldn't forget.

We did.

When it dawned on us, we all made a mad dash for the oven, Dennis setting the pace. Through the gate in the corrugated iron fence, up the stairs, across the Wade's verandah, around the end of the dividing slatted balcony and across our verandah. It was serious, but it was fun.

Bursting through the door into the kitchen we beheld, horror of horrors, smoke puffing out from the sides of the oven door. Without even a hint of hesitation, Dennis grabbed the little steel oven knob, twisted, pulled the door open, grabbed the baking dish and yanked. Bare handed.

Miraculously, our parents appeared right behind us. But too late to stop the boiling fat splashing over both of his forearms.

Ouch.

That's why Dennis's arms were bandaged.

o O o

Dennis had a lot of pluck, but up to this time there had only been glimpses of it. In later life, 203 appearances in first grade for Queanbeyan Rugby Union Club and an OAM for his services to rugby put more than a seal on this.

The first stoush I remember him being in was when, in the backyard at our grandparent's home at Tharwa, some half-sloshed uncles and aunts taunted him and Roger, his uncle (though only six months older), but also far and away his best mate, to have a minor difference of opinion out with their fists. It hadn't gone far before my mother arrived on the scene and firmly put a stop to it and the urgers to deserved shame. Dennis and Roger walked off arm in arm, no doubt wondering what in the hell that was all about.

Dennis generally brushed off the lesser bullies with a few words and a shove or two back. They weren't sure enough of him to press the point. In time, however, this wasn't good enough for the ranking bully, Jimmy Esplin.

Quiet, easy going, lean and lanky Dennis looked every bit of a pushover. A likely mark for your average bully.

One afternoon, inevitably, Esplin and his toadies were waiting for him half way down the lane behind Lowe Street on our usual route home together.

To Esplin's surprise, Dennis neither backed off nor looked especially frightened. He didn't have to be as I was frightened enough for both of us. Esplin was bigger and meaner and there was nothing a third-grader could do to help against a bunch of sixth-graders. They circled each other in the ring which the Esplin toadies had formed and Dennis eventually got a bloody nose. But the outcome was a standoff. No one bothered him at that school again and Esplin's reputation diminished.

o O o

In my early childhood, my grandfather, Bob Kirchner, had a horse and cart – of a kind that was called a dray – which he used during the week to do running repairs for the government on the dusty dirt roads around and in the vicinity of Tharwa. On the weekends, he odd-jobbed on the big nearby sheep farms, principally Cuppacumbalong and Lambrigg. In time, the horse and dray were replaced by a dark blue 1928 model Dodge truck, in which he would occasionally turn up in Queanbeyan for those goods which couldn't be got from the Jeffries' little general store in Tharwa. He would set out early for the seventeen mile run and if we kids had word that he was coming, we would keep an eye out for him from the front window of that flat above Koorey and Wade's shop in the main street and hurry down with our mother to greet him.

Saturday mornings were the busiest for shopping. The main street, Monaro, had one concreted strip down the middle, which was flanked by graveled verges down to the gutters and the broad, tarred, footpaths along the front of the shops. Hitching rails and watering troughs for horses were dotted along the street and there were few spaces left at the big one outside Morton's bakery down where the old arched timber bridge spanned the bewillowed Queanbeyan river.

Queanbeyan had for the past hundred years or so been the supply center for a large district of the southern tablelands, including, in more recent times, the fledgling Canberra.

Everyone dressed up a bit for Saturday mornings. The main street was dotted with clusters of people catching up and the men dipping their hats to the women. The children were on a lighter leash.

o O o

Tharwa was a thrilling place for us. It was there that Nanna and Grandad Kirchner's modest cottage, facing the bush with its long timber-planked and banistered verandahs down two sides, overflowed at Christmas with uncles, aunts and cousins.

From either our green Ford or its succeeding black Hudson, both built like tanks and just as heavy, how excited we were to be the first to spot the bridge over the meandering Murrumbidgee river from just beyond the gates to Lanyon Station. Lanyon – its vast paddocks rolling away from the dusty road down to the river beyond. Down to the Wiradjuri's Murrumbidgee – 'big water'.

How much of an adventure it always was to be let loose on the village Common where for a very modest fee everyone grazed their cows and where we would join Nanna for the early morning milking. And how, back in the spacious country kitchen with its floor of expansive blue granite slabs and its big black iron pots and kettles on the wood-fired stove, we would relish scoops of still warm yellowing cream straight off the top of the milk bucket for our bread and jam.

At the Christmas gatherings, there was plenty of food for all and a nine gallon keg of beer for the men towards the corner of the verandahs – tapped from about midday. They were mostly left to it by the women who drank tea and fussed over the food preparation while we kids were left to roam free.

Ham and vegetables, roasted chickens freshly caught from the chicken run that morning, beheaded on an old stump down the back yard and defeathered after being ducked in boiling water in a big old tub. Plenty of home-made boiled Christmas pudding with shiny silver threepences awaiting discovery. Extra helpings for full stomachs sometimes discreetly taken outside and ditched over the fence after rummaging through it for more coins. What a treat it all was.

o O o

Dick Hopman was the schoolteacher at Tharwa's little one room primary school. He was the brother of the already famous Australian tennis coach, Harry Hopman, and he lived in the little fibro cottage next door to my grandparent's place. He had two children of our age, Margo and Richard.

Dick was a good man – quiet and unruffled. He taught us for a few months in the latish 1940s while our mother was in the Royal Prince Alfred Hospital in Sydney and we had been left in the care of Nanna and Grandad. We didn't know it then, but at barely twenty four she was having a kidney removed – a major operation for that time – for the condition that may have caused her death just before the first forms of dialysis appeared.

Dennis shared a room with Roger, Barbara was in the back room at the end of the verandah and lucky me had my bed *on* the verandah. Corrugated iron roof overhead, open across the bannisters to the crisp night air of the dark bush and guarded by Roger's surly red kelpie, Chester.

Very early one morning I awoke with someone gently stroking my cheek. Glowing in the soft morning light and the fresh aroma of the bush, she was back.

How my heart leapt!

o O o

Our father's tiny shop in Crawford Street, just over from the bus stop outside the public bar of the Royal Hotel and alongside a narrow service lane which ran down to Chilla Burns's billiard room and SP bookie establishment, had got under way a few years after his return from the war. He had gone to Sydney on the train with the grand sum of sixty pounds ($120) and returned with a bag full of hard to get buttons. The shaky little business had gone well enough after a year or two for him to move to a larger shop around the corner in the main street which was owned by Constantine Georgiadis, a well settled member of an earlier wave of Greek immigrants.

The owner of the café next door, Nick Cassidy (also from that wave of immigrants), helped vouch for him with his countryman, and to stake him for the fitout. Others of the influential Greek community, Minosa Poulos and George Nano were also somewhere in the mix, as were their kids up there with us at the primary school. One of the Nano kids used to love calling we Debenham kids 'ham and eggs'. Nick was given to calling me 'little Frankie' – after my father. Occasionally, it was worth a free milkshake.

Soon, it became possible for us to leave the little flat above the butcher shop. For eighteen hundred pounds ($3,600) our father bought a three bedroom fibro house, of a reasonable size for those times, near the top of Erin Street opposite the Queanbeyan District Hospital. It had good views across Queanbeyan to Mount Jerrabomberra and weren't we sitting pretty!

Erin's land was large enough, front and back, to stir memories in my father of a few of the skills and disciplines that had been bored into him during his time at Barnardo's farm school in Picton. During our first year there, when we weren't quite big enough to be co-opted, he grew potatoes and melons everywhere to help loosen up the shaley soil. But he had bigger plans and Dennis and I were going to be a part of them.

It wasn't so bad, but the labor which we sweated and blistered out over a few years – me from the age of nine – with picks and hoes and rakes and wheelbarrows – in transforming that hill of resistant shale into an immaculate garden did not seem like a lot of fun at the time.

More difficult though, was what was becoming my father's prod, prod, prodding disapproval of how we performed at this and just about everything else.

Family life at Erin Street nevertheless settled into the predictable routine of many a country town childhood, with his niggly edges softened as best she could by our mother. Settled too into a baffling mix of parenting – his of censure and threat, hers of comfort and refuge. The puzzle for me was that she so adored him – almost to the end.

o O o

Two of the highlights for us of those years were the Easter Show in Sydney and the hunting.

Not that we three children ever went to the Show. That was the only time of the year when our father and mother could close the shop and have four days to themselves, and we didn't begrudge them this. They were sometimes joined by our most liked and often seen uncle and aunt, Tod and Vi. They would stay in one of the better hotels in the city, wine, dine and dance at Romano's and go to Royal Randwick for the big Easter horseracing carnival – really living it up for a few days.

Our England Nan would come in from Canberra to look after us while they were away. We had come to know her as a gentle soul and for us the change of routine which she brought was entertaining.

When they returned – she absolutely beaming – there would be Easter Show bags loaded with goodies for each of us, tales of the wondrous cattle and produce exhibits and, from our father, news about who had got absolutely flogged in Jimmy Sharman's boxing tent.

The Hunting

The hunting started a bit later, when I was about 12, and became an annual event for the next few years during the May school holidays.

For us, it was high adventure and a time during which my father usually showed a better side. Uncle Tod, who was a principal chef at the Royal Military College, Duntroon, was a keen shooter and something of a marksman.

Making a start before dawn, Tod, my father, Dennis and I and our cousin Brian, a year older than me, would head off northwest of Queanbeyan to some of the outer reaches of New South Wales which my father had known in his days with Barnardos.

The dirt roads started just outside Canberra. Some were good, others were terrible. We always headed out through Yass and on up through Young, Murrumburrah/Harden, Forbes, Parkes, Peak Hill and Dubbo. Always a long day and with my father in his tense, hunched-up driving style, doggedly determined to go as far as he could and keep the pee breaks spaced almost to bursting point.

From Dubbo, we sometimes headed well north to Walgett and the Barwon and Namoi rivers. Other times, it was out west to places like Carinda on the Macquarie Marshes and Warren where my father's war time mate, Ray King, had become Railway Station Master for the end-of-the-line, one-train-a-week service – primarily for the needs of the giant sheep stations like Haddon Rig, Buttabone and Raby.

On the first trip, in what would have been 1955, with our provisions packed solidly into a little open trailer which fish-tailed along behind us on the loose dirt and gravel roads, kicking up an impressive cloud of dust and gravel, we drove into one of the big sheep stations on the Namoi, stopping to say hello at the homestead and then driving out into the paddocks to find a camp site on the river.

At that time of the year the river had dried up into a string of muddy waterholes and as we drove down to the likeliest looking one, lined as it was with typically scrubby gums, an impressively sized family of feral pigs, which had been minding their own business cooling off in the water, charged out grunting and squealing their surprise and annoyance. Up the bank on the other side they went and off in their powerfully ungainly way into the scrub.

It was the kind of campsite which, at the end of a long day’s ride, would have warmed the heart of many a true bushman – like Sid Kidman.

We pitched Tod’s spacious jungle green canvas army tent, set up a campfire, fetched some water from the pig wallow and boiled the billy. Boiled it well. A green gum leaf or two in the brew and a green twig across the top of the billy to keep the smoke out and we were away. Town water had never tasted this good. It just didn’t have the body.

Walking through the bush early in the morning and late in the afternoon when the pigs were out was fine, but the shooting was gory. They were using standard army issue .303 caliber rifles with their vicious looking standard issue hard-nosed bullets which made an awful mess of the pigs. Very clean entry, but with guts and gore hanging out of the gaping exit wounds. It wasn’t hard to imagine what these weapons had done to men.

We stumbled across an emu’s nest with quite a few eggs in it, but had gathered only a few when the big hen suddenly appeared – unexpectedly and furiously. Although they had seemed to have no qualms about shooting everything – pigs, roos and emus, my father and Tod left this one alone as we beat a hasty retreat.

One evening, Tod, half reclining on his canvas stretcher, reached out to grab a canvas haversack passed to him at a stretch by Dennis and his shoulder (the right one I think it was) collapsed in front of our eyes. In his inimitable fashion, my father gave Dennis an instant serve. But good-natured Tod, wincing with pain, explained through gritted teeth that this shoulder had a habit of popping out and he could fix it. He sat up, grasped it in an odd way and, impressively set of jaw, worked it back in. 'No problem Frank. Don't worry about it Den. Not your fault. Right as rain'.

On the last trip, maybe two years later, we camped in one of the corrugated iron shearers' huts at Quambone Station on the fringe of the vast Macquarie River marshes. We would have been able to get in on the evening of our arrival had it not been for a sharp downpour that had turned the road out from the little village of Quambone into a black bog. We would try again the next morning, but in the meantime we had to find somewhere to stay. The owner of the only pub in town let us camp out the back on the pub's kitchen floor.

Late that evening there was a terrible row outside with people fighting up and down the street. The owner ducked in and said everything was OK – it was just the usual Friday night stoush. My father and Tod knew better than to go out for a closer look.

We made it into the Station next morning, slipping and sliding down the road, but amazed at how quickly this stuff dried out.

We were greeted cordially at the homestead. Responsible pig shooters were welcome to help the farmers keep down the huge pig population which, apart from making a mess of available pasture, sometimes helped itself to the odd newborn calf or lamb.

The shearers' huts were next to an inviting bore-fed dam and we boys were quick to take a dip. Quicker still to get out when we discovered how hungry and how fast the leeches were. Over the following days, the challenge between us was to see who could dive in, swim to the other side and clamber out with the least number of leaches aboard.

Our nights were pervaded with the unforgettable odor of the acrid smoke from cow dung burning outside the open door of the hut. While we didn't doubt that this would dampen the enthusiasm of the bloodthirsty clouds of mosquitos, it was a toss-up as to which of the two was the worst.

Two things happened on this particular trip which were to put me right off hunting. Both involved the courage of the animals we were after.

o O o

The first was when we had surprised a huge black boar on the edge of a boggy area. He was plowing away from us through shallow water when my father brought him down just as the pig had clambered out of the water onto a bank. For some reason he left a double-barrelled shotgun with Dennis while he skirted the water to come around on the other side and have a closer look at his handiwork.

The pig was down on its haunches and very still, presumably with the awful .303 exit wound out of sight on the other side. Careful, I thought, he hasn't rolled over yet.

Sure enough, just as my father was almost at the boar's side, about seven or eight metres from us, it stood up and lunged. My father was stumbling backwards, fumbling with his rifle, struggling to stay upright, when there was an almighty clap of thunder right next to me.

Dennis, who a few days earlier had been allowed to fire one practice shot with this gun and, to the amusement of my father, was favoring a deeply bruised shoulder for his trouble, had not hesitated. Amazingly, the pig was down for keeps and our father was still up.

For a while, Dennis may have wondered if he had got the right one, as our father, typically imagining a worse outcome and no doubt embarrassed by his foolishness in waltzing up to such a pig, tore a strip off him. The boar would have made minced meat of him, but that didn't matter. Anyway, of the two as far as we were concerned, the pig had been the smarter and the more courageous one.

o O o

The second was about an instance of even greater bravery by another animal.

On one of the forays of the great white hunters, way out in the flat paddocks on the edge of the marshes and coming around some thick bush into a clearing, we surprised a big red kangaroo buck with his doe and a small joey which was out of the pouch.

Caught unawares out in the open not that long before the growing heat of the morning would have driven them into the scrub and out of danger, they were only about fifty or sixty metres away.

We stopped and, startled, they sat up and froze. Someone fired and missed. The doe and the joey took off for the scrub and the big buck came at us. I did not doubt for a moment that this was a deliberate, instinctive, ploy to give the doe and the joey time to get away.

Alongside me, my father, fumbling with his bolt-action .303, was missing the buck. I was rooted to the spot, transfixed by the spectacle of the buck bearing down on us – wondering who, as sure as God made little green apples, was going to get creamed. Tod turned and brought him down with barely a few metres to spare.

It was horrible to see just how hard a magnificent animal like that could go down from such a blow – at one moment a picture of perfect grace, power and courage, at the next, a quivering, lifeless heap of blood and gore on the ground.

It was the last time I went on one of those 'sporting' hunts.

School Days

Canberra
1950s

With 4th Class (Junior School in those days being broken up into six Classes and Senior School five Years) at the Queanbeyan Public School almost out of the way and with the long Christmas break in prospect before having to face up to the fearful (or so we thought) Earl Tankey's 5th, my father announced that Dennis and I were to start at Canberra Grammar the next year, 1954 – Dennis in 2nd Year and me in 5th Class.

As far as he was concerned, we were to have only feelings of joy about joining the privileged ranks of those whose fathers could afford to send them to the one and only private school in sight. Never mind the emerging clarity of my position in the various pecking orders at QPS or that the QPS girls were just coming into focus. The boys-only Grammar School it was going to be. In truth, we were pretty agnostic about the whole thing and any kind of change was going to be, in any case, an adventure.

o O o

Despite the huge events and changes that were afoot, we kids were, in the 1950s, oblivious to anything outside sleepy country-town Australia. The world stage was being set for a roiling evolution out of a few centuries of white Western imperialism and belief in its racial and religious superiority. In the context of which, the German experience through the Hitler years had been but one of the more odious.

Against all odds and with the help of a few fumbles by General George C Marshall, then as US Foreign Secretary, Mao Zedong had swept away Chiang Kai-shek's Kuomintang and, at the expense of Korea, the West had tasted Russia's ambition and China's emerging military power. There, General Douglas MacArthur had presided over a brutal phase of America's approach to friendly non-combatants in their first Asian war and, with the help of an exasperated Truman, was about to fade away. Against all odds, it would not be MacArthur, but his former 'clerk', Eisenhower, who would throw his five stars into the US's presidential ring.

The Liberals' Robert Menzies was firmly back in control of Australia's parliament after having to yield to Labour's John Curtin and Ben Chifley during the war years. A part of Labour's success in turning Menzies out of office had been their characterizing of him as 'Pig Iron Bob' for his sanctioning of iron ore sales to pre-war Japan. Menzies had now turned the tables on Labour by implying that it was soft on communism – at a time when Western alarm was growing about the post war posturing of the USSR's Joseph Stalin. Menzies was able to turn up his volume upon the ascendance of Herbert 'Bert' Evatt to the leadership of Labour's parliamentary party because of Evatt's unapologetic leftist profile and the political fuzz surrounding the defections in Canberra of junior Russian Embassy staffers, Vladimir Michayklovich and Evdokia Alexeyevna Petrov.

Australia's affairs overseas were managed by London and, with our humble acquiescence, Britain's careless and secretive atmospheric nuclear testing was on at Maralinga in remote South Australia. It was not at all remote though to the evicted aborigines of the area who had called it home for a long long time – The Pitjantjatjara's ancient Maralinga Tjarutja.

Eisenhower and Stalin had made the British Prime Minister, Anthony

Eden, and the French pay for the folly of their response to Nasser's bold assertion of nationalism in Egypt. Here, in the run up to their military invasion of Suez, Menzies, as a reliably pompous envoy for Eden, had dropped in to Cairo to make a fool of himself with the assured Colonel. In the derogatory British and colonial parlance of the time, Menzies confided to his diary that 'These Gyppos are a dangerous lot of backward adolescents full of self-importance and ignorance'. In other words, they didn't know their place, daring though they had been (with some help from the USA's CIA) in prising themselves out from under the heel of the British. Perhaps Menzies would have been more at home with Britain's buffoonishly decadent puppet, King Farouk. The one who Nasser had so rightly deposed.

Attlee's Britain had hastily handed a partitioned India back to India on the one hand and Pakistan on the other in a fashion which, led by every blue-blood's darling, Earl Louis Mountbatten, had brought about an epic bloodbath of Muslim, Hindu and Sikh.

Good old Britain was as well turning viciously on Kenya's hapless Kikuyu in a fashion which may have eclipsed all but the worst excesses of the Germans and the Japanese in the recently concluded world war. The French and the Belgians had been as bad in Algeria and the Congo, and pre-apartheid white South Africa was doing some on-the-spot checking and taking of notes.

British lies about their behavior in Kenya were not at all new and they were not at all on their own in this respect among the other colonial powers who shared their lordly distaste of the damned heathen or, in reality, anyone who didn't look like a white European Christian. An attitude which was not that inconsistent with what Le Carre would later describe, though in another context, as being no more than 'Saint George's children going forth to save the empire'.

The Australian economy was still mostly about wheat and wool and our immigration policies were unapologetically and securely racist – as were most white Australians. Very little was known about the plight of our ancient indigenous peoples and most white Aussies could not have cared less. They had few rights and were mostly vilified as dirty, ungrateful, fringe-dwelling 'Abos'. What was left of them, that is.

Christian America's utterly relentless annihilation of its Indian peoples was glorified week after week to cheering school kids at the Saturday matinee movies about cowboys and Indians.

God Save the Queen was the national dirge and Menzies led the gushing adoration of the royal family and all that Britain stood for. While this wasn't so hard to understand in the glow of their extraordinary stand against the Germans under Churchill's most extraordinary period of leadership, it paled considerably as more of the real story about Britain's brutal colonial history became known. Boy, had they shown the other Europeans how.

The big names in horse racing were Redcraze, Rising Fast, Todman and Tulloch. In an Ashes-centric era, the big cricket names included Cowdrey, Dexter, Truman, Miller, O'Neill, and Davidson with a nod towards rampaging West Indian bowlers like Wesley Hall and batsmen like Frank Worrell. Other cricketing nations were hardly worth a mention. Our world beating swimmers included John and Ilsa Konrads, Dawn Fraser, Murray Rose and John Henriks. Though pressed by Marlene Matthews, Betty Cuthbert was unbeatable in the sprints, as was Shirley Strickland in the hurdles, and Hec Hogan was hard to beat in the men's sprints. Britain's Roger Bannister had broken the four minute mile just before John Landy, and Dave Sands (who the extraordinarily gifted Sugar Ray Robinson was ducking) and Jimmy Carruthers were household names in the boxing world.

Performance enhancing drugs were unheard of, with Frank Sinatra's *The Man with the Golden Arm* reminding the lovely Kim Novak and us that recreational drugs were confined to a few really hard cases in the American underworld.

Anyway, little would be known of or could be learned about any of this until long after we had left a school system fixated as it was on the assuredly wondrous and heroic example of Britain the Great.

We did, however, get to see and hear Black Rhythm and Blues get converted into and claimed as White Rock and Roll. In the USA, high quality black artists such as Nat King Cole, The Platters and Little Richard were widely reviled by right-thinking whites.

The Queanbeyan of those days had a population of around seven thousand and was experiencing a lively infusion of new kinds of immigrants. Still exclusively white and European of course, but with many of the new kids in town coming from places we had never heard of, such as Romania and Lithuania, and most having very little English. They just sat in class and picked it up. There was a matter-of-fact acceptance of them and they weren't deliberately excluded from anything. A lot of games could be played without English. The grown-ups of the established Aussie community had little to say about the newcomers, most likely because of what some of them had seen or heard of the plight of others during the desperate war years.

Berzins, Meszes, Grass, Kalnins, Van Keulen and Satrapa all mixed in benignly and productively with Freebody, Ryan, Woodger, Morton, Murphy and Maxwell. The odd Bradley or Ebsworth stirred the pot, but it usually wasn't about new Australians. One of them had in any case got a hiding one balmy evening in the late '50s by an innocuous enough looking Serb while we all looked on from a visiting roller skate rink on the vacant block of land where the Queanbeyan Swimming

Pool is now located. Me holding hands with the gorgeous Frances Gudgeon.

o O o

John Lazdovskis, from the new Latvian community, joined me at Grammar from my class at Queanbeyan. In the interesting immigrant custom of the time, his father had built half a house, which looked exactly as though the other half was waiting somewhere to be stuck on later. It would turn up as earnings permitted. Theirs was a large block just off Urriara Road with a huge chicken run and a few goats for milking. I had not seen a goat before then and it didn't take me long to work out that they knew what to do with their bloody hard little horns.

Although classmates, especially like Elizabeth Hill and Inta Grass, would be missed, Ellie Van Keulen did join us later at the Grammar Schools from our year at QPS. Blonde, smart, and with a winning smile, Ellie was from the small Dutch community of Queanbeyan. Tragically, one evening years later, not that long after Ellie had begun university and quite a few of us had only recently partied at her place, her younger, intellectually impaired, brother killed her at their home with a single shot from a .22 rifle.

o O o

Way back then, Quodling's school buses out to Canberra, with their long floaty gearsticks, challenging gear changes and mostly grumpy drivers, started at about eight o'clock from the old Royal Hotel on the corner of Monaro and Crawford Streets, just a few doors in one direction from the affable John Gray's news agency and a few more in another towards my father's shop. After collecting the Cassidys outside their house a few blocks up Crawford, it was our turn at the end of Erin Street and then on to the Hotel Queanbeyan which was at that time owned by Terry Snow's parents and managed by Brian Koorey's – both also new Grammar boys of about my age.

Winding up along Urriara Road and sweeping over the railway line, which at that point formed the border between NSW and the ACT, and down past the *Harman* Naval Base, the bus rambled along the '50s road to Canberra through patchy avenues of various wattles and gums before weaving away through the grassy paddocks of Fyshwick. Then on up through the poplars of Canberra Avenue near the small bridge over Jerrabomberra Creek and past the fibro and weatherboard settlement of old Narrabundah – which, though established in the 1920s to temporarily house the early builders of Canberra, is still there.

To the west, open grassy paddocks rolled away, interrupted by very few signs of habitation, towards the distant Brindabella Mountains.

The first drop off was at Saint Eddie's College at the gateway to one of Canberra's original suburbs, Griffith, and the second was at our little timber bus shed opposite the old Kingston Power House on Wentworth Avenue. Here, the Grammar boys mingled with the Grammar and Saint Clare's girls or, perhaps more so, eyed each other off, for ten minutes or so until we connected with the Canberra buses to our schools. It wasn't that simple with the Grammar girls, as they made the shed theirs, whereas the Saint Clare's girls, every bit as appealing, hung around outside with us.

o O o

In 1954, Grammar's collection of two-storied red brick buildings was out on its own at the bottom of Red Hill where Flinders Way ended and Mugga Way began its journey northwards. Open grassy paddocks swept lazily away to Mount Mugga Mugga on the southern side. To us, the buildings were other-worldly and there were just enough of them to form what I was told was The Quadrangle or, once you got the hang of it, The Quad – then the focal area of activity outside the classrooms. Toss in a quaint timber-shingled bell tower, a big brass bell and a cloister or two and we were about as close to the Old Country as any good old Protestant parent dearly wanted us to be.

The dusty driveway up to the front of the school from the just as dusty Monaro Crescent, which skirted what was then a swamp, followed the same course as the spruced-up driveway of today, flanked by the same pines, but in those days looping on past the front of the school around the top of the oval and onto Flinders Way. The oval too was flanked on the Flinders Way side by the pines that are still so grimly hanging on there today.

The quaint little pine chapel and Fred Fage's Farm-Mechanics shed behind it, both somewhat removed from the main buildings over near the roughly formed open-air stage on the western side of the school, helped connect the aloofness of the ivied main buildings to what then lay immediately in the wide brown beyond – country Australia and the bush.

Getting into religion in the chapel – more especially learning how to belt out the hymns – and, on the odd clear summer's day lazing through a lesson or two under the gums near the open-air stage caught on quickly.

The tuck-shop was in a small brick building out the back of the main classroom block and alongside the Headmaster's house – which was in the style of a modest English manor. It was a treat, for about two shillings or twenty cents, to be able to occasionally order a brown paper bag lunch from the cheery volunteer mums who ran it. The dining hall, replete with a good sized stage at one end, full length drapes and all, was grand, though only available for use by the boarders other than for speech and play nights and the odd assembly when it was raining.

Rugby beckoned and, at age 11, I was soon to find myself in the 4 stone or 5 stone 7's – I can't remember which. Queanbeyan had offered none of this kind of extra-curricular stuff and I was hooked.

Winter mornings in the Canberra of those days, nestled east-west between Mt Ainslie and Red Hill and running south-north from Narrabundah to Ainslie, could be bitingly cold with thick frost encrusting everything in the early morning and often remaining in the patches of shade cast over the edge of the Grammar oval by the driveway pines until midday. Waiting for the early morning school bus in Queanbeyan, the hills around were often so deeply frost encrusted that they might as well have been covered with snow.

Most classrooms had open brick fireplaces which were all in use at the time. All classrooms were fitted with more efficient iron pot-bellied stoves by the winter of 1956 and this remained the only form of classroom heating through to 1960 when I finished at Grammar. The trick was to be neither too close to nor too far from them. The close-ups had their jumpers off and shirt sleeves rolled up while those on the outside, especially in the early morning, kept everything on, including at least one glove (for the non-writing hand).

The boarding dormitories were neither heated nor insulated, but that was normal at the time and it didn't bother anyone, even though one of the housemasters insisted that the windows should be left open at night. We were young and hardy and whenever it was necessary a warmer jumper or a wind jacket would do the trick. Blessedly, hot water was always available for the boarders in the dormitory shower block. Showers of any kind were not available for dayboys until 1959 when the you-beaut gymnasium was completed.

Winter was an especially hard time for being caned. The Director of Studies and Deputy Head-Master, John Tyrrell, and one of the maths teachers, Ron Morrow, were the preferred dispensers. Neither Tyrrell, who only caned on the backside, nor Morrow, who used a deliberately ineffective broad and flat blackboard ruler, again only on the backside, put a great deal of heart into it. For those connoisseurs among the onlooking mates of his victims, Morrow's ruler provided bonus entertainment by way of the gusts of fine chalk dust which his initial whacks liberated from the ruler. Both Tyrrell and Morrow were well liked and thus inflicted less pain in this way than by their admonishments.

But some others allowed their anger to get the better of them, using whippy knotted canes on the hands when there was no time to warm them first, and with sufficient force for the bruising to last for days. Though of little consolation, a modicum of honor did attach to taking it with as little flinch as possible. This kind of punishment could be dispensed for just about anything, however minor, so that few boys missed their share. Some were quite entertaining about it, dancing around and causing enough misses to stir more annoyance and lead to more 'cuts' as they were known.

Once, when I was in first year (1956), Ted Knox – Knoxy – an accomplished pianist who had branched out of Music into Business Principles, sent me off for what he and I expected to be a caning by Tyrrell for having referred casually to him, Tyrrell, in class by the name every boy spoke of him – fondly: Jack. I failed to see the point and fortunately, following a heartfelt explanation, neither did Jack. Out of all the opportunities I gave the caners, it was the only reprieve I ever had. I suppose it was to Knoxy's credit that he was averse to doing any of the caning himself.

o O o

On one of Canberra's crystal clear winter's days we were all let out of class onto the oval to see the fly-over of a British Royal Airforce Vulcan bomber. With its full delta wings, it made an impressively low pass right over the school. Like most Australians, we knew little of its role in ferrying out British materials for their infamous surface testing of nuclear bombs at Maralinga in South Australia. Little wonder that the Brits didn't have much to say, initially, about subsequent French surface testing out in the Pacific. These tests were, of course, about as far away as you could get from both Britain and France.

Many years later, when I was Australia's High Commissioner to Sri Lanka and the Maldives, I visited what was by then the defunct British airbase on the southernmost island of the Maldives, Gan, at which these secret Vulcan flights had refueled en route to Australia. In the early 1990s, the old airstrip had been converted by Australian aid into a modern domestic facility for this glorious archipelago of islands way out in the middle of the deep upper Indian Ocean.

o O o

There wasn't much physical bullying at Grammar, although there were the odd standouts. Big Billy Hawke, a class or two ahead of me, was one of them, but he calmed down after a while – most likely helped along by his sporting pursuits. Billy was one of those who, along the way, came off second best in having a go at my tougher, if less likely looking, brother Dennis out the back near the tuck shop.

I managed to avoid a straight-out fight until I was in 6th class when I had had enough of Max 'Red' Hall's cheek. Red haired, freckle-faced and a stirrer. I didn't know what he was on about, but with a little egging on by Dennis, we set to at the bus stop down on Flinders Way one afternoon.

I had pretty well bluffed my way out of trouble up to this point, so it was new territory for me and I didn't really know what to do until he gave me a good whack in the ear and the years of play fighting with Dennis took on a new relevance. He was gone but, lacking viciousness, I wasn't sure how to finish it when a big 5th Year prefect with the impressive name of 'Jesse' James appeared and broke it up. Typical of the outcome of these kind of scraps was that, afterwards, Red and I didn't dislike each other anywhere near as much.

I got through the rest of my years there with only a few minor scrapes – other than in my final year when a classmate who I had long admired for both his academic and sporting prowess spat the dummy when I stole the ball off him while he was in full flow with one of his stylish lay-ups during the usual lunchtime muck around basketball game in the gym. I instinctively came up through his flailing charge with a lucky one which finished it. My feelings were, though, probably more hurt than his bloody nose and I left the gym unhappy with myself and shaking off those idiots who were trying to congratulate me.

o O o

We were joined in 6th class, 1955, by Paul Murphy – who was to have a significant career with the ABC and SBS. Paul had a beautiful singing voice which was memorably deployed that year in Ron Morris's school play production of A A Milne's *Toad of Toad Hall* – otherwise known as *The Wind in the Willows.*

Paul played Mr Rat and delivered a crystalline rendition of

'Somewhere over the Rainbow'. Judy Garland's version wasn't in the hunt, but his soprano must have been on its last prepubescent legs. How Ron managed to inject this particular song into that particular play is still a mystery to me, but it worked. The ebullient and cheeky character of Richard Ferris-Guy worked brilliantly in the lead role of Mr Toad. Chris Hayden, as Mole, had such an awful case of stage fright on the first night that he was barely into his first few lines when he exited left with a faint 'oh sir' as Morris caught him just before he hit the deck. Tony Hunter read Chris's part that night, but Chris bounced back for the other performances.

My opening night Mr Badger elicited a chuckle in the *Canberra Times* for having been so obviously laughing his head off in a lounge chair behind a newspaper when he was supposed to be tut-tutting over Toad's crashing of a make-believe racing car while under his stern care. The stoats and the weasels put much more into their stoush on the opening night than was called for in the script or noticed by the audience – with a nice little backstage spill-over featuring an aggrieved Charlie Cooper. The show was taken to Queanbeyan for a night or two of sellouts in the old town hall down on Rutledge Street – which had been the scene of my eisteddfod triumphs when I wasn't much more than a baby.

We had a wonderful time rehearsing and playing, and we saw only the best of Ron Morris. I too had an agreeable taste of boarding when I would sometimes overnight in one of the dormitories after rehearsals and have a go at the boarders' cold-set porridge the next morning.

o O o

At an assembly one morning in 1954 we were told that Lindsay Pearce, a few years ahead of us, had been killed by an unexploded mortar round which he had picked up while playing around with his friend, Terry Birmingham, on the RMC firing range out behind Mt Ainslie. Terry survived with, as we saw a few days later, nothing more than a small gash across the bridge of his nose.

o O o

So on to High School where my sporting interests flourished and my academic performance faltered. I found it hard to deal with what had become the unrelenting negativity of my father's attitude towards me and my increasingly important homework. Nothing was good enough for him even though I had been more than holding my own in the classroom and with the teachers. The prospect of submitting everything to him for scrutiny and criticism, and his daring of me to disagree with him filled me, increasingly, with gloom. I became defensive about my home study to the point of either not doing it or doing only as much as I could sneak in without his interference. Which, oddly, seemed to suit him.

I even gave up writing letters to my childhood mate, Phil Wade, and one or two pen pals overseas, as he would insist on critiquing my letters and requiring rewrites before giving me the few pence needed to post them. He even insisted on seeing their replies.

Slipping grades passed with little comment from him or the school. The concept of counseling was unknown at Grammar in those days. Everyone was treated as if they were equally happy and safe and as if grades were only an outcome of whether you were by nature a good or a naughty or a lazy boy. At school, my transition from a standout in the first of these categories occurred more or less seamlessly. Not that I didn't enjoy some aspects of the second.

But even had counseling been available, I would certainly not have risked my father's reaction to my having either sought it or responded to it. It had been bad enough when in First Year (today's 7th) I had arranged with Knoxy to get me started with piano lessons in the lunch breaks. I would figure out how to break this to my father in due course, possibly having to drop some subject or other to accommodate it. The problem being that piano for a boy tended to be regarded then as being a bit sissy. But just as I was getting the hang of it, Knoxy rang my father out of the blue to tell him that I was going so well off my own bat that it would be a really good idea if he could arrange for me to practice somewhere after school.

The sky fell in.

Goodbye Chopin.

Marbles anyone?

Bugger!

Back then, unless you had been blown to smithereens by a bolt from the blue or torn into gory shreds by a marauding pack of feral dogs, the school did not initiate contact of any kind with parents. As some of them were nonetheless occasionally seen wandering around the school, individual initiatives must have been tolerated. But my father was not one of them.

When, years and years later, my brother admonished him for similar disinterest in my appointment as Australia's High Commissioner to Sri Lanka, he said he thought that congratulations would be more in order when I had been appointed as an Ambassador. There was nothing to be gained from pointing out to him that High Commissioner was in fact the title applying, for boring legal reasons, to Ambassadors to Her Good Majesty's British Commonwealth Countries.

Anyway, I became disconsolate about my schooling and I came

Dennis and the copybook rugby tackle.

to envy the borders and their lives away from home. In a way it was fortunate for me that back then academic achievement was measured solely by one intensive run of examinations at the end of the year. 'Fortunate', because I was a good swatter. Which is to say that although my teachers were unimpressed with my lack of attention to homework or 'prep' throughout the year, as well as with the emergence of a bit of smart-arse stuff in the class and elsewhere, I was usually able to get through the defining exams with a few highly intensive days and nights of hitting the books.

o O o

1st Year (Year 7) in 1956 meant our own home room and a different teacher for every subject. Sweetly demure Miss Ayreton, normally at the Girls' Grammar but filling in for someone down the road at our place, got us twelve year old prospective pubescents into our compulsory novel, C S Forrester's *The Ship*, from which we took turns, in the classroom, reading out passages.

This was going along more or less the same as any ho-hum class reading until we got to what for us was a pretty erotic part, though this was not universally recognized until the reader stopped abruptly in mid-sentence.

Had 'breast' really been mentioned? In front of a woman?

A hush fell over the now wholly attentive class. All eyes were on Miss Ayreton.

Had her lips parted and, if so, what did this mean?

Would we read on? Hope beckoned, however feebly.

Bless her heart, she blushed, thoughtfully but firmly closing her copy of the book. Which was the signal for us to do the same, however reluctantly.

Next day she explained, with the best air of indifference she could muster, that, terribly sorry, we had been given Third Year's (Year 9) book by mistake. So would we please hand in all of the copies. Now. Thank you.

By then we had of course had enough time for a few re-reads and some thoughtful discussion.

Who knows what the name of the replacement novel was.

o O o

My early high school years at Grammar included being in some awe of the achievements of what became the (Leaving) Class of '57 – my brother's. This year swept all before them – swimming, rugby, tennis, athletics, cricket and leadership. The inter-school competitions in those days were between all the local schools – Grammar, High, Telopea, Saint Edmunds and Queanbeyan.

That's all there was. Canberra was a small place. No Woden, no Tuggeranong and no Belconnen. Well, they were there of course, but not populated, other than by the odd farmer or two and lots of cows and sheep.

Saint Patrick's in Goulburn did, however, come into the mix fairly early on and in our senior years we had annual rugby challenges against the 'Cordies' of the Royal Military College at Duntroon and the naval officer cadets at HMAS *Creswell* in Jervis Bay – all Navy bases on land being registered as ships. Saint Pat's, well stocked as it was with some pretty robust borders from country towns and farms all over the State, usually gave us the hardest time. Along with Saint Eddie's, these two Catholic schools had the best rugby coaches.

Anyway, of that Year of 1957, Wally 'Rollo' Hasluck dominated the swimming pool. In rugby, Tony May was an accomplished outside center with a good step and an equally good turn of speed. Arthur Roberts, school captain, was a flying winger, Dick Pickburn the other, and the formidably sized Phil Nadin was somewhere in the forwards. (When we were old enough to play the Old Boys, Phil brought along his equally formidable older brother, John). Tony Hewitt was a standout breakaway and fullback John Cooper knew how to hit the line.

From this rugby crucible, my brother, Dennis, who scored two tries in the First XV's win over Sydney's Newington in 1957, went on to a stellar rugby career for Queanbeyan in the ACT competition.

In the sprints, I remember that the Roger Bannisterish upright style of Arthur Roberts was unbeatable and that Tony May excelled at the middle distances. Peter Firth was the champion miler at that time.

It was a very cohesive year in which the boys, as a group, were great role models for those coming behind them.

But they weren't a bunch of good old boys by any means. They had their moments and their close scrapes. One involved the invasion of one of the two Year of '57 classes by the other when a strong body of invaders on one side of one of the classroom doors met spirited resistance from an equally strong body of repellers on the other.

Back and forth they surged until, without warning, the door, complete with its frame, succumbed – tearing away from the wall and crashing to the floor. Instantly united in their quest to avoid retribution from above, the whole structure was wedged back in place just in time for them to be at their desks before the arrival of the master for the next lesson – the flashy Ted Knox.

Given to theatric entries, Knoxy bounded up the stairs, grasped the handle and flung the door open, upon which the whole precarious ensemble thunderously resumed its position on the floor.

Knoxy stood transfixed in the opening. The boys rushed to his aid, sharing his amazement with such a shoddy piece of craftsmanship and pumping up the impression he had made. What a guy.

All other doors and frames in the block were duly checked for their soundness.

o O o

A problem for the Queanbeyanites in their enjoyment of the school's sporting regime or, for that matter, any other extracurricular activity after school hours, was that if you missed the 3.45pm school bus just below the school on Flinders Way, you had to walk to Kingston to get the 4.20 or 5.00pm buses home – invariably having to stomach a hassle from the drivers (except for Bill Green, who was always good to us) for using your school pass on a non-school bus.

As neither option worked when fuller sports training didn't finish until 4.30pm, hitch-hiking became the only option. If you were lucky, you got picked up on Canberra Avenue between Manuka and St Eddie's. But this was so rare that I sometimes cut through suburban Griffith and Narrabundah to come out on the more prospective stretch between Eddie's and Fyshwick, where the construction of Canberra's first light industrial area was getting underway. Quite a bit further away, but only a bother when it was raining.

I had a particularly awkward time of it once when, at rugby practice, nuggety Phil Parry accidentally came down hard, sprigs and all, on the top of my left foot. Sister Sorby rang my father, but he couldn't get away to pick me up. With my foot ballooning and throbbing, I hobbled off for my hitch into the crisp Canberra night wearing an old oversized slipper that the good Sister had rustled up for me. How I envied those boys who could walk or ride their bikes home, or who had someone who was willing to pick them up. After his own cursory poking and prodding, my father did not entertain the idea of seeing a doctor. Muscle-up son. The foot did mend – eventually – but it still doesn't like a cold day.

o O o

Geoff 'Brod' Broderick arrived on the scene in about my second year of High School – 1957. His parents had broken up and he lived with his mother who, as far as we could tell, was very supportive of him.

Of unremarkable build and shortish like me, he was probably the most gifted athlete the school had seen up to that time. He was an all-round fast-bowling, handy-batting, cricketer, a natural sprinter on foot and in the pool, a champion diver (matched only by Phil Parry) and hockey player, a courageous rugby fullback and, in gymnastics, with the potential to reach the top. His interest in gymnastics was inspired by the first generation of Grammar gymnasts, notably Jeff 'Bandy' Carpenter and the muscular Ted Usher, who were a few years ahead of us.

In those days, before the gymnasium was built, the school's gym equipment, which was pretty well confined to a rickety timber vaulting horse, a set of parallel bars, a high bar and a trampoline, was taken out of the old sports shed and set up on the oval whenever it was required. There weren't quite enough mats to help soften the landings – which once cost the fearless Brod a broken arm.

Our sports master, Vern Davies, knew something about gymnastics and later went to the Rome Olympics as a judge (but maybe this was for swimming or diving). Brod was a godsend for Vern and together they took the school to new heights. There were other talented gymnasts of course and they notably included John Boddington, Peter Cochran and 'Ernie' Munro, who I especially remember trying his heart out on the rings. It was Brod though who made the Iron Crosses look easy.

Brod's star quality and carefree style made him popular with everyone – students of all ages and teachers alike. Or so we thought. But half way through our final year, 1960, he was suddenly expelled by the new Headmaster, Paul McKeown.

We were all stunned. Although he had taken his studies pretty lightly, we felt that with the right support at school, which some of the teachers were providing, Brod could become a fine achiever. With his air of easy bravado undiminished, Brod told us that he had come to McKeown's attention on his way home from school with his tie undone and smoking

Canberra Grammar School 1960.
Howard, left end of second row. Front row: R. Sowell, John Tyrell, Paul McKeown, Roy Morrow.

a cigarette. Big deal. As neither McKeown nor anyone else told us anything to the contrary, we concluded that one-off Brod had simply been an obstacle to McKeown's cloning aspirations.

Unless of course he had been hanging out with the School's idea of the wrong kind of women. And, unlike the rest of us, not only in his dreams.

Geez Brod!

It was not until a long, long time later that I discovered while living in Brisbane that life had not, in fact, worked out that well for our schoolboy star.

o O o

It was upon the departure of the much loved Canon David Garnsey after the 1958 academic year that McKeown, a not so old boy of the school, was appointed Headmaster. He still held an athletics record or two at Grammar and brought new energy and new management skills to the school. Skills which ultimately laid very strong foundations for the Grammar of today. But he also brought an uncommonly harsh demeanor. Old school discipline and a hectoring style replaced the supportive Garnsey legacy. Morning assemblies invariably amounted to tedious harangues.

In the second year of his incumbency, 1960, the end of May to be precise, the Masters of the two senior boarding houses asked, in the evening assemblies just before dinner on a Sunday night, that the smokers put their hands up. The Head wanted to deal with this issue, they said, and would like to speak with these sinners the following day. Man-to-man. Names were taken. My mother had died very shortly before this and I had just arrived for my first night of boarding. Of course I had smoked. Who hadn't? But I still had enough of my wits about me to smell a rat.

Sure enough, the next morning, McKeown, a big and well-proportioned man, so exuding as he was of his own self-importance, dispensed with the pow-wow stuff and let his cane do the talking. A brief lecture and six of the best for each boy in the long closely supervised queue.

What a guy.

Most of us – those who were duped and those who weren't – were simply angered. Few were intimidated. No one stopped smoking. For many, to continue doing so became a badge of honor and, for most, McKeown assumed in their esteem the lowly position he had so earned. Perhaps, combined with his energy and the diversity of skills which he reputedly brought to education, and which he reputedly continued to grow over the course of his long career at the school, this early bit of fooling with the minds of his students helped shape, more positively, his remaining twenty five years at Grammar.

o O o

1958 saw an athletic performance which stunned me and everyone else who saw it.

Chris Hayden, a 3rd Year (today's 9th) colleague – studious, lean, unassuming, with no top finishes, but capable of setting his jaw – put his name down for the Open 440 (quarter mile) in the inter-house sports. What on earth was he thinking? He would be up against the 5th Year (Year 11 and the final high school year in that era) mob among which Dave Gillett was the accomplished performer at this challenging distance. Bigger, stronger and with a great record.

Canberra Grammar School, 1960 – First XV Rugby Team. Howard, front row, first from the left.

Canberra Grammar School, 1960 – First Basketball Team. Howard, front row, first from the left

1958 – Howard with Brian Koorey at Kings Point near Ulladulla, NSW

*1960 Canberra Grammar School –
Ray Mildren, Howard, Tony Prance and John Lazdovskis*

But Chris hadn't let on to anyone that he had a plan. He would start with a sprint and let the rest look after itself.

OK, so he was a mile in front at the half way mark, but who wouldn't have been? He was going to die.

Sure enough, he was struggling by the 300 and seriously wobbling at the 400 with Dave reeling him in on the short home straight. Rigor mortis got him over the line in a retching heap. Champion Dave breasted the line beautifully, but had not caught him.

It was an epic win.

o O o

At McKeown's behest, a marathon run of about fifteen kilometres was introduced in 1959. Everyone in the final two years of high school, 4th and 5th, would have to do it. It was, in his mind, the kind of challenge that maketh the man – ready, able or not. For the less able or physically endowed, it was just another source of annoyance or humiliation.

Able I was, but also feeling rebellious about the style of McKeown's exhortations. I nevertheless felt I had betrayed myself more than a bit by not taking it seriously the first time round, having wandered in with a bunch of rebels and smokers near the tail end of the field with our 'protest' attracting not the slightest bit of attention from anyone at all.

I resolved to do better in my final year, 1960, and on this occasion I was within sight of the few front-runners about half a kilometre from the finish when both my knees cramped painfully enough to put me down. I should have had a second bowl of cornflakes for breakfast. Our champion miler, Ernie Munro, and someone else passed me before I could get going again, hobbling on to a finish still near enough to the top handful.

Completely out of the blue, lean and lanky Terry Snow who, though ballsy, had never before featured in any of the school's athletics programs, put on a remarkable performance to win it. He was starting to show colours which were to bloom prodigiously over the coming years.

Apart from the self-esteem thing, my prize for this finish was to have to forgo the opening game of the rugby season for an interschool cross-country run. I did alright, but rugby was my thing and I wasn't going to qualify for more of this nonsense at the expense of it.

o O o

The route of the marathon had been the wholly rural setting which is now a thoroughly built-up Woden Valley. We started out south from the entrance to the school along the as yet unsealed extension of Monaro Crescent, heading towards what is now Canberra's main rubbish dump and along the eastern side of Mt Mugga Mugga. Then, turning west, we wound our way up the steep, deeply rutted dirt road to the saddle on its southern side which is now part of the link road between today's Isaacs and the Monaro highway out near Hume. At the top, we would grab our carefully allotted glucose tablet or two from the one teacher who was out there to deal with our travails. A sip or two of water would have been handy.

Some distraction from what was happening with the legs and the lungs was afforded by the bucolic vista of grazing properties – Bill DeSalis's 'Weston' and others – rolling away down to the Murrumbidgee and its languid course along the foot of the hazy blue Brindabellas.

Maybe Bill's lovely raven-haired daughter, Adrienne, who I had danced with at one of the rare and closely supervised get-togethers between the boys and the girls Grammar Schools, was down their somewhere too.

Not that this was helping my rhythm.

Anyway, on we would go along what seemed to be the only road in the valley – narrow, winding, rutted and dusty. An Aussie icon.

Here appeared, as we struggled on, the occasional farmhouse and shearing shed. There, bemused, the odd farm animal or kangaroo. Mount Taylor dominating on the left, Black Mountain off in the distant north and, eventually, the Federal Golf Course on the right.

On and on, still ever on, rounding the northern end of Red Hill. Legs leaden, grinding it out along the newly formed Stonehaven Crescent of leafy Deakin. Girls Grammar and Anne, Ingrid, Judy, Pam and others in blurry imaginings off to the left beyond what might as well have been some Great Wall.

Would it have helped my hallucinating passage into the final stretch along leafy Mugga Way had I known that soon enough one of them would be disclosing to me the joy of pert, made-for-life, 32B's?

o O o

Our year didn't get up to as many antics as some of the teaching staff may have imagined. But there were some.

Such as in 1960 on a night trip back from a hard game of rugby in the middle of winter at St Michael's Agricultural College at Inverolachy, somewhere out the back of Lake George, when the usual suspects thought they could get away with lighting up at the back of the bus. Of course we had got a window partially ajar for the subtle egress of our smoke. But not subtly enough for our coach, Mr Shaw, who appeared, egregiously, among us from what we had thought was his distant enough perch at the front of the bus.

Given the incident of the mass caning and Geoff Broderick's recent expulsion, we braced for what we were likely to get when we got back.

But it didn't happen. Shaw was one of the Housemasters who had, in good faith, lined the boys up to have their chat with the Head back in May. He took us aside, gave us a verbal boot-in-the-bum and sent us packing. He was one of the few who, after that, we occasional criminals felt we could go to if we needed some help or advice. Over his years at the school, he put a lot of energy and ability into rugby, camping and hiking, and the establishing of an army-cadet-style 'Group X'.

He even had a go at getting a boxing group underway until McKeown found out about it. Oh no, not at Grammar, not boxing! Which was a pity, as it looked as though it was going to give some self-professed tough guys, such as Billy Cheung, a chance to put up.

o O o

1960 produced the infamous incident of the paddle pop sticks. Yes, paddle pop sticks. At a full school assembly. In the gymnasium.

The gym was still so new and so little money had been left over that it had simple straw bundles attached under the high metal roof for noise and heat reduction. The change rooms and showers underneath had been a great boon for us after sport and the lockers became receptacles for desperately unwashed gear such as the infamous jockstrap.

Anyway, the morning assemblies had moved from the quadrangle to the gym. The teachers would assemble on the stage and the French teacher, Mrs Jessop, a person of considerable ability and charm, would accompany the daily hymn on the piano. How struck I used to be by the silliness of the words of some of them, such as in *Onward Christian Soldiers*, but how we loved belting them out to the stirring tunes.

Some of us high adventurers had discovered that the strategic weaving of a few paddle pop sticks through the piano wires behind the keyboard produced a most satisfying and surprisingly on-key honkey-tonk effect. How could we share this gratifying artistic discovery with the school community and how could we achieve the greatest effect?

Easily!

On that fateful morning, Mrs Jessop got herself and her flowing black academic gown just right at the piano stool and set off, pedals-a-pumping, with her usual upright élan. She had played more than we expected before she, the teaching staff up there on the stage with her, and the whole student assembly twigged.

Hands frozen in mid strike above the convulsing keyboard, disbelieving for but a moment, she stood up sharply, knocking the stool over with a crash. Flushed and breathing heavily, eyes flashing, she hitched her gown over her hips, swept the hair off her fevered brow and completely went for it.

Our very own Jerry Lee Lewis in drag. Honky-tonk rock personified.

The teaching staff rose as one and, with a beaming and hooting McKeown in the lead, conga-lined off down the stage stairs, around and up the centre aisle through the wildly applauding student body. Man, it was more than just wild – it was far out.

Anyway, back on planet earth where her hands were frozen in mid strike you could have heard a pin drop. Then – pandemonium as a sustained wave of laughter from the assembly washed over everything. Most of the teachers were trying to swallow grins and we were about to resume breathing when Mrs Jessop, at first bemused, quietly stood up, adjusted everything, left the piano stool standing and staged a stiffly dignified walk-out.

No more hymns today.

The assembly was over and the perpetrators were invited by the completely unappreciative, po-faced, Head (not, unfortunately, back from his conga-line) to own up after the assembly dispersed.

Most oddly, we thought, we were referred to John Tyrrell and good old Jack wasn't too hard on us – even though, sorry, it *hadn't* been him we had imagined leading the conga-line.

It had been a reasonably deserving prank – if only Mrs Jessop hadn't been so upset by it. A deputation apologized to her and she graciously, with a hint of recovered humor, though not quite of the expansive Jerry Lee Lewis kind, pardoned us.

o O o

Apart from nearly rolling my father's two-toned blue Holden FC station wagon on the old level Scott's Crossing of the Molonglo River on my final day of school – with who else but Ray Mildren, the son of Australia's reigning Grand Prix champion, sitting alongside me – my life at Grammar tailed off with few bells and whistles and devoid of conscious goals or, for that matter, much enduring camaraderie.

School was out and I could not have been more completely clueless.

Just another kid heading off down the road.

Maybe with a wistful notion of me and some kind of *Moon River* in my head, but with nothing to get on board and with not even a hint of some inviting bend in sight.

A Life in Australia's Foreign Service

The untold want, by life and land ne'er granted,
Now voyager sail thou forth to seek and find.
–Walt Whitman

Starting Out

I joined the Department of External Affairs through the back door in about April 1961.

The front one was reserved, rightly, for university graduates. Even had I chosen that route, at not even 18 I neither had a degree nor had set myself on a path to obtain one. In fact I hadn't set myself on any kind of path other than, vaguely, to find some clear sky following the uncertainties brought about by my mother's sudden death and a realization that there wasn't much going on in the form of family support.

o O o

Such was the confidence of his hold over me that my father had arranged my first job without bothering to first discuss it with me. It was to be with a friend of his, Ken Hardwicke, who ran a small accountancy business around the corner from my father's shop in Garema Place in Canberra's Civic Centre. Also at his behest, though with the kindly Ken's encouragement, I would study accountancy at the Canberra Technical College. What else could the youngest son of a businessman want to do?

Well, what I really wanted was to get away from him. Which became all the more pressing when, upon leaving Grammar, I had moved in with him at his new house in Campbell over near the Australian War Memorial. A house which he had bought as the bridal home for his new wife – who was but six or seven years older than me.

When she went back to her mother in Sydney soon after, I again found myself home alone with him, having to endure another round of his epic self-pity. Me, with my anguish over my mother's death still pretty fresh, comforting him over her bloody successor!

It wasn't long before I packed my very spare possessions in a little bag and left for Sydney to look for work there and to stay with my brother in a tight little boarding house half way down Coogee Bay Road where we shared a room with one other guy. The three beds filled the room, but we managed. The landlady was an elderly and motherly kind of soul who fed us well. In addition to hearty hot breakfasts and dinners, she packed us wholesome lunches.

I had made the break and I found work soon enough in the office of a car parts manufacturer, Duly and Hansford. They were, however, at Marrickville which was a bit of a hike from Coogee. Having first enrolled at Ultimo Technical College in the City and then at St George to continue my accountancy studies, this meant that on College nights I didn't get back to the boarding house, via trains and buses, until close to midnight. College assignments were done at weekends on the floor of our crowded room. Which did not really bother me that much. At least I didn't have my father badgering me with his censure and his self-pity.

Anyway, I moved with my static little bundle of possessions to a boarding house in Marrickville. Close enough to walk to work, but with not enough in my pocket after paying the board – which included one modest bowl of cereal for breakfast, carefully doled out by the po-faced landlady, and a pretty lean dinner – to do anything else except maybe splurge on the odd mushy, however Aussie iconic, meat pie.

After a while, finding that I didn't even have enough change to buy toothpaste and toothbrush, and thus having to resort to pinching some salt from the spare breakfast table for use with the odd burred green twig off a nearby gum tree, something had to give. It dawned on me that the only way any youngster with zero resources and backup could survive on seven pounds twelve and sixpence ($15.25) a week, with five guineas ($11) of it coming out for the miserable bloody boarding house, was if they were still at home with mum and dad.

Dennis's own money problems had obliged him to leave his promising Woolworth's management cadetship for the better pay of being a builder's laborer. But when he was sprung by the Builders Laborers Federation for not being a member and not having an avenue available for becoming one, he picked up traps and returned to Queanbeyan.

OK, I was on my own again with hardly a penny to bless myself with but I wasn't the only one in that boat. Better speak to the boss or start looking for another job. But the boss was more than a bit stony-faced about it and better paying jobs for unqualified young men like me were not exactly abounding.

One thing led to another and my father, perhaps having been rebuffed by Dennis who, upon his return to Queanbeyan had moved straight in with our grandmother in her old fibro house up on a lower slope of Mt Jerrabomberra in Queanbeyan's McIntosh Street, suggested, in the plaintive way which he could muster when it suited him, that I should come back, stay with him and help him out with the business.

Oh god. Surely there was another way out.

But there wasn't.

So, stuck as hard as I was in Marrickville, I would have to give his plan a go. If only, I hoped, once I got there I could find somewhere to stay other than with him. But as far as I knew boarding houses in Canberra would not be any more affordable than in Sydney, and offers from the wider family around Canberra to take me in were not exactly thick on the ground.

Heavy of heart, but emptier of stomach and with the condition of my paltry wardrobe more noticeably diminishing, I yielded.

I took a train back to Canberra with the ten shillings and sixpence ($1.05) which he wired me for the exact fare and with not enough in my pocket for much other than the bus to the railway station. He was too busy to pick me up, so, hefting my suitcase onto my shoulder (well, I wouldn't say it was that heavy), I got off the train at Queanbeyan, just short of Canberra, and walked down the mile or so to his store in the main street.

Too proud to tell him how hungry I was, I waited until we went back, hours later, to his empty bridal home out in Canberra to see if he had anything in the cupboard.

I started with him in his business the next day. Me, still seventeen, with all of the clumsy uncertainties of early manhood, selling women's clothing.

Perfect.

Bras madam? Why of course. Let me give you a hand.

Soon enough, I found myself with very little of interest or substance to do in the business and very little space to myself at 'home' which came to accommodate his new, distractingly vivacious, girlfriend who wanted to know more about my love life, still mostly imagined, than I was prepared to let on. But soon enough too, this resolved itself with her entirely predictable return to Sydney and his sudden declaration that he was going to sell the business and go to England for, well, who knows son, a year?

Would I therefore please find myself somewhere else to live.

Gladly.

Anyway, by this time, I had already left his world of high women's fashion for what else other than Canberra's dominant industry, the Commonwealth Public Service. For a stay which I figured, however vaguely, would be long enough for me to get a bit of a grip. And maybe, because the starting pay was so much better, to get a new pair of trousers. I was in fact even able to buy a fake horn-toggled navy-blue duffel coat complete with brown quilted lining, which not only kept me warmer than I had ever been through Canberra's nippy winters, but survived to come in very handy later in the '60s during the more challenging winters of craggy Korea.

As I was also already back at the Canberra Technical College, continuing with the bloody accountancy, I moved into a government hostel within walking distance of the College. Despite the disruptions, I was holding my own with the law and theory units, but could just not warm to the thrill of double-entry financial accounting.

Narellan House was one of the less permanent, weather-boarded, government hostels (now long gone). Typical of the time, it was a rambling one-level, three winged, fairly neat affair strung around a central unsealed car park and a do-it-yourself laundry. A narrow corridor down the middle of each wing had rooms on each side which wouldn't have been more than five square metres apiece. No sound-proofing in the walls or insulation in the ceiling and thin linoleum on the board floors. But fitted at least with a little washbasin and running cold water in the corner over near the window and plenty of hot water in the shower block. Canberra's frosty winters were relieved only by the bring-your-own electric bar heater. Mine was a single bar, but it was enough and it could toast a slice or two of bread for a late night snack.

Narellan wasn't too bad really. What it had to offer at that time was in fact the norm for many young people setting out in the public service in Canberra. I had my own space, I was getting three squares a day for a weekly rental that didn't break me and no one was bugging me. I even managed to fit in a little table for my college assignments.

It also provided some privacy for the odd assignation, however much these were barely in prospect at that time and however much they might have had to be a bit quieter than the boisterous bench marks being set by the much envied older guy in the room next to mine.

Kiap or Diplomat?

In 1961, joining the Public service had been as simple as going to the Public Service Board on leafy Kings Avenue on the site where Harry Seidler's besiloed monument – originally to the hallowed agricultural beginnings of the Department of Trade – now resides, breasting up to the counter and filling out a simple application form.

The sole lady at the counter asked me which Department I wanted to work in. I had absolutely no idea, but the sort of meaningful look she was giving me indicated that I should. Two sprang to mind because of the places where I knew the fathers of school mates worked, so I said External Affairs or Air. Her face brightened. She made one phone call and then told me that I had an appointment the very next morning to see the Finance Officer, Bob Johns, at the Department of External Affairs.

Which happened to be just across the road from the Board in the Administrative Building – so named because it was big enough, and government was then small enough, for it to accommodate many of its Agencies. The building had, in fact, only been completed in the late 1950s after its huge defective initial foundation blocks had lain extracted and strewn forlornly around the site for years. With plenty of room to spare, External Affairs barely occupied just one of its four wings.

Kindly red-headed Bob, an accountant, was not only taken with the fact that I was doing accountancy at the Tech but, so it seemed, that, like him, I was an Anglican in what he saw, good naturedly enough, as External's bastion of Catholics. The public service in Canberra was like that in those days and for a few decades beyond. I didn't let on that some of my best mates were Micks and that I was in any case already pretty well tipped towards atheism.

Anyway, Bob said that he was keen to have me, but that I first had to see someone else, one John Stone, who was then the Department's sole security officer and receptionist. John explained to me that there were some forms to complete and some checking to be done by the police and others (ASIO? What was that? Charles Spry? Charles who?) before I could start at External. In the meantime, I would be placed somewhere else in the Public Service. OK, I thought, how long could such a simple thing take for such an abidingly ho-hum local boy?

Well, time soon started to drag, especially given the monumentally boring job I was given in the filing section at the Department of Works over behind the Public Service Board in what was known as the Riverside Buildings. 'Riverside' because they were located on a bluff above a languid stretch of the Molonglo River, just south of what became the western approach to the Kings Avenue Bridge. It wasn't long before this job and my boss, a Mr Weiss, started to grate and I started looking around for something else.

And so it was that I ran into Tony 'Sam' Voutas, who had finished Grammar a year ahead of me. Sam was in town on a stint of leave from his cadetship as a Patrol Officer in Papua New Guinea. Over a coffee or two at his father's popular café in Manuka, we talked about how it was going for him up there. I was intrigued. Sam colored in for me some of what I already knew about PNG through Colin Simpson's *Plumes and Arrows* which my brother had brought home a few years earlier, and my follow-up reading of the tales of Ion L Idriess and one of the great pioneers of patrol life up there, J K McCarthy.

Soon after my encounter with Sam, during a lunch break from Works,

I walked across the road to the Department of External Territories, then also located in the Riverside Buildings complex, and applied for a Patrol Officer cadetship. My timing was impeccable as the process for recruitment of the next intake of cadets was just getting underway. They worked pretty quickly with these things in those days and it can't have been more than a month or so before, still in that great job at Works, I was summoned over to be told the good news. I was elated.

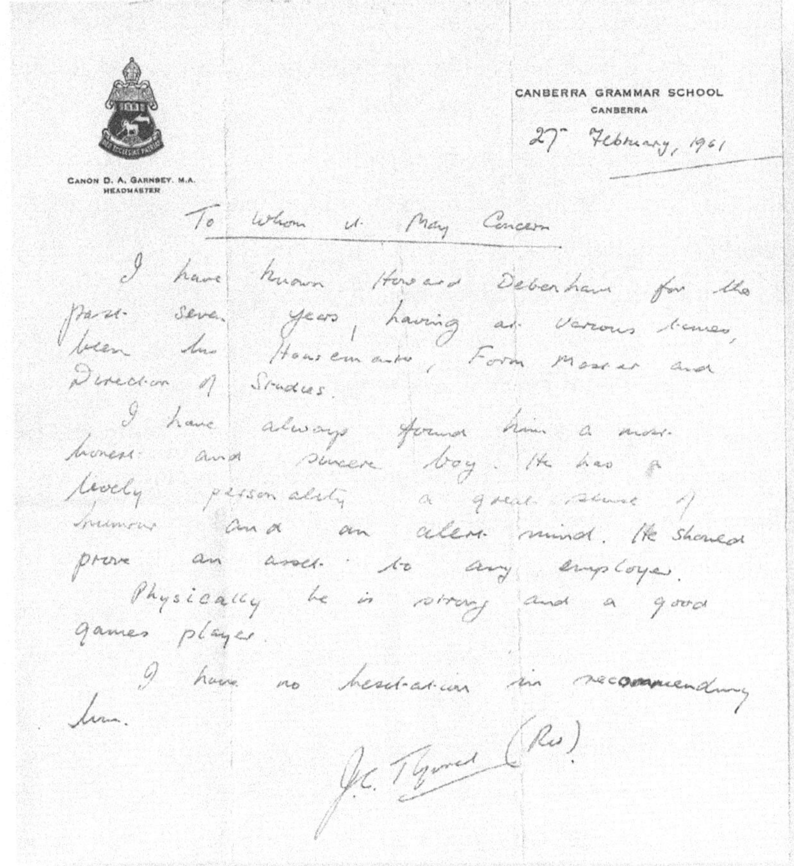

CANBERRA GRAMMAR SCHOOL
CANBERRA

27th February, 1961

CANON D. A. GARNSEY, M.A.
HEADMASTER

To Whom it May Concern

I have known Howard Debenham for the past seven years, having at various times been his Housemaster, Form Master and Director of Studies.

I have always found him a most honest and sincere boy. He has a lively personality, a great sense of humour and an alert mind. He should prove an asset to any employer.

Physically he is strong and a good games player.

I have no hesitation in recommending him.

J.C. Tyrrel (Rev)

My very first character reference. By the Reverend John Tyrrel – in support of my candidacy for the positon of Cadet Patrol Officer, Papua New Guinea.

Suddenly, and still not 18, I was on a course to pull out of dreary Canberra for exotic Port Moresby, via the School of Pacific Administration in Sydney, on a package which, I was assured, would feed me, clothe me and provide me with as much adventure as any young buck could handle.

You beauty! And I wouldn't need to bother about Duffel coats any more.

All at once, my security clearance for External Affairs came through and they wanted me over there straight away. To me, the choice was a no-brainer. I was off on the big adventure! I was needed up there and I was going. Wild horses couldn't stop me. I could already see myself out there on the frontier, trudging through a wilderness of rainforests and gorges, setting up camp in remote villages, interacting with wildly colorful, resourceful, if sometimes dangerous, people and generally doing really really good things. Being alive! Being challenged!

But with it all about to be deflated.

A few level heads weighed in with their damned view that I should definitely *not* go to PNG. That External was by far the more sensible choice. Their cruncher being that more than enough noise was being made in the United Nations, most notably by the Russians, for the withdrawal of Australia's mandate in Papua New Guinea and, thus, careers for Australians in colonial type administration. That was news to me. Nothing of the sort had been alluded to by the recruiters at the Department of Territories.

I wasn't convinced. Not by a long shot.

(The influencers – most notably Tom Eckersley, a former senior Australian diplomat with the kind of demeanor and understated knowledge which even a crass teenager could warm to – played a key part in this process. But my relationship with the Eckersleys, which had given me a take on how warm some Anglo families could be, is another story.)

OK then, what will you have achieved, they posed, if the plug gets pulled on Australia's mandate after five or even ten years? Who will want an Australian colonial administrator, a 'Kiap', semi-skilled in bringing someone's idea of white-man's (the ones with the guns and the money) order to tribal cultures which had survived the ages?

Well, I supposed, what about the value of getting out of the hometown rut now, getting into the Great Unknown now, getting into high adventure, slog and sweat, even danger? Taking a chance. Roughing it more than a bit. Having to make do out in the bush. Getting to understand and learning to help remote communities. The Sepik, the Kuka Kuka, plumes and arrows, full on outward bound, however abbreviated!

Not to mention, after a long trek in from the bush, breasting the bar in Moresby for a beer before ducking out to have the odd arrow head removed from sundry parts of my anatomy.

The making of the man! Surely all that would count for something?

Why even bloody Paul McKeown would be parading my virtue to all those mightily impressed little buggers back at Grammar.

Yes, but when it's over, as over it will be, you will have to start all over again instead of being otherwise well on your way with a real career in the Foreign Service and the possibility of lots of adventure, however different to that of a Kiap in deepest darkest. And not of course forgetting the travel.

Travel?

Yes.

Really? How much?

Lots. That's what they do.

Where?

Everywhere.

Oh.

For how long?

A couple of years at a time.

Oh.

And so it was that I turned up at that back door.

Three years later I was in fabulous India.

The Road to Sariska
India 1965

The narrow, patchy, road out in the parched and timeless wilds of Rajasthan, a long way from Delhi, had been deserted when I bounded out of my car to help the bike rider I had knocked down. But now, crouched over the bloodied and unconscious man, I found myself looking up into the sullen faces of dirt-poor Rajasthanis who had materialized in their swirls of ragged clothing with a smouldering resentment of the ages in their eyes.

o O o

I had arrived in New Delhi on my first Foreign Service posting in January 1965. I was twenty one and, at a time when the world was so far from Australia and overseas travel was still such a hugely expensive novelty, beyond the reach of most, I was excited to be in a country of such kaleidoscopic diversity. Those of my Foreign Service colleagues who craved postings in the modern cities of the Western World could have them. I would have preferred Timbuktoo to that.

India's first Prime Minister following the collapse of the British Raj, Jawahalal Nehru, had only recently died and been succeeded by the diminutive Lal Bahadur Shastri. Shastri's brief tenure would soon end, however, with his sudden death in Tashkent, capital city of the USSR's Uzbekistan, following an historic meeting with President Ayub Khan of Pakistan about ongoing tensions between India and Pakistan. A meeting

Passport number D-3744, issued on 20 January 1965.

which had been mediated by the USSR's Prime Minister, Alexi Kosygin.

From the front gate of our High Commission office, or Chancery, which was in a large house we rented from the Nawab of Pataudi on Sardar Patel Road, just below The Ridge – on which British forces had been almost wiped out during the so-called Sepoy mutiny against British rule in 1857 – I watched Shastri's casket being brought back into the city from Palam Airport. He was quickly succeeded by Nehru's daughter, the deceptively demure Indira Gandhi, who Kumaraswami Kamaraj and the other powerbrokers of the mighty Congress Party expected would do their bidding until they sorted out who their real leader should be.

Tall and lean, balding and gracious, Sir James Plimsoll, known by his friends as Jim Plim and much admired by the Indians, was our High Commissioner. But he soon exchanged places with the Secretary of the Department of External Affairs, Sir Arthur Tange, after Sir Paul Hasluck (with whom Tange did not have the best of relationships) became Minister for External Affairs. Although he came to be just as admired by the Indians, Tange was cut from a different cloth to Plimsoll, with most of the staff of the High Commission regarding him with awe or fear or both. But he took a paternal kind of interest in me and I was thus able to see the better side of him.

o O o

Cars of any sort of reliable quality had to be imported into India and this took time. In the meantime, with the help of new friends, I was able to see some of the sights in and around New Delhi. Something of what I was in for started penetrating and my impatience to be able to range freely and further afield was growing fast. Everything about the place – good or bad, beautiful or ugly – tugged at my senses.

o O o

As in China, civilizations of immense grandeur and cultural diversity had been flourishing across this land while the comparatively primitive Europeans were sorting out their boundaries and their ethnic mixes and setting out tentatively in their puny little ships for the feared horizon.

Directly descended from Genghis Khan and Tamerlaine the Great, the Mughals (Persian for Mongols) had conquered a vast swathe of the sub-continent in the early part of the 16th century, creating there an Empire of contiguous princely states and achieving astounding power and wealth, cultural and artistic vibrancy and, remarkably, religious harmony. After an extraordinary run of enlightened and talented leaders, their dynasty began waning in the middle of the 18th century when the less well-endowed, though cunning and powerful British were already around and ready to make their move – masquerading as Robert Clive's British East India Company.

But what did this this matter to a callow young Australian who had only ever been told that all things great and wondrous, just about anywhere, had been brought about by the British? What else was the term British Raj supposed to conjure up? Well, the bleedingly obvious fact for anyone who cared to have even a cursory look around over there was that the Brits had had nothing at all to do with Delhi's Red Fort and the Jamma Masjid (except to have a good go at destroying them), Jaipur's Pink Palace or Agra's Taj Mahal. And that these were but a small sampling of Mughal greatness which was either in or within day-tripping distance of Delhi.

No, something outside of your average Aussie's consciousness had definitely been going on here and I for one was not going to miss it or misunderstand it. The British Raj? Sure. Well done chaps. But I'm sorry, it seems to me that this is by no means the whole story.

Delhi itself was fascinatingly kaleidoscopic. A hugely sprawling and rowdy mess where great misery and great wealth lived and went about its business cheek by jowl. But a mess in which surprises and reminders of the soaring pre-Mughal and Mughal past abounded. Often breathtakingly so. The acclaimed Scottish historian, William Dalrymple, describes Delhi, in part, in these terms (p8 *The Last Mughal,* Bloomsbury Publishing Plc):

> … of the great cities of the world, only Rome, Istanbul and Cairo can even begin to rival Delhi for the sheer volume and density of historic remains. Crumbling tomb towers, old mosques or ancient colleges intrude in the most unlikely places, appearing suddenly on roundabouts or in municipal gardens, diverting the road network and obscuring the fairways of the golf course. New Delhi is not new at all; instead it is a groaning necropolis, with enough ruins to keep any historian busy through several incarnations.

And:

> For miles in every direction, half collapsed and overgrown, robbed and reoccupied, neglected by all, lay the remains of six hundred years of trans-Indian Imperium – the wrecked vestiges of a period when Delhi had been the greatest city between Constantinople and Canton.

o O o

Four hours or so by road to the north of Delhi, tucked into the foothills of the mighty Himalaya, was the old town of Dehra Dun where the so called 'White Mughals', the British, had at different times fought pitched battles with Ghurka and Sikh and had come to so admire the courage and tenacity of both that, in time, they co-opted them to spearhead what they were given to calling, in their imperious way, the 'native' forces of the Raj.

Further into the Himalaya lay the fabled Vale of Kashmir and in yet another direction the ancient Grand Trunk Road so well-trodden by the Kim of Rudyard Kipling's flawed fancy. Tales of every Britisher's notion of their heroic Raj, such as those concerning Robert Clive or recounted by Francis Younghusband and John Masters abounded.

Tiger, leopard, bear, the outrageously raucous and colorful peacock, monkeys of many kinds, including the impressively fanged Langur, deer ranging from the large and languid Sambar to herds of skittish Cheetal or Spotted Deer, and the powerful Nilgae antelope, abounded. All could be encountered along the road, but in greater and more convenient concentrations in the nominally protected game reserves.

o O o

Anyway, early on in my posting, I had heard about a wildlife sanctuary at a place called Sariska, about two hundred kilometres from Delhi into neighboring Rajasthan. Though at increasing risk from poachers, tigers were, so it seemed, still there in reasonable numbers. Basic forest accommodation in the form of what the British had provided for the convenience of their travelling officials all over India – dubbed 'Rest Houses' – was available as well as tours guided by the resident game warden. With luck, tigers could be seen from a stone tower in a nearby ravine – lured to the site at night by a pathetically frightened calf, bleating for its mother, which would be tied to a stake for the tiger's convenience and the gory entertainment of visitors.

Not long after finally taking delivery of my car from Canada and driving it up to Delhi along Kim's Grand Trunk Road from Bombay, I set out for Sariska early one morning with two Australian companions from the High Commission – Margaret and Anna.

At about the halfway mark we were well out into the countryside, which at that time of the year was at its parched and barren best waiting for the monsoonal rains to usher in a flurry of planting. Prone to flooding, the hand-built road was raised a metre or so above the fields and the only trees to be seen were the scraggily knarled and well-spaced ones alongside the road.

There was nothing else in sight when, through the usual pungently rising haze, a bike rider began taking shape several hundred metres ahead in a long, lazy, left-hand curve of the road. In a country where everyone and everything uses the roads – from walkers and bike riders to elephants, horse carts and the huge 'Tata' trucks driven mostly by Sikh highway warriors – I already knew something about the virtue of driving defensively.

At about one hundred metres, I could see that although he was traveling in the same direction as us, the bike rider was doing it on the other side of the road. Never mind – it was his road. I slowed down, and even more when I noticed that he had the wobbles. Who knew why? He was dressed in the swirls of the well-worn greyed cotton shirt and dhoti (sarong) of the dirt poor and he may have had a rare good night. That was his business. Mine was to get us past him safely.

I had slowed to maybe twenty kilometres an hour and was almost abreast of him when my horn blowing suddenly registered. Maybe I should have tried to ease by without making a noise, but that wasn't the system. If you had a horn you blew it at everything.

Suddenly, he wrenched the bike over, glanced off the right side of my front fender alongside the headlight and jackknifed into the laminated windscreen with sufficient force to cave in a small patch just in front of me. He tumbled forward over the hood and onto the road in front of the car and we came to rest a bare metre or two apart. He wasn't moving.

Horror stories about the outcomes of these kinds of incidents were a part of everyone's initiation into India and they were running through my head. But I couldn't help obeying my natural instinct to jump out of the car to help him.

At a glance, the immediate countryside was in any case deserted. Margaret and Anna were right behind me. While I was greatly relieved to find that he was breathing, I was horrified by the deep abrasions on his arms and legs and even more by what appeared to be blood in his mouth. Margie thought this might be betel juice and, sure enough, the wad was spilling a little from his open mouth. Out in the Indian countryside in 1965 there was no way to call for help and no question of waiting for anything resembling an ambulance.

My mind was on getting him into the car and to the nearest town for help when I looked up into those smouldering eyes. About a dozen pairs of them. In any other situation, I would have been impressed by the ghostly materialization of our company. But now my stomach started melting.

Some hesitated because they could see that we were trying to help, but others were picking up rocks from the side of the road. Right or Wrong was not the issue. It was Rich versus Poor. The bike rider was stirring, but we were going to cop it.

Suddenly, there arose a blood-curdling wail from the parched field to our left and everyone looked around. A man, clad only in a dhoti, was running wildly from the field brandishing a large rock over his head. Everyone was momentarily transfixed, but I managed, under my breath, to urge Margaret and Anna to move back to the car. The crowd paid no attention to them as they did so. All eyes were on the poor wild man and the rich sahib and I could not risk taking my eyes of him.

As he arrived I could see he was in such a rage that his eyes were actually starting out of his head. Funny, I thought, that this wasn't just a figure of speech after all. Anyway, he propped near me and hurled the rock at my head with as much force as his wiry body could muster and, twisting away, I took it high on my left shoulder. It turned out to be mostly clod and exploded fairly harmlessly.

Margaret and Anna had made it into the car and I now wasted no time making a dash for it. Everyone else leapt into action, but I had a few seconds on them and in the confusion of the wild-man's performance they had not thought to grab me.

I had left the keys in the ignition and the car started immediately. As I nudged forward to find a way through what was now a swirl of angry people and dust, thinking that I might have to actually bump some of them out of the way, I wondered why Anna, in the seat next to me, was slowly raising a rug up in front of her.

The first rock, a pretty big one, hit the windscreen right in front of her and, despite the lamination, did so with such force that it broke through and slid down the blanket to the floor. My god Anna! Well done!

The bike rider was back on his feet and out of the way, but as I moved away, hand pumping the horn, another rock broke through the rear window and more bounced off other parts of the car. Everything seemed to be happening in slow motion.

Down a long shimmering stretch of the road we went. Mute. Stunned.

Off in the middle distance was a bullock cart carrying a huge load of grass with the usual family of six or seven on top. Comforting in a way, wallowing along as it was in the timeless fashion of many an ancient vehicle on such a typical piece of rural Indian road. Slowing, I eased a little onto the shoulder to give it room. But as we came abreast, those on top of the load rose as one and rained rocks down on the car. Seeing the commotion from however afar had been enough – the rich had to cop more.

Down the road we went again. More mutely, more stunned, soon sweeping down into an area of rocky outcrops and ravines. A huge noise, like a dozen steam trains coming down an unseen track grew closer and closer, but we could see nothing. Around a particularly craggy outcrop we went and on our right an ancient steam-operated rock crusher suddenly appeared in a ragged quarry – in full grunt. Which was a relief – until a dog suddenly ran under the car. It had to be dead and there was in any case no way that we were going to stop.

o O o

India being India, meaning that you had to live with the way things were rather than the way you wanted them to be, we decided against looking for the nearest police station. We didn't want to risk being found there by an angry mob and we didn't want the police charging around the countryside bent on punishing the pitifully poor. We thought it more prudent to keep going to Sariska and lie low there until it was safe to go back along the same road to New Delhi in my battered car. We knew there was nothing we could do now to help the injured man.

Rattled as we were, Sariska lived up to its reputation. The humble

Rest House deep in the forest, the cold bucket baths, the richly flavored curries, the hawk-eyed game warden with his impressively bristling moustaches, and the three tigers that came around on our night of roughing it in the stone tower on the side of the ravine, got our heads sorted and our feet back on the ground. The journey back to New Delhi a few days later was without incident.

Naturally, it all had to be reported to the Indian Foreign Ministry. Which, about six months later, calmly advised the High Commission that an investigation had not found any trace of or anyone out there connected with the incident.

o O o

Ten years later, I was on my second posting to New Delhi, this time married and with our two young boys, when the Sariska incident was brought vividly back to life.

We had been returning home from a day trip to historic Meerut and were slowly threading our way through a throng of people attending some public celebration behind the old Ashoka Hotel in Chanakyapuri, when a small child ran out from between two parked buses at full pelt and bounced off the front of our virtually stationary car onto the road. He jumped up straight away and seemed unhurt, but was sobbing.

The bystanders surged, the angry eyes were flashing and my stomach was fizzing again as I got out of the car. What else could I do? Suddenly the child's mother materialized, scooped him up, gave him a bit of a whack on the backside and disappeared with him in her arms.

The crowd heaved a sigh and melted away. As did we.

Saigon
Vietnam 1967

The good sense of my Thai International 707's steep slip-sliding approach into Saigon's Tan Son Nhut airport – a maelstrom of joint civilian and military use – became suddenly apparent as on its short final approach we swept down over a ravaged moonscape of rocket and bomb craters. Ground skirmishes, I thought. Intense, but surely not intended for incoming commercial aircraft.

Having completed my Delhi posting, I was on my way back to Australia for some briefing and a little R & R before taking up my new two years assignment. And for a pretty clueless 23 year old it was shaping up to be a cracker. Why, I might even be there for the victory parades. A few days in Saigon en route would seal the deal. There were a few personal issues which had to be sorted out along the way, but I was not overly concerned about them.

It was April 1967.

o O o

I was pumped about having been assigned to our embassy in Saigon where I would be close to what was clearly a just war against those vicious commies up North – backed as they were by every right-thinking person's bogey-men, the Russians. I was as wilfully ignorant as so many others then about what was really going on in Vietnam. Whatever the Americans were saying at this time was broadly sucked in through the rosy prism of their defining role against Hitler's madness and their stance against what was seen as the new threat, post WWII, of communist USSR and its excesses in consolidating and exporting its power – including, that is, in Vietnam. That the American led West was doing exactly the same kind of thing was not on anyone's radar in the West – or at least not enough to be noticed.

It was a time during which the West had successfully downplayed the extraordinary significance of the USSR's crushing defeat of Herr Generalfieldmarschall Paulus's Sixth Army at Stalingrad and the ensuing destruction of Germany's floundering resistance in its bitter retreat all the way to Berlin. A destruction which had paved the way for a small – in comparison to the appalling scale of what had been done to the Russians during the German advance – payment in kind for the cowering citizens of East Germany. And, of far greater significance, a destruction which had virtually assured success for the advancing Western allies.

It was also at a time when, following the humiliation of French colonial forces at Dien Bien Phu and the flight of the French from Vietnam, few in the West knew or cared about the political agreement which had been struck in Geneva in 1954 to help pave the way for country-wide elections in Vietnam in 1956 – known as the Geneva Accords – and Eisenhower's zealously covert determination to undermine them.

Surely – or so it seemed at this time of huge military build-up against the North in 1967 – the South Vietnamese could trust us. We were there to save them. We, the Aussies, were on the side of Right and Might. The Right that was being so deftly prosecuted by that man's-man, Lyndon Baines Johnson – our very own Prime Minister's number one pin-up boy. 'All the way with LBJ' was the catch-cry so wittily coined by the toothily beaming Harold Holt. All this and still with the darkly unbalanced Nixon and his deeply fawning National Security Advisor, Kissinger, yet to come.

In 1967, the hype and the irresistibility of the American war machine was such that Hollywood's amply willing propagandists were just as surely girding their hawkish loins to cast for the defining post-war epic. Jimmy Stewart as Johnson and John Wayne as General 'Westy' Westmoreland – or vice versa. Peter Sellers as Dr Henry A Strangelove *and* Barry Goldwater. An Englishman, yes, but great with accents – including of Kissinger's deeply guttural kind. If he could be found, Fu Manchu would do Uncle Ho Chi Minh, but the high cheek-boned and skinny enough Frank Sinatra might also be able to pull this one off – with bonus renditions of *Strangers In The Night* and *I Did It My Hue*. A shadowy and bloated Marlon Brando would somehow do the durable arch villain, General Vo Nguyen Giap (about the equivalent of Jabba the Hutt doing Fred Astaire). Grace Kelly or, if some décolletage was needed, Marilyn Monroe, along with Bing Crosby and Bob Hope would swing in with a rendition of *The Road To Danang*. And some kind of 'I love the smell of napalm in the morning' scene would be ghetto-blasted in with Wagner's *Ride of the Valkyires* (a sentimental favorite of Adolph Hitler). That emerging excitement machine, Francis Ford Coppola, would work it all out and, given his abundantly worldly persona, a worthy title could no doubt be built around some catchy word like, well, how about *Apocalyse!* Whose apocalypse would not become clear until later on.

Anyway, few had yet paid much attention to cautionary works of authors like Bernard Fall who Noam Chomsky, among others, would come to regard as being 'the most respected analyst and commentator on the Vietnam War' – thus naturally attracting for both of them the close attention of J Edgar Hoover and his virtuous G-Men.

In the West, dissidence had been growing, but most of the more visible kind was at that time about the cost of the war. The cost, that is, in terms of budget and the lives of Americans and those who they led, not in terms of whether the cause was just. The shootings by the Ohio National Guard at Kent State University were still three years away.

At the time of my arrival, Daniel Ellsberg – a complete unknown outside US intelligence circles – was only a few weeks shy of completing his two years assignment at the American Embassy 'evaluating pacification in the field' (www.ellsberg.net) and returning, with some misgivings about the war, to his highly sensitive work at The Rand Corporation in Washington DC which at the time was a major contracted provider to government of intelligence and analysis on the war. There, he would have access to the most highly protected information on just about everything the White House, the Pentagon and others were doing in relation to Vietnam. Ellsberg would, within four years, be driven to leaking the so-called 'Pentagon Papers' and becoming one of the most honoured dissenters in American history. Over four decades later, he would become a vocal supporter of another very significant whistle-blower – Edward Snowden.

But back in 1967, macho Kick-Ass was still the big winner with your average American or Aussie – as long as it wasn't *their* asses that were getting kicked. Dien Bien Phu? Dean Bean who?

Also around Saigon at this time and already making a name for himself was an Australian cine-cameraman and war correspondent by the name of Neil Davis (see his biography by Tim Bowden – *One Crowded Hour*). He was doing what I had, as a keen photographer, merely fantasized about doing. I got to know Neil years later in Bangkok where I was Australia's Consul-General and he was based working for the American television network NBC. Considering the number of front-line scrapes he had been in, he had a most satisfyingly easy air about him but, like me, didn't care that much for small talk. He swore by the durability of Nikon cameras, describing how well his had survived mud, water and the bumps and scrapes of headlong dives under fire – and I haven't bought any other kind since. Dressed however casually for around Bangkok, he would not be seen out of his signature red socks. I fell out of touch with Neil after leaving Bangkok at the end of 1983, but this did not diminish my shock over his senseless death at the hands of trigger happy Thai troops in the streets of Bangkok during a military coup on 9 September 1985.

o O o

My last three or four months in New Delhi had had its moments. I had been conflicted about a warm relationship with Margie, a lively colleague at the High Commission who had returned to Australia a few months before my time was to be up, and an emerging relationship with an appealing Chinese nurse, Agnes, at the American Embassy. But I had also had the first illness of any consequence in my life when I had come down with a bout of heat exhaustion and couldn't seem to shake off its effects. This I found hard to fathom, because I had always managed Delhi's bugs and scorching summers better than most. My limit had apparently been reached through the amount of time that I had spent running around the countryside and on the site of our new Chancery building pushing for its completion. A site where I had never ceased to be fascinated by the little community of low-caste laborers – men and women – who toiled away in all kinds of conditions, often appalling, for a hand-to-mouth living in their squalid little village of juggies (shanties) on site. There was of course plenty of that and much worse around every corner and down every road and alley in the country, which included children who had been deliberately disfigured or wounded for begging appeal.

At the beginning of it, I had been flat on my back for days before it became obvious that Agnes's soft ministrations weren't helping. She rounded up Dr Earle Chawla and he got some serious treatment and rehydration underway. But, weakened as I was, I succumbed to a series of ailments and recurring dysentery which kept me more or less knocked down, if not completely dragged out, for a while. A sustained loss of appetite didn't help. Fortunately, the cool season had begun and I slowly picked up. Also, my posting was coming to an end, which meant that I would be out before the heat started again. Chawla thought that this was fortunate and that I should, furthermore, avoid a hot climate of the Delhi kind for a few years.

OK, I thought, I'll take it on board, but there's no need to break this to anyone dealing with my career path. That is until My High Commissioner, Sir Arthur Tange, asked me to stay for another year. Not being known for gestures of this kind, he was not that chuffed by some hesitation on my part. I had not wanted to raise Chawla's advice but, having done so, Tange's view was that a young bloke like me would get over this sort of thing quickly enough and I was inclined to agree. So was Agnes.

Then Canberra weighed in out of the blue with its decision (there was no discussion about these things in those days) that I was just the right man for a Saigon assignment. Now thanks – on your way mate. Single, dispensable and why not!

This was more appealing to me than marking time in New Delhi. It also offered career brownie points for working in a full-on war zone and a little time in Australia en route to put the health issue to rest and see where I was up to with Margie.

So – Saigon, via Australia, it was.

o O o

After a night of partying and a warm final embrace from Agnes out in the crisp early morning at Palam International Airport, I boarded a British Overseas Airways Corporation flight for Bangkok.

It was the first time for me on BOAC and I couldn't get out of my head the joke which had been hammered into me over the past few days of it having been dubbed 'Bend Over Again Christine' – because of the currency of a scandal in London involving a good-time girl, Britain's Defence Minister and a Defence Attaché at the Russian Embassy in London. The so-called 'Profumo Affair'. Actually, I thought that Christine Keeler's friend and sometime partner in her adventures, Mandy Rice-Davies, was the more appealing of the two.

Feeling tired, hung over and a bit melancholy, I settled in for a quiet leave-me-alone-please flight.

Up, up and away, levelling-off, getting ready for some quiet time and a nap.

'Tea love?' asked the beaming, creamy complexioned hostess.

'No thanks.'

'Oh, but you so look like you need one.'

She had expressive deep blue eyes which brightened with my impression of a submissive grin.

'There you are love – and with some nice warm scones and jam.' She leaning over to shake out the napkin, pat it down nicely onto my lap and arrange things just right on the tray in front of me. Straightening up to admire her handiwork. Awfully, charmingly, English.

'Thanks very much' I said. And what an ample bosom you have inside that prim navy – blue jacket. How comfortable I would be snuggled up in there. Maybe I wasn't feeling that bad after all.

Tea and scones successfully aboard, I settled down for a nap … at last. The lumpy little cushion would have to do.

'More tea and scones love?'

Resigning myself to being fussed over, I opened the blind to see off to the north, now that we were way up above the smog and the dust of the Deccan, the magnificent, the raggedly beckoning, Himalaya.

One day, I thought, one day.

o O o

About mid- afternoon, the Thai International flight on the short haul from Bangkok came to a halt near Tan Son Nhut's little civilian passenger terminal. The stairs were wheeled over and a few officials came on board. At their bidding, everyone put their passports into the little baskets they were handing around before we disembarked and made our way across the sullenly steaming tarmac to the terminal. Odd, I thought.

We squeezed into the packed and chaotic terminal like so many more sardines. Everyone seemed to be yelling – passengers, officials, baggage staff and mothers anxiously herding their children. It took me awhile to make out a few Embassy mates (we all knew each other in those days) making their way toward me. I was a bit concerned about ever seeing my passport again, but they assured me that this was the go and that all we had to do was to keep an ear out for my name above the bedlam when it was called out. I eased over towards a wall and, with my back to it, sank down to the floor on my haunches and nodded off.

Was Earle Chawla already mumbling some admonition in my ear? No, it was John Albietz giving me a bit of a shake. 'We've got your passport mate – all stamped and ready to go. Come on, we're getting out of here.'

Not good, I thought, clambering up. The oppressive heat in that sardine can had hit me like a bomb. But it will pass I thought. It had to.

Off we went. The embassy car was air-conditioned, the conversation was lively and the excitement level bucked me up.

I was going to be put up at John’s place rather than at a hotel, so we went there, freshened up and took off for a few beers with the others. I was more or less OK as long as I was on the move, but when we returned a few hours later I crashed for as long as I could before we set off for dinner.

After being checked through a deeply sandbagged and heavily armed entrance to a US military building of some kind, we went up to the flat rooftop – at about level seven I’d say. Though it was roofed, its open sides afforded panoramic views over busy downtown Saigon. There were no Vietnamese in sight in this strictly ‘round-eyes’ enclave. We ordered thick T-bone steaks from the barbecue and a round of beers as the night closed in and Saigon came alight. By the time the steaks arrived I was starving. I hadn’t felt like eating since the scones of early morning and the transfer of flights in Bangkok. Here they came – on sizzling platters – and I hoed in.

I hadn’t got very far with it when someone said, ‘Check this out Howard – *Puff the Magic Dragon*.’

‘Pardon?’ What did that sweetly wistful folk song of Peter, Paul and Mary’s have to do with any of this?

But he was pointing out beyond what he said was the Saigon River, maybe a kilometer or so away. We went over to the balustrade on that side of the roof. I had never seen anything like this before. Two wickedly long tongues of solid yellow fire were licking hungrily down to the ground in sustained bursts from separate points high in the dark sky. Above the din of the city, I could make out the drone of some sort of lumbering aircraft and the zip-crackle of those tongues of fire. Soon, I could see that the two were connected and that they were obviously tearing out paths of death and destruction on the ground over there. Not in some jungle, but in what seemed to be a closely settled though poor neighborhood.

We went back to our table and steaks, but the 'show' over there went on for a while longer.

Someone else said, 'This is how it works Howard. The VC come out at night and on this night they have been detected getting up to something over there. The Dakotas (they were McDonnell Douglas DC II's) have been brought in – two of them flying in concentric circles – and from their open side doors they are hammering them with their mounted mini-gun tracer.'

'There must be a bloody lot of VC over there' I said, because the fire seemed to be waving around all over the place.

'Yeah, there'd be more than a few, but the trouble is that the VC mix with the civilian population at night, so there's usually a fair bit of collateral damage.'

' "Collateral damage"? – that's a new one on me' I said.

'Yeah, it's when non-combatants get killed because of their proximity to the action. Can't be avoided.'

'You mean innocent civilians?'

'Yes, the poor bastards, and sometimes lots of them. The VC do it deliberately to show how brutal and uncaring the Yanks can be, but no one's fooled' he shrugged.

'Oh', I said. He must be kidding.

I put my knife and fork down and took a long pull on my icy cold Bud. I wasn't hungry anymore.

o O o

We went on to a hostie bar. There were po-faced Vietnamese guards armed with automatic weapons on the door. The girls were pretty but painted up and pushy. The air conditioning was chugging along and the western music was throbbing at volume. Apart from a few alert and tough looking Vietnamese men who didn't seem to be there for fun, the clientele was exclusively foreign, though few were evidently military. Some were already unsteady and a few were openly pawing the women. In a huddle over our beers someone wanted to point out, helpfully, what could go wrong in these bars.

'Such as?' I asked.

'Such as the lobbing in of the odd grenade and such as what the odd clever VC girl can achieve with a sliver of razor blade inside the hollowed centre of a small potato inserted in an entirely unexpected place. Most are 'good' girls though and very sexy, but there's no way of telling who the bad ones are.'

'Oh – you mean until you're shredded?' I asked – with sufficient disbelief to evoke much knowing laughter.

The night was almost as hot as the day and I was folding. I was carrying the sleeping sickness around with me as quietly as possible. But every time I sat down – almost anywhere – I wanted to sleep.

We got out to some military airport early the next morning to hitch a shortish ride on an RAAF Caribou transport – first to Australia's Task Force Base at Nui Dat in Phuc Toy Province and then on for a dip in the surf at Vung Tao. After scrambling up the rear loading ramp, we strapped in on the tin benches along the sides. With no discernable acoustic insulation of any kind we roared and clattered down the runway and were off in what we were told would be a spiraling ascent – to evade small arms ground fire – and an equally spiraling and probably ear-popping rapid descent into our destination. Ear muffs were pointed out and I took a pair, but they didn't make a whole lot of difference.

'Wake up Howard, we're here.'

'Eh, where?'

'Nui Dat mate. Christ you can sleep!'

We scrambled back down the ramp. A squad of soldiers was already examining the fuselage for bullet holes.

After a quick tour of the inner part of the base, we headed off to Vung Tau for a taste of the beach life. It wasn't much and most of the soldiers – Australians and Americans – seemed to be happy just having a break lying around on the beach with the sand between their toes and a beer in hand, rather than bothering with the flat surf and the muddy looking water. Given what they were living through, they probably didn't pay that much attention to the two helicopter gunships doing their continuous crossover runs, at about one hundred feet up and down the shore line, with their flack-jacketed crews at the ready behind mounted machine guns pointed in our direction.

'It's just for show Howard. The VC won't have a go here as long as they are using the other end of the beach for the same purpose. This will be a resort town in a few years' time when all of this is over.'

A few beers and a few sandwiches and we were on our way back to the Caribou and a restful (at least for me) return flight to Saigon.

Emerging from the car back at John's place, we were struck by an invisible remnant of a nearby tear gassing and a goddamned Phantom jet streaked overhead with an appalling roar at what couldn't have been much higher than the rooftops – which was obviously intended to intimidate those mindless enemies of the deadly musical chairs of the country's Catholic leadership and their American masters.

'Inside quick and close the door' he said. 'Keep the gas out.' He explained that this did happen a bit around here, as we were near a significant pagoda to which activist Buddhist monks sometimes marched in protest against their oppression. 'Why', he revealed, 'they sometimes march right down this street and occasionally one will douse himself with gasoline at the pagoda and burn himself to death for the cause.'

Something's going on here that no one is bothering to explain, I thought. Something that I would have to discover for myself. Something that surely has more to do with the kind of belief and desperation which was unknown to us than madness.

There wasn't much time left for me to see beyond what my well-meaning mates assumed would be of most value to me in preparing for my Saigon assignment – namely the reassuring omnipresence and power of Australia's mates, the Americans, and the rampant availability, if risky in more ways than the usual one, of cheap sex.

OK, they are entitled to their assumptions, I thought, and maybe this is what it comes down to in a city like this where the war is by no means confined to a front line out there beyond the suburbs and where on any given day anyone could get unlucky.

Don't they mix with normal Vietnamese? I thought. Don't they have neighbors and business associates? Couldn't I have met some of them? Isn't there any sporting or other kind of social opportunities for interaction? Perhaps they had not had time to work some of this into my few days. Anyway, war or no war, I was sure there must be much more to Saigon and the Vietnamese and that I would find it all out for myself soon enough.

As we drove around from this or that well defended American club or bar or past an array of government offices and the walled villas of the wealthy, I had noticed that life did seem to be going on behind the veneer I had been shown. That regardless of what was being served up to them and how they felt about it, the ordinary people of this city seemed to be getting on with their lives with what was, even from the casual observance of a young foreign passer-by, considerable calm and normalcy. Of course it wasn't that simple, but the air of it being so was impressive, even reassuring.

From the deep phalanxes of motor bikes and scooters that came at you down the broad boulevards, and in the shops and on the sidewalk cafes and eateries along the side streets, the Vietnamese seemed to me to be just like anyone else in getting on with their lives. Better perhaps than some as they seemed to care about their appearance and there seemed to be humour and courtesy in the ways they interacted with each other. This certainly hadn't been the case in India – so divided as it was by religion, caste, language and culture. Sure, I hadn't even scratched the surface here and was smitten by the grace of the Vietnamese women in their demurely flowing Ao Dais, but it was sufficiently encouraging and inviting. Surely there would be a grand culture to discover – theatre, art, costume and food – even if there would be none of the freewheeling around the countryside that I had become accustomed to over the past few years in India.

o O o

I slept most of the way to Hong Kong and, fabulous city though I knew it was from the few days I had spent there en route to India, I couldn't be bothered doing much on my stopover day. I put it down to the amount of beer I had consumed over the past few days. So what harm could some more sleep do?

Arriving in Canberra a few days later, I checked into the old double-brick Lawley House government hostel over in Barton as winter closed in. I bought another one bar electric radiator and, for my walking to and from my place of work, I unpacked and aired the duffle coat which I had not seen for two years. Like my home of two years ago at Narellan House on the other side of Canberra, my worldly possessions still fitted comfortably into a small room with a cold water washbasin in the corner over near the window.

Despite the cool weather, I promptly relapsed into my sleeping sickness.

The extended sick-days off and a resumption of weight loss landed me in front of a government doctor and brought on the reluctant production of Earle Chawla's diagnosis. Amoebic dysentery was suspected, but eluded firm diagnosis. Further mandatory examinations led to the Saigon assignment being cancelled and an expectation that I would take courses and courses of remedial medicines and vitamin supplements.

Damn – now what?

I didn't want to be stuck in Canberra and my restlessness over this led to a bit of dogged in-your-face partying. Staid Lawley wanted to kick me out, but relented after I ate a bit of humble pie. Where else could I go? I decided that I had better take it easy for a while.

The personal relationships side of my life became even more awkward with the return to Canberra from London of a sweet friend of my youth. So … Ingrid was in Canberra, Margie was in Sydney and Agnes was writing from Delhi.

Until not so long ago, I had been as sure as I thought I could be that Margie was the one. We had been good together. She the smart, with-it extrovert, me less assured but coming along. Marriage had been in serious prospect. But at barely 24 it was dawning on me that I was still too restless to be any good at this. Too restless and as yet altogether too ignorant.

Before long, I was offered an assignment in non-tropical Seoul, where I would arrive in the middle of its serious kind of winter, and I jumped at it.

Destination or Destiny? I would have to wait and see.

Left to right: Howard. Colonel Bill White, Ambassador Alan Loomes, President Park, Chung Hee, Foreign Minister Choi Kyu Ha.

Korea
My Story
Late 1960s

I was thinking I knew what a broken shin felt like when, in 1961, at 17 and as a center in my first year of first grade rugby for Queanbeyan's 'Mighty Whites', I went down from a full-blooded mis-aimed kick from an opponent while I was toeing a ball through against an Illawarra selection at the busy coastal steel town of Port Kembla. But the grasping pain and the rippling bruising subsided, the sock was pulled back up and I rejoined the fray. Although the off-the-ball stuff was much more willing then than it is today, no one had actually tried to kill me and the game rolled on.

Later in the '60s, a long long way from the rough and tumble of fair-go Australian rugby, I was scrambling to get up off a bed of rocky rubble on the side of a country road in Korea thinking I knew what a broken nose felt like. But this time I was at the center of a desperate sort of game that wasn't rolling on and I had a bad feeling that some people *did* want to kill me.

o O o

In the still comparatively fledgling Department of External Affairs, not a great deal of information or support had been available in preparing for a posting to anywhere, let alone to a country which in 1967 was as apparently inconsequential to Australia as South Korea. The bitter

Korean War of the early 1950s had not been forgotten but, in Australia, very little else was known about the place. Historians still liked to refer to it as the Hermit Kingdom, a once isolated tributary state of China and, until recently, a colony of Japan.

The war had reached its stalemate in 1953 without delivering a peace agreement and the combatants had withdrawn to their respective sides of the ceasefire line, the 38th parallel, to lick their appalling wounds and to plot their next moves. President Truman's sacking of the commander of US and UN forces in Korea, the imperious General Douglas McArthur, had faded away, as had they. The ravaged communities of the peninsular were left to pick up the pieces as best they could with little help from those who had fought over them. The Americans had little change to spare for the Koreans from their expensive plans for stabilsing the post Second World War economies and politics of Germany and Japan.

John Kennedy had come and gone and Bobby's run at the presidency still had six months to play out before he was to cross paths with Sirhan Sirhan behind the ballroom of the Ambassador Hotel in Los Angeles. In Vietnam, the Americans, still licking their wounds over the unsatisfactory outcome in Korea, were about to have at least the political stuffing knocked out of them by North Vietnam's massive and completely unexpected Tet Offensive. Daniel Ellsberg, had not yet decided that this war was unjust. And Richard Nixon's tough guy xenophobic persona – so dependent as it was on pitting his country against the commies, and so revved up as it had been by the likes of the Dulles brothers, Alan and John Foster, and his good old buddies Joe McCarthy and J Edgar Hoover – was flourishing as much as Lyndon Johnson's was starting to wobble.

While North Korea, the other part of the Hermit Kingdom, was building an ever stronger cult around its charismatic leader, Kim Il

Sung, the South appeared to be faltering through, in the early post war years, the self-serving and corrupt leadership of Syngman Rhee (as he was known in the West). A strong US led United Nations force was installed on the peninsular eyeballing the North across an agreed no-go demilitarized zone.

The West's frontline bulwark of democracy and capitalism against what was seen as the seamless red monolith of Chinese and Russian communism had moved from Japan to Korea – now the ROK or the Republic of Korea. The South Koreans, having emerged from thirty years of brutal subjugation and exploitation by Japan and now desperately dependent on foreign aid, however meager, were trying to find a way ahead, but it was obvious that Rhee had to go.

In 1960, following a sustained period of civil unrest known as the 19 April Revolution, Rhee, who had been President since 1948, was spirited away to exile in Hawaii – reputedly in a CIA owned DC4 aircraft. The ensuing power struggle was resolved through a bloodless military coup d'état in 1961 which placed Major General Park Chung Hee in power.

Among other issues, the military believed that the North held some attraction for southerners who were tired of what had become Rhee's brutal autocratic ways and who, during the war years, had in many ways been treated better by the forces from the north than by those of the predominantly US led United Nations forces.

This was the South Korea I was sent to in late 1967 at the tender age of 24 in the middle of an icy, snowing and slushy winter. It was exactly what I had wanted. So different, so mysterious, so exciting.

o O o

The Seoul of those days was much smaller than the sprawling metropolis of today, mostly confined as it was to the bowl between the Presidential mansion, known as the Blue House, beneath the craggy ridges on its northern perimeter and Namsan (South Mountain) on, yes, its south.

Further south from Namsan, towards the impressive Han river, fledgling urban development had sprung up to support, primarily, the massive US 8th Army garrison. I remember there being only one bridge over the Han for people and motor vehicles and one for trains. Beyond the river, well out of town, was Kimpo airport, which serviced both military and civilian needs.

After a brief stay in a cozy little cottage in the suburb of Itaewon, where I had shivered through my first night out of the hotel – Christmas Eve – without heating, I made way for our new Deputy Head of Mission, the amiable Rick North, and moved to a dingy semi-detached house in downtown Myongdong behind the popular Jingogae restaurant. It was very convenient to the town Centre and comfortable enough, though the rats were the biggest I had ever seen. In the winter, even with their thick coats on, they didn't mind wandering into the little living room to sit and preen at a discreet distance from the heating system – a pot-bellied wood-fired stove in the middle of the room.

After once catching one in the prescribed little timber cage with a morsel of cheese inside and a spring gate to snap shut behind, I proceeded to try to despatch it by the prescribed method – immersing the whole thing, rat, cage and all in a bucket of water. But the poor little critter squealed so loudly and struggled so bravely that I relented and let it, a bit bedraggled but none the worse for wear, out the back door. The one who wandered in the next night looked pretty familiar if a little less cocky.

I became very fond of the Jingogae food, especially the slim strips of marinated beef called bulgogi which were cooked at the table on little conical, brass barbeques over pre-heated charcoal embers. Complimented principally by the Korean staples of rice and various kinds of heavily spiced and fermented kimchee.

From here, it wasn't far to my place of work at the Embassy down through busy, narrow, Myongdong to the main thoroughfare running from the ancient South Gate, turning off left just before the Blue House and then, on the right, a few hundred metres up a winding unsealed road to the quaint old house which was our Embassy office – the Chancery.

There weren't many of us. Six Australians and about ten Koreans, including drivers and maintenance staff. The Ambassador at the time was professional enough, but far too crabby for a little office in a place which had its challenges. Happily, he was succeeded fairly soon into my posting by a calm and thoughtful kind of soul, Allan Loomes, who was close to retirement. His wife, Nan, was as motherly as he was fatherly. Which suited a youngster like me just fine.

The Embassy had adapted as well as it could to the residential layout, though my 'office' was oddly placed in an anti-room which was open to the inner side of the main lobby and this turned out to be fortuitous. From my vantage point I could see, if I liked, anyone who presented themselves to the receptionist, Miss Noh, in her little alcove on the other side of the lobby just inside the tight entrance to the Chancery.

About mid-morning one crisp sunny day a month or two after my arrival, I could not help noticing the arrival of a striking red-headed, evidently American, woman with an equally striking figure. It was hard not to take more than a few glances, but I needn't have bothered as Ms Noh, having invited her to take a seat, gave me the lady's application for a visa to visit Australia. She was the famous stripper, Gypsy Rose Lee. The very one who had taken stripping to a new, respectable, level of art. In conducting the required interview, no doubt with a pathetically transparent attempt at aplomb, I fell completely under the spell of her unaffected manner, her radiant smile and, especially, her remarkable emerald green eyes. Her performances on base must have sent the GI's crazy.

All such and other encounters were, though, a mere prelude to the appearance in early 1968 of another visitor. Evidently already known to Miss Noh, she had, as it turned out, come to the Embassy to renew contact with Korean staff who had some years earlier helped her obtain travel documents to go to Washington DC to resume her role with the children of a former Australian Representative to the United Nations Commission for the Reunification and Rehabilitation of Korea (thankfully known as UNCURK). She had stayed in the States for five years, returning to Korea from Hawaii to reconnect with her family before taking up an invitation to become a permanent resident of the US.

We saw each other and exchanged smiles. Trim, finely featured and quite a bit more than appealing in her snug mustardy corduroy midi coat, it occurred to Ms Noh to introduce us.

Her first name was Joosik and we soon got to know each other better.

o O o

Ted Evans was an Australian living comfortably enough in Seoul within a network of mostly American civilian suppliers of goods and services to the US's 8th Army – at that time commanded by General Charles H 'Tick' Bonesteel III. How American can a name be! As one indication of the intensity of the militarization of South Korea at the time and the US's domination of this status, Bonesteel, as Commander of United States Forces Korea, was also Commander-in-Chief of all United Nations Forces in Korea.

I later had two close encounters with the good General. The first was when I was among a few embassy people who were waiting for a ride out to a visiting British aircraft carrier on a dark and stormy night in Inchon harbor, when he appeared with his impressive entourage and invited us to join him aboard his amply proportioned Commander's launch. The second was when our Defence Attache, Colonel Bill White, and I were about to return to Seoul by road from a visit to Panmunjom,

'Her first name was Joosik and we soon got to know each other better.'

on the Demilitarised Zone, when Bonesteel invited us to join him in his big helicopter. Halfway back to Seoul, we had the uncomfortable experience of being moved out of the way so that a couple of anxious engineers could get at a flow of lubricant down the main propeller shaft and hearing them telling the pilot to lose altitude.

Anyway, Ted, became a friend and during the summer we occasionally spent weekends at a cottage of his up at Cheongpyeong Lake – a leisurely drive into the beautiful hilly countryside northeast of Seoul. Cheongpyeong itself was then nothing more than a sleepy little village at the end of a dirt track a few kilometres off the Seoul road. It was on the southern shore of the lake behind a dam which had been built in 1943 for the purpose of flood mitigation and the generation of hydro-electricity.

On a sunny early Saturday morning in May 1968, Ted and his mate Bob Stilson in one vehicle, Joosik and I, and a colleague from our Embassy in mine, arrived at the southern shore of the lake. Transferring our stuff into his boat under a bright blue sky, we took off across the clear deep blue of the lake to his cottage which was perched on a steep and well wooded hillside above a sparkling little bay on the northern shore.

Over the weekend, we skiid behind his amply powered boat, picnicked, ambled around and generally got some of the intensity of curfewed Seoul out of our systems. Beyond Sunday afternoon, Ted and Bob were going to stay for a few more days to complete some chores around the place, and so the rest of us set off for Seoul late on Sunday afternoon in my sedately black diplomatic-plated, car. My pride and joy – AMC's Rambler, the successor to the original Nash Rambler.

We had no idea what we were in for.

o O o

The following account of what was to have been a relaxed and familiar drive back to Seoul is drawn from the written explanation which I gave to Ambassador Loomes the day after our return to Seoul. To my relief, he calmly reassured me and did not doubt my account of what had happened. He attached my written version to a formal diplomatic note which he personally delivered to the Korean Foreign Ministry.

It began:

> … Ms Cho and I spent the weekend of 10 and 11 May at the cottage of Mr Ted Evans at Cheongpyeong Lake. We left Cheongpyeong at about 6.00 pm on the evening of the 11th and had been proceeding back to Seoul at a leisurely pace when after about ten miles on the open road we came up to a convoy of eight late model black sedans travelling at about twenty five miles per hour. As the road was winding its way through a hilly section I followed them at their pace until we came to a suitable length of clear road. As all of the cars were close together and did not increase their speed, this could have been achieved quickly and safely …

My fuller account continues:

When I pulled out to pass the rear car it blocked my passage by pulling out alongside the next car and staying there. I managed, eventually, to ease past these two and drew up to the other six which had gone on ahead. They were still travelling very slowly, so when the coast was clear I pulled out to pass them. But the last two cars pulled the same stunt as the first two which now drew up abreast of each other behind me. Boxed in, I could neither speed up nor slow down. I could see in my rear vision mirror that the occupants of the cars were laughing and egging their drivers on. A brief respite provided by cars coming in the other direction allowed me to step on the gas and get past them all. It had been a bit annoying, but the fun for these bloody idiots seemed to be over and we simply wanted to get away from them.

But it was not to be.

One of the cars put on an impressive set of four headlights and, surprisingly, two flashing red lights, and set out after me. It came up fast and alternated between tailgating and trying to pass. I could see that the occupants still thought they were having fun. To my mind, stopping wasn't an option as all the other cars would have arrived quickly and, surrounding us out on the open road, could have done anything they liked to us. So I drove on, careful not to get into a race, but just as careful not to let him pass. I didn't want him to be trying his hand at forcing us off the road and they were being stupid enough for this to be a possibility.

Just when they seemed to be losing interest, we came to a small town, in the middle of which had been some sort of accident which was blocking the road. People were milling around and there was no room for me to pass. I had to stop and the chaser came hard up behind me.

In my rear vision mirror I could see that the driver still thought it was a big joke, so I thought – OK maybe this wont be so bad, but if they do want to try something the focus should be on me – not Joosik. So it would be best, I thought, if I was on my feet out of the car. At least now there were others around to see whatever it was they might want to get up to.

As I emerged from the car, the occupants of the other were laughingly urging their driver to get out. He did and I took a few steps in his direction. There was no use saying anything and I was not about to ask Joosik to come and translate.

Anyway, urged on by his masters and quite rightly thinking he saw a little hesitation on my part, he lunged at me. I grabbed him with both arms and pulled him to me, but he struggled hard to get free. Not, obviously, for the purpose of having a chat.

We waltzed around a little while his people were piling out of the car and egging him on. We had reached the edge of a nearby stone-walled culvert which I didn't want to go over with him – so I let go, took a few steps back and then leaned into his windmilling rush. What else could you do with such an idiot? Anyway, his face collided with a pretty willing left and down he went over the bank as outraged suits, now from all the big black cars, came swarming in.

It's funny how clear the options can become in a crisis and without having a fair-minded set of rules or a referee on hand or a ball to set off after. Especially when you have become the ball. These suits were so obviously of a mind to do me over if I stood to reason with them that I thought … let's see if we can keep it to a fair fight. So over the bank I went to have it out, if that's what he wanted.

A bit hot-headed? Maybe. A good plan? Maybe not. But when instinct takes over who the hell gets a chance to think? And in any case, what else could I do? Run?

Anyway, it was all immediately blown away by the hot arrival of a bunch of brown uniformed guys who flowed over the wall and who turned out to be police from a station which happened to be directly across the road. They grabbed both of us before we could get into it.

So – it looked like everyone would get a chance to cool down, have their say and be on their way. Good. They weren't waving rule books or blowing whistles, but they did look tough enough and determined enough to sort things out.

Think again.

The policemen holding the driver were pulled off him by the suits and the policemen holding me did not react quickly enough. With my arms pinned behind me, the driver, fairly heftily built and really pissed off, landed a good one.

Which was when I thought I now knew what a broken nose felt like.

My police guys let go of me, but in their rush to grab him they pushed me back onto the rubble and down I went. The suits swarmed around as I scrambled to get up. Slipping and sliding, I sensed as much as I could see that above and behind my left shoulder, silhouetted against the setting sun, one of them was raising a large rock over his head. Crazy I thought, but there it was.

Suddenly, from my right side, someone flew over me in a furious blur and plowed into the suit. Down he went, rock and all, as did the blur. Momentarily, everything stopped except for another of the suits who landed a kick on the blur. The blur clambered to its feet with me, grabbing my arm, long black hair streaming, almond eyes flashing defiantly.

Jesus, it was Joosik! All forty five kilos of her!

I wasn’t the only one who was stunned by this as we stood together, surrounded, waiting for someone to make the next move.

Had it been a man, any man, who had done this – bowled over the guy with the rock – the melee might well have got even nastier. But some rule seemed to have come into play through the totally unexpected intervention of a brave young woman. Everyone drew breath, giving the police a moment to have another go at taking control and this time they succeeded.

Would they invite us all over to the station for a nice cup of tea and a lecture on good behavior before waving us off? Not a chance. They instead hustled Joosik and I over to my car and made no bones about telling us to get in and be on our way. Ka, ka!! Go, go!!

OK, whatever. It was over and we were still in one piece. Though sore, Joosik shrugged off the kick, and my broken nose feeling had subsided. He had in fact hit me a little too high for that and the only thing I had to show for it was a small graze on my forehead just above the nose. Much better, I thought, than the bloody gash which he was sporting high on his right cheekbone.

Fortunately, my Embassy colleague had held the fort at the car, unaware of what had been happening out of sight and which would have only taken a few minutes, start to finish. So he didn't have to be rounded up.

Whatever had caused the road block had gone and so away we went out past the edge of town and in the fading light onto a long straight stretch of road toward the next fold of hills. A stretch which, as was then common around the country, was raised a metre or so above the surrounding paddy.

We were, otherwise, pretty damned quiet, but with our blood still sufficiently up to be more annoyed than worried. I looked at Joosik. Quietly taught, but with her eyes bright and her jaw firm, she was indeed more stirred than shaken. Our eyes met and she reached over and squeezed my arm – firmly, surely. Steady Howard, it said, we're OK. 'What a remarkable person!', I thought.Anyway, we were fairly sure that it was over.

It wasn't.

We had barely gone a few hundred metres when a few of the black cars burst out of the town obviously bent on catching us. Being not just big shots, but drunk and angry big shots, they had evidently brushed the village cops aside and were going to have another go.

I put the foot down, but then could see in my rear vision mirrors an extraordinary sight. The cars were being overtaken by three large motorbikes and they were gaining fast – three abreast. Frankly, this did not bother me too much as my car was a good size and I couldn't see how they could do much to us, unless they had weapons.

As the pursuing cars seemed to have backed off to see what the bikes could do, I let one of them get alongside so I could have a closer look. There was no flourishing or appearance of weapons, though they may have thought that the ridiculous black Z's tattooed on their foreheads would cow me into yielding. One pulled in front of the car and started throttling back with another coming abreast on my right and the third pulling in behind.

OK boys, but we obviously haven't been watching the same movies.

Even had his horse – Toronado – been such a bike, I was pretty sure that Zorro would not have tried such a stupid stunt. I put my foot on the accelerator, the palm of my hand on the horn and left the rest to fate. Theirs. Zorro One had nowhere to go other than, for me, in a most satisfying arc out over the bank on the left hand side of the road and into the bog of the paddy. His dumb amigos stopped to help him out and we didn't see them again.

Those in the big black sedans who had rejoined the chase pulled over to check out their deflated heroes and it looked as though we would have a clear run into Seoul. There still wasn't a lot for us to say, so I started thinking about who these people were, what they were going to have to say about all of this, and how I was going to explain the whole bloody thing, as I must, to my Ambassador and, no doubt, Canberra.

This little reverie did not last that long, however.

Shortly after joining a line of cars in a section of sharply winding road through the last range of hills before Seoul, one of the black sedans appeared from nowhere and recklessly passed everyone before disappearing. He didn't try to stop us, but I knew something would be waiting for us soon enough.

Sure enough, just on dusk, as we came out of the hills and into a straight stretch of road with the city emerging from the haze off in the distance, a big, well built, American military policeman and his Korean counterpart were waving us down. In those days, both US and ROK military police maintained joint 'round-the-clock roadside posts all over the place to keep a sharp eye on comings and goings.

I pulled off the road onto the broad, dusty, verge and the American, very politely I thought, asked us to come over to the nearby post with him. Stirred as we were, his manner was reassuring. Having evidently been told by the occupants of the crazy car, who were lurking nearby, that we were Americans, he was surprised to find that we were not. It transpired later that our idiot antagonists were shaken by the revelation that we were in fact Australian (well, except for Joosik) and not the Americans they had thought they were baiting and in respect of whom they had assumed they would, at the least, be cut some slack.

While the suits were circling outside with a few of their equally idiot mates who had caught up, we gave the MP's our version of what had happened. They listened attentively and the American asked if it was alright if he called his command and the nearby Chung Yung Hee police station. This seemed sensible to us and I asked if I could also contact my Deputy Head of Mission, Ric North, to have him meet us at Chung Yung Hee.

Sure sir, that would be fine.

The American said it would be OK for us to wait in our car, but as we were leaving his hut, a few of the suits, still mightily agitated, put it to the MP's with more than a bit of aggressive accompanying body language that they should stand aside so that they, the suits, could take us away.

Here we go again, I thought.

But the big American put one big hand firmly on my shoulder, unclipped the holster flap on his big black square handled army issue .45 with the other hand and firmly declared us to be under his protection.

He wasn't mucking around.

Which was fine with us.

The suits skulked around until a police Captain, who spoke passable English, and a few handy looking helpers arrived and escorted us to their police station. I hadn't seen the driver with whom I had had the fight until we were in the corridor leading to the Captain's office, but he suddenly appeared and took a running swipe at me. This time my arms weren't pinned behind my back and he didn't come close. Though tempted, I thought better of giving him another one, especially given how that even more impressive looking gash on his cheek seemed to be nicely pulsating.

Anyway, getting on with the interview, the Captain was doing a good job of maintaining order and taking statements when the suits came out of a bit of a huddle and spoke quietly and pleasantly enough, in Korean of course, with Joosik, who was sitting alongside me. She stiffened and responded briefly but firmly before turning back to me. She told me they had said that although they were sorry to find out that I was Australian – as Koreans had a special regard for Australians – I had nevertheless wronged them and that she, as a good Korean, owed it to them to take their side with the police. She said she had told them that truth rather than nationality was the issue and that they should be ashamed of themselves for what they had done. It had still not registered with these fools that she was not easily intimidated. They were a bit taken aback and the good Captain, who had heard it all, seemed to be warming to us.

Ric North arrived and confirmed that two of us were indeed diplomats from the Australian Embassy. We were all allowed to leave and the Captain assured us that the others would not be given the opportunity to follow us. He did not have jurisdiction over we two young diplomats and my concern about whether or not he might want to detain Joosik quickly evaporated.

o O o

Less than a week after the Ambassador had delivered his formal Note on the incident to the Foreign Ministry, he ducked into my office to tell me he had been summoned to the Foreign Ministry to discuss it. He seemed to be relishing the prospect, but I was, to say the least, apprehensive. At my lowly level, I could only imagine the sort of pressure that influential people could bring to bear to get the outcomes they wanted. I did sense though that Loomes was well regarded in most of the right places in the Korean government and that his say would carry some weight.

When he returned, he asked me up to his office and I was greatly relieved to find him smiling. In fact he could hardly contain his delight with the outcome, which he said had been conveyed to him personally by the Foreign Minister, Choi Kyu-Hah (who later served as Prime Minister and President). An outcome which would not, however, be formally conveyed to the Embassy, given issues of 'face' which the government had to deal with in its own, Korean, way.

Not a man of many words, Loomes more or less chuckled his way through what he had been told. The carloads of suits were, it seemed, assorted, well connected, members of the Lyons Club of Seoul who were returning from an outing in the countryside. Included among them were several members of parliament and they had all had a fine day out eating and drinking.

In those days, no one doubted the effect on the participants of such a fun day. Koreans love a good party and a group of Korean men love a good party even more.

But how, it had been posed to them, good party or not, could they explain eight carloads of mature men in responsible positions attacking one twenty four year old Australian? Loomes said that in response to some huffing and puffing from the suits, the all-important 'face' issue had been dealt with by way of a suitably elegant implication that such a comparatively little thing would be nothing compared to what the Korea Central Intelligence Agency might choose to take up with some of these guys if they didn't pull their heads in.

In those days, you didn't mess with the KCIA.

What a relief!

o O o

I loved my two years in Korea. I travelled the length and breadth of the country and in winter traipsed the craggy hills and reemerging forests (which had been all but disappeared by the Japanese during their long and bitter period of colonization) for the delicious ring-necked pheasant. Many a friendly little thatch-roofed village had sat me and my mate, Ray Dury, down for a few steaming makolis – a suitably alcoholic, milky colored fermented blend of rice, wheat and water – with the men while the ajimas (the older women) relieved our belts of a few birds and cooked us up piping hot earthenware bowls full of pheasant stew in their chilli hot homemade broth before cheerfully waving us on our way.

I became very fond of all manner of Korean food and custom and had found the Koreans to be universally warm and friendly – willing to share a joke and a drink and the odd tear. I didn't learn much of the language, but this didn't seem to matter a lot. I would find out in a later career incarnation that in this way they were a lot like the Italians.

As a youngster, I didn't know it all that well at the time, but I did come to realize that, given their pretty harsh history, the Koreans have a very well-developed sense of what is right and what is wrong and an equally well developed sense of not letting an injustice go unchallenged.

o O o

Joosik and I married in early 1970, but in our hearts it had happened much earlier than this.

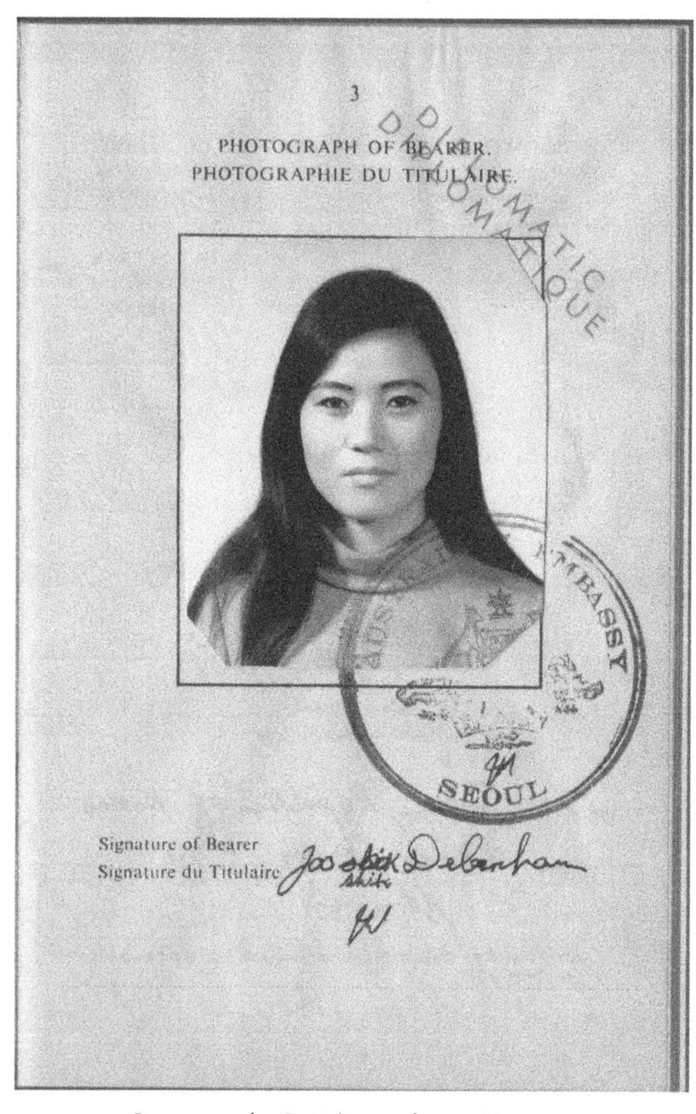

Passport number D-3049, issued on 22 May 1970.

Korea
Her story to the late 1960s

Little Changwoo Shin's life with her family would soon be over. As the second born, the years of her part in caring for the ever growing number of her siblings, helping out with household chores and, in more recent times, getting involved in some bits of the mixed farming of their landlord's fields surrounding their tiny hamlet was about to end.

Born in 1915, she was about to turn twelve and so would soon be leaving.

Forever.

Having hardly ever been beyond the hills and the forests surrounding the humble timber-framed and mud-walled cottages of their hamlet, deep in the heart of the Korean peninsula, the idea of leaving filled her with dread as she would, for the rest of her life, be going to live with a family she did not know in a place she had never been to. Also, that she would then be far enough away from this, her home, to make any future contact with her parents, her siblings and her friends uncertain. She had tried to put it out of her mind until closer to the time of her departure, but this was now fast approaching.

She turned her mind to comforting things like the field of red sweet potatoes, which would soon be ready for digging up and carrying in by the women in their simple straw baskets, or in bigger loads by the men on their home-made timber A-frames slung over their shoulders with thick ropes of woven straw. As there had never been a lot of space available for the cultivation of these potatoes on the gentler nearby slopes of their part of the countryside, the crop would not be large and would be harvested without the help of the children. But she liked the bustle of it and would find a way to get involved, if only by carrying cool drinking water from the old deep stone-walled well of the hamlet up to the fields.

It had been a good year for their chilies, which were drooping in their twisted shiny red abundance on the vines up beyond the potatoes in the sunniest and best draining patches of the hillsides. This harvest was already underway and she would soon be helping to sort them and lay them out to dry on the airy thatched-straw roof of their cottage and on straw mats in various sun-bathed spots on the ground. Being careful though, as stinging eyes had taught her when she was younger to keep her hands away from her face during this task.

In the run up to the approaching winter, she would soon have been helping with the picking of the succulent cabbages and radishes from the richer flats down along the stream, to be followed by the preparation and putting down of the family's winter kimchee. The earthenware pots for these were still much too large and heavy for her to handle by herself, but she had always enjoyed helping her mother and her older sister with the elaborate process of opening up and folding in among the fleshy leaves of the cabbages, freshly ground chilli powder, garlic, coarse granular salt and, if they were available and affordable, a sprinkling of anchovies. A most deliciously pungent brew. For the past year or so she had been permitted to use a sharp knife to help with the dicing and shredding of the radishes and then mixing in the same rich ingredients before tipping dishes of these into their own kimchee pots, which, having been thoroughly scoured and cleansed, had already been returned to their tombs in the ground of the little mud-walled courtyard just outside the back of their cottage – with only their snuggly fitting lids showing above ground. Once the pots were filled and the lids were tightly on, the cold ground of winter would slow down the essential fermentation process and thus keep the vital supply of staple kimchee fresh, if progressively richer in flavour, up until the early spring.

Getting the kimchee down would mark a time of relief and satisfaction for the family, signifying as it did that, along with their share of the rice and other harvests, they would survive another winter.

Last year's winter had been harsher than usual, with the snow deep and the ice hard and the stream frozen over for long periods. As ever, the deep well water had remained reliably accessible for all needs throughout, including for the regular challenge of washing with its clear icy water from a bucket in the privacy of their walled courtyard.

There was no reliable way of telling what the next winter would be like.

She would miss being gathered into the women's group for this work, but then perhaps, she thought, something of the same kind might be waiting for her to join in at her new home with her new family, and that this might help her settle in. It cheered her up a little.

After getting the kimchee down, she would have been going out into the forest with her mother and older sister, a few of the younger ones tagging along for the adventure, to start gathering the fallen branches and brush required for fuelling the warming of the simple, but uniquely Korean, *ondol* floors of their cottage through the coldest parts of the winter. The men too would be going out to cut and gather heavier firewood. This was not a chore she would miss that much, especially in view of the mounting restrictions being imposed by the colonial masters of Korea, the Japanese, about where they could and could not do their gatherings. Changwoo was not to know that these restrictions would in time grow into a ravaging and calamitous deforestation of the country in order to provide building materials in Japan, and to preserve Japan's own forests.

With a deep sigh, she knew that all of this was over for her here, in her home, and that the short time which she now had left would be mostly taken up by caring for the growing number of her siblings – so far all girls – coming along behind her. Carrying the smallest ones around in a sling on her back, helping with their feeding and their cleaning and their changing, and at all times keeping an eye on the more mobile ones.

Her formal schooling, such as it had been, was over and it had not pointed her in any direction other than the village and the role of women in it. Yes, theirs was an honoured and important role, largely free of exclusion or discrimination, but one with little prospect of variation, year-in and year-out.

Like most rural Koreans, let alone those of her tender age, she knew nothing of how the takeover of their country by the Japanese had been so profoundly, yet, on the world stage, how furtively, promoted by that man's man of an American president, Theodore Roosevelt. And how this, as only one act of betrayal of the Koreans – let alone the Chinese who had already suffered mightily through decades of western greed and power and proselytising – would propel Japan into the powerful and arrogant juggernaut that would in time turn on its benefactors and have to be confronted in an horrific Pacific war. An outcome of which would, in the ensuing war over Korea, see it and its people further devastated as mere pawns in the calamitous posturing of big powers at the outset of the Cold War between the USSR and The West.

No, all that mattered at this time to Changwoo was that this part of her home and family life was about to end.

And yet … there would be one last joyous celebration with her family. For all Koreans, it was the most important festival of the year – *Chuseok*

– and it would be starting in just a few days' time.

Along with everyone else, she loved the busy three days of *Chuseok* when ancestors would be honoured in a variety of customary historic rituals, and a successful harvest would be celebrated. The great King Sejong too.

On the morning of the first day, she would visit with her family the grassed high-mounded earthen graves of their ancestors, some of which were in small cleared patches out in the serenity of the forest among the blazing autumn colours of the deciduous trees which so richly mingled and contrasted with the shining swathes of evergreen pines and firs. Everyone would help in the happy process of clearing the weeds and other growth from around the sites and then, having kneeled and bowed – three times for the girls and the women, two for the boys and the men – would offer food and drink to the memory and the spirits of these ancestors. For the adults, the preferred drink offering would be the clear, highly distilled and potent alcoholic beverage, *soju*.

After returning to the hamlet, the men would gather to drink from small bowls their home-made *makgeoli* – a much less potent milky rice beer, naturally fermented and unfiltered.

Over the ensuing days of *Chuseok*, the thematic commemoration of ancestors would continue in a variety of ways, including the preparation of delicious and colorful traditional foods like *hangwa* (biscuits made from rice or wheat flower and dipped in homemade corn syrup) and *songpyeon* (small bite-sized rice cakes stuffed with a variety of ingredients such as sweet red bean, sesame seed paste and crushed wild chestnuts gathered from the forest). Apart from feasting to the extent that could be afforded, the festive atmosphere of the whole hamlet would release everyone from the usual routines and chores, and Changwoo would be an enthusiastic participant in games for the children.

Also celebrated at this time was King Sejong's introduction, in 1446 CE, of *Hangul*, a phonetic alphabet system for the native Korean language. Long before this, Koreans had adapted to their spoken language the Classical Chinese literary system of vast numbers of characters, derived as they were from pictograms (pictures) and ideograms (ideas). For the ruling classes, an important advantage of this enormously complex system of writing was that the subservient and uneducated classes – that is, the great majority of Koreans – could more readily be deprived of knowledge and the dissemination of ideas and opposition. The enlightened Sejong, who was also sufficiently gifted militarily to push the country's northern border further into Manchuria and put down Japanese raiders and pirates in the south, overcame strong opposition in his Court to his determined goal of literacy for all Koreans.

Compared to the festive nature of everything else that was going on around them during *Chuseok*, the greatness of Sejong didn't mean that much to youngsters like Changwoo. But through stories such as his they were, by the start of their teenage years, beginning to understand and value their national identity and thus, in this instance, the intensity of feeling all around them about the virulence of Japanese opposition to the use by Koreans of their own language. The more the Japanese forced the adoption and exclusive use of Japanese, the more Sejong and being Korean were celebrated. And the youngsters were also beginning to see that the more the Japanese ignored the historic resilience and courage of Koreans, the more troubled and perilous would be their occupation of Korea. The youngsters of this time were growing up with their Korean identity being even more strongly stirred in their blood.

This year, the hamlet was very proud that one of its men, stronger and heavier than most, would be travelling to a larger nearby village to engage in a district *Ssireum* wrestling contest, where the winner would receive a much prized ox. His training sessions in the cool of the late afternoons with two other young men of the village had been an exciting spectacle for Changwoo and the other children, a source of merriment and encouragement for everyone and, for the men, an opportunity for more *makgeoli*, boisterous prodding and singing.

o O o

Changwoo would be leaving all of this because, in the honoured ways of Korean antiquity, she had been promised in marriage, years earlier, to the son, Youngsik Cho, of another family. She had been too young for this to have meant much to her at that time, but now she had reached the age where she was to be taken to live with that family until she was of suitable age for marriage. In her mind, there were no thoughts of any kind of resistance to this, because she had been brought up to respect the rights and wishes of her parents in these matters and to understand that this was the way the lives of men and women were arranged; that her betrothed, who she had not yet either seen or met, had no more to say about it than she had; and that her future home life would somehow work out for her the same way it had for her parents and others through many many generations before them.

It was 1927 and she had just turned twelve.

Throughout Korean society at that time, love was a concept which, while recognised and admired, was not regarded as being relevant to such an important arrangement as marriage and the survival of family. A matter of this gravity could surely not be left to youngsters who knew nothing. It was, clearly, the responsibility of the parents and the elders to make suitable matches before their children reached an age where like or dislike, love or otherwise, might intervene.

Changwoo fretted about leaving behind everything and everyone she had ever known up to this point in her life – everyone she cared for and everyone who cared for her.

She had not been at all unhappy at home. She had been aware that they were poor and that they lived a more or less hand-to-mouth existence. But that was the way of life in her village and that was the way it had been for a long time. She had never gone hungry, she had always been clothed well enough and their little cottage was warm and cozy in terms both of the shelter it provided and the care of her parents. She had come to understand that the welfare of the hamlet was at all times subject to the whims of the owners of the land for whom they worked, and that they had not always been assured of their fair share of the crops, which they laboured year-in and year-out to produce. But, even as a little girl, she already understood that, like most Koreans, they would not allow themselves to be too downtrodden without a fight, and that landlords overlooked this at their peril.

She wondered if, in her parent's anxious quest for a son, her mother would ever stop producing sisters. This had become a real burden – of children to feed, protect, clothe and shelter. She understood, however ruefully, that she would now be one less mouth for them to feed. Yes, she was jealous of the two girls in the hamlet, older than her, who had not been sent off and were to remain with their families, but she accepted the fairness of this being attributable to each girl being the only girl in their family, one with three strong brothers and the other with two.

The view of her parents and the close knit hamlet community was that the match made for her had been a most fortunate one, because she would be going from their somewhat lowly class to a family of the Yangban class – the land owners – who were second in status only to the Kingdom's rulers. She had a vague comprehension of the fact that if the match worked out well it might help improve, at least in some small ways, the security and influence of her own family. But this was, really, of little comfort in her churning anxiety about the complete unknowns of the place and the people with whom she would soon be deposited.

The fateful day of her departure finally arrived.

o O o

She awoke much earlier than usual and for a while just lay there on her blanket in the corner of their communal room letting the soothing sounds of the stirring hamlet drift over her. Sounds which until now she had taken for granted. The birds and chickens, the cows and the oxen rustling about in their nearby enclosure, and the faintly discordant sounds of someone getting started in their narrow little earthen-floored kitchen nearby.

She emerged from the cottage just as the first sparkling shafts of sunlight were playing with the tops of the fir trees high on the surrounding hills. Soon, they would begin their bright journey down into the village to deal with the misty early autumn chill.

The *haraborgi* (old man) next door was squatting contentedly on his son's doorstep drawing deeply from his darkly stained little wooden pipe, but she hardly noticed him as she submitted to the embrace of the familiar and reassuring scene. He turned his rheumy gaze her way knowing, like everyone else in the village, that this was the day. She was a willing and cheerful girl who had been happy to stop and talk with him since his days in the fields had come to an end, and he was ready with a word of encouragement should she turn his way. But, lost in her reverie, she turned back into the cottage and he again drew, with a knowing sigh, on the comfort of his old pipe.

She busied herself with the stirring household and then turned to helping her mother prepare the family's simple breakfast, normally of clear broth, plain boiled rice and kimchee. To her delight, her mother produced dishes of small boiled eggs, shredded beef and some curds and told the other children that Changwoo was to take her helpings first. She and her mother exchanged misty looks of warmth and sadness and they took their time enjoying these treats. Her father ate sparingly and was very quiet.

By the time they had cleared away the utensils and the washing-up had been done, the sun was warming the cottage.

Changwoo took up the stiff brush broom which was leaning against the front doorstep and set to busily whisking up the eddies of bright autumn leaves which the cool evening breezes had arranged on the dry ground outside the front of the cottage – as if this were to be just any other day in her home life.

But a familiar figure cast its long shadow over her work.

She looked up into the kindly face of her father as he gently took the broom from her hands.

'Come my little one', he said, 'it's time'.

And so it was.

o O o

After bidding a brave farewell to her sisters and her mother, who was heavily pregnant with her next child, hoping fervently that it would be the much awaited first boy, Changwoo set off with her father.

Most of the *halmonies* (old ladies) and some of the other *Omas* (mothers) had gathered to say goodbye to their spirited little companion and some of them, reminded of their own such journeys of so many years ago, shed tears for her and for whatever her fate may be. Her sisters and most of her friends walked along with them until they reached a point where, as they would soon be out of sight of the hamlet, they were turned back by her father. Here, at the final point of parting, the goodbyes were more tearful, with the little ones, hitched up on their sisters' hips, wide-eyed and wondering. Changwoo vowed to herself that she would remember the older ones, but knew that she would never really know the others.

Their journey would take up most of the day and would be as much over fields and skirting paddy and hills as along any kind of rough road or foot-worn path. They had some food and water with them, but other hamlets such as theirs would be encountered along the way and their inhabitants, no longer busy out in the fields, would wish the travellers well and, in a time-honoured tradition, offer them rest and refreshment.

Her father carried some items of clothing for her wrapped neatly in a simple but prettily patterned cloth. He had not been able to afford one of the handsome little lacquered wooden trousseau boxes which she knew, though without resentment, were so proudly gifted to the daughters of more fortunate families on the occasion of their sending off.

Changwoo was small, but strong, alert and agile and not at all bothered by the prospect of the long walk. Soon enough, her somber thoughts turned to the new scenery along the way and the chatter of her father as he now reflected on losing her. Up to this point, he had been stoic and taciturn when the subject of her arrangements had come up. But now he was speaking in an affectionate way which, though pleasing to Changwoo, did not make her feel any happier.

In the wilder parts of their journey, she recalled the many stories she had heard among the adults about encounters beyond the hamlets with boar and wild dogs, and even the mighty tiger. But then, too, she thought, they might come across the elegant and fleet-footed red deer which were especially prized on the rare occasions when one had been caught and shared among the pots of the hamlet. She drew closer to her father whenever they took to the narrow winding tracks over the wooded hills which connected this or that little community down in the stream fed farmlands.

Her anxiety returned as the day wore on and, as later in the afternoon, they neared their destination. Coming across a broader road, she was astonished to behold a very great truck bearing down on them in a cloud of swirling dust. She clung to her father as the appalling roar and clatter of it passed by and disappeared around a bend. She had seen trucks before, but not anything of this monstrous size or sound or speed. 'Is this what it's going to be like?', she thought with a shudder. But after only a short distance they turned onto a smaller road which soon took them to the outskirts of what was to be her new home town – Mungangmyon. Off in the distance, her father pointed out, was the big town of Quesan.

That she was in the central province of Chungcheongbuk-do was of no consequence to her at all, other than in terms of a vague understanding that it was better to be here than in the more mountainous and less fertile regions way up to the north. Here, the surrounding farmlands were larger and richer looking than she had been accustomed to and she wondered whether its owners, among whom her new family were prominent, would be as aloof and, at times, as mean as those for whom her family had worked so hard back at home. She couldn't help wondering whether she would be taken in as a full family member or treated more as a servant. She did know, though, that she would be powerless to influence how things would work out. She was a mere girl, she was betrothed, this was to be her family forever and she would just have to cope with however things worked out. She had not yet discovered the inner strengths that would, in time, help her and her own family through – the family which she would make with the boy who was to become her husband.

The Chos of Mungangmyon were ready for them and, following the observance of solemn ceremonial introductions which included her deep bowing on bended knees to the head of the family, she and her father were fussed over with reassuring warmth and generosity. The house, though naturally in the thatch-roofed rural style, was grander than she had anticipated, spread as it was around a central courtyard and with an adjacent barn for the cows and oxen, plenty of chickens and, wondrously, a number of much prized large, plump, pigs and their piglets.

The mother and father of her betrothed were robust in appearance and seemed to be of a kindly nature. And she was able to see, by way of guarded glances, that her betrothed, Youngsik Cho, was not unpleasant in appearance and nature, as were his younger brother and older sister. Appropriate to the occasion, a feast, the likes of which she had not seen before, was laid out and she was gathered, with less restraint than she had dared hope for, into the celebration.

As an honoured guest, her father would rest comfortably in the house of her new family overnight before leaving her the next day for the long walk back home loaded down with gifts. Then, she thought, she would see more truly whether or not the warm and welcoming appearances of her first hours there were an illusion.

After her father left, she was filled with uncertainty. She fretted and fretted about whether she would ever see him and her family again. She was here in Mungangmyon, but her heart, along with her childhood that was now over, was far away in that little hamlet.

As it turned out, her first impressions of the Chos had not at all been an illusion. Changwoo was taken wholeheartedly into the family. Both the mother and father of her husband-to-be were kind and inclusive towards her. They came to admire her energy and quiet determination, and were well pleased with their choice for their first son. More than once, they gave thanks at the temple.

The handsome Youngsik and his betrothed, the pretty Changwoo, were in due course married in an elegant and suitably lavish Buddhist ceremony and their first child, Joohee, a gorgeous girl, was born in 1936, just before Changwoo turned twenty one. At first, Changwoo worried about whether she, like her own mother, would have to produce a lot of girls before a boy came along. But, to her relief, in a farming family where strong boys were an essential asset, the next two, Chanjoo and Changjoo, were boys. Then, for good measure, two more girls, Jooningee and Joosoo (who, at her grandfather's wish became known as Joosik), and then yet another two boys, Younjoo and Kwangjoo. That made seven children. There had actually been eight, but the next born after Joosik, a boy, had, to the family's great grief, died soon after birth.

o O o

The slim volumes of bound registers, prominently arranged in a richly black lacquered set of shelves in a corner of the main family room of the Cho house had been noticed by Changwoo soon after her arrival. She knew what they were because, given the deeply venerated Buddhist tradition of honoring ancestors, many families, rich or poor, had them.

They were copies, printed on fine rice paper, of the official records of the family's births, deaths and marriages – the orderly keeping of which had been mandated throughout the country early on in the Goryeo Dynasty (918 – 1392 CE) – a Dynasty which had been preceded by Korean Dynasties dating all the way back to that of Old Chosun (2333 – 194 BCE) – and through which communities of sophistication and culture had flourished while the Europeans were emerging from their Dark Ages.

Jajang Cho was the first name in these registers of Changwoo's new family. The entry was not dated because the formal recording system had not got underway until five generations later when the first birth date of official certainty had been registered, in 1145 CE, for Inpyung Cho. So that Jajang would have been born around one hundred years earlier, in 1045 CE.

This was during a century in which, a hundred years before the birth of Genghis Khan, China's disintegrating Song Dynasty paid tribute to keep at bay both the Tangut of Tibet and the Khitan of Manchuria; a new warrior class, the Samurai, was emerging in Japan; the Turks conquered Persia; France's Normans under William 1 invaded England and ended Anglo-Saxon rule; and Jerusalem fell to Christianity's bloody Crusaders.

Inclusion of the five undated entries – from Jajang and Inpyung – had been made possible by the prominence of Jajang as governor of Sunchang County in the province of Jeollabuk-do. His influence had been of such significance that the Chos had been officially awarded Clan status. They became the Sunchang Cho Clan.

As was then naturally the case, not only in Korea, property and wealth grew from power and influence and it was thus Jajang's wealth, power and influence which caused the elevation of the Sunchang Cho Clan to the landowner, or *Yangban*, class – second only to the ruling class.

Inpyung Cho consolidated the early power and influence of the Clan through his role, in 1176 CE, in the putting down of a revolt known as the Mange and Mongsoe. This was during a period when the power of the Goryeo dynasty had been seized – for the first time – by the military under Chunghon Choe (1149 – 1219 CE). Inpyung Cho must have exercised skill and agility in surviving this dangerous time as, having

'... emerged into prominence ...' Chunghon Choe '... proceeded to rid himself ... of all who disobeyed his orders, even though they might be among his own supporters.' (p141 *A New History of Korea*, Lee Ki-Baik, Harvard University Press.)

Two or three hundred meters from the seat of today's Sunchang Chos – the property bequeathed in the traditional manner to the eldest son of Changwoo and Youngsik, Chanjoo, across the now handsomely stone-walled banks of the nearby river – is a beautiful shrine which honors yet another period of notable contribution to Korea by the Clan. It is nestled into the foot of a steeply rising and heavily wooded spur at the southern end of a spine of rolling hills which runs up the eastern side of a picturesque valley of farmland. All of which once formed but a part of the Clan's land holdings. Comprised of three handsome and meticulously maintained buildings – two of them walled inside one compound – it was erected in 1975 by the provincial government of Chungcheongbuk-do as part of a national project to memorialize significant contributions to the development of Korea. The inscription on a tablet at the front of the shrine, in both Korean and English, reads as follows.

> 'Chilchungsa Shrine measures 3 kan (a unit of measurement referring to the distance between two columns) by 2 kan and has a gable roof. The shrine keeps the mortuary tablets of the seven leading royal retainers from the Sunchang Jo (Cho) Clan: Jo Jong (1437 – 1506), Jo Bok (1525 – 1592), Jo Deok-gong (1547 – 1597), Jo Deok-yong (1567 – 1638) and Jo Gi (1584 – 1661). The shrine was built in 1975. There is a pavilion named Pisijeong (literally 'pavilion for a hermit') in a dense forest near the shrine. Jo Sin, one of the aforesaid seven, lived here as a hermit following the fall of Goryeo. A wooden structure having a hipped and gable

roof measuring 3 kan by 2 kan has several frames containing letters hung on the wall.'

o O o

Joosik Cho was born in 1947.

In some ways this was fortunate, because as a little girl the world of the brutal and lordly Japanese colonial masters had just passed, and in 1952 she would be barely five years old when the devastating whirlwind of the Korean War was over. Although it had swirled around them for three years in vicious paths up and down the peninsular, and the behaviour of the United Nations forces toward non-combatant Koreans had been feared more mightily than that of the North Koreans, Mungangmyon had been one of the very few communities on the peninsular spared from ruin.

She was too young to have comprehended the hiding away of village girls when the *Migooks* (Americans) and other *Wehgooks* (foreigners) were around. She would have seen the heavily armed United Nations soldiers passing through and at times either helping themselves to valuable possessions and food stores or viciously laying waste to them on the pretext of denying them to the enemy. But she would too have seen and heard of the many kinder *Migooks* and *Wehgooks* and what some of them had had to endure in their shallow dug-out positions along the ridges of the hills immediately behind and in front of her home which, as they had been laid more or less bare by the Japanese, provided rugged observation eyries and free fire zones.

But, as a little child in the arms of her family, none of this had meant that much to her at the time and none of it would be recalled.

She was fortunate too that, unlike in her mother's time, the custom of arranged marriages had disappeared – although it may have endured a little longer in the poorer and more remote hamlets and villages.

Her father and his younger brother, who lived in his own house just behind them in Mungangmyon, had not gone off to war. Their job had been to help keep their armies fed and they did this to the best of their ability. But although the war was comparatively brief, it brought devastation and ruin to the country and its people. As well, the country had been split in two and a great deal of ominous sabre-rattling continued. North Korean refugees flooding into the South put further pressure on a fragile nation and the South's profoundly corrupt leadership of the immediate post-war period offered no relief. Its political opponents were being crushed.

So the future of the farming Chos would depend entirely on their own resourcefulness and resilience in rebuilding without any kind of assistance whatsoever. Joosik's father, much worn down in the aftermath of the war and a man too kindly for his own good, was showing early signs of faltering. Her mother's natural shyness and patience wore thin over time as she discerned with growing apprehension the gathering cost to the family of the carelessness and generosity of both her husband and his father. To the children, she became the task master and the disciplinarian – now with a quick enough temper to watch out for.

In his time, Youngsik had been influential and distinguished. A successful farmer and builder, his accomplishments for the community of Mungangmyon included paying out of his own pocket for electrification of the village and its surrounds. Without any government assistance, he had organized and purchased all the materials and the construction resources to run electricity lines four or five kilometers from Quesan and had helped each villager connect their cottages and houses to it. He had also acquired and widely shared machinery for ploughing and for easing the backbreaking task of husking the rice harvest.

Joosik's eldest (by twelve years) sister, Joohee, though worked pretty hard by their mother, made the time to help look after her two little sisters. When Joosik she was still small enough for Joohee to carry around in a sling on her back, any undue squirming or cheekiness would be dealt with by a firm pinch on the backside. Which she as often as not took as encouragement for more of the same. There was much merriment between them and they grew very close.

Getting to and from school at distant Quesan from a young age was a challenge, but one which she mostly relished. It was exciting to be in such a big town and a big school. There were no buses and certainly no regularly available family means of transporting the children to and from. But apart from the last few hundred meters up a moderately steep hill to the school at the top, the long walk was relatively flat. After heavier falls of rain, the narrow, low-lying dirt road would be breached by overflowing creeks which, as there was never any question of turning back, had to be forded. On the worst days, this involved taking off shoes and socks and as much clothing as the conditions required to be able to wade through, dry off and then put them on again the other side. Ice and snow in the winter added to the challenge.

She thrived at her school and was as happy at home as any fortunate child – until Joohee married and moved to Seoul with her kind and handsome husband, Taedok. Under the stern eye of her mother, Joosik remained dutiful enough and there were aspects of farming life which she loved, such as the wonderful time of the rice harvest when all the neighbours banded together to bring in the crop one farm after the other, with communal lunches provided boisterously every day by the women in the fields. But she was not finding sufficient outlets for her buoyant spirit and energy, and her longing for Joohee did not diminish.

Joohee came to the rescue.

In the hard and uncertain times of Korea's 1960s, she and Taedok were doing well enough in distant Seoul where they had worked very long days to set themselves up in a smallgoods shop with just enough living space attached. Missing her lively little sister, Joohee suggested that Joosik come to stay with them, continue her schooling there and help out with her new babies. It was a common enough arrangement in Korean families and their mother acquiesced.

o O o

A chain of events now began which would see Joosik move with much enthusiasm to Seoul, then live in the USA, first in Washington DC and then in Honolulu. In these American cities she would, through her care of the children of two families of diplomats – the first Australian and the next American – become a much loved member of these families.

For five years she lived away from home, spoke very little Korean, furthered her education as best could be managed and seemed headed for some sort of life in the USA.

The defining moment in this trajectory came when, in late 1967, Robert Fearey arrived home at their spacious house in Makalapa Drive, Honolulu to lay out in front of Joosik the paperwork required for her to obtain residential status in the USA. For Bob and his wife, Shirley, this was the natural next step in folding Joosik into their family, and they had planned it as a big surprise for her. Regarded more as a daughter than an employee, Bob had not only taught her to drive, but had helped her to buy what every dad would like to buy his eldest daughter – one of the more coveted sports cars of the day, a sparkling white Austin Healey

Sprite with red upholstery. He had also helped her obtain a glider pilot's license and she cherished the hours which she was able to spend soaring, solo, on the warm thermals which so reliably and so majestically carried her up the western side of Diamond Head and the sharp ridges of Maui.

In his State Department role as Political Advisor to the Commander in Chief, Pacific Forces (CINCPAC), Bob advised Admiral Ulysses Simpson Grant Sharp Jr until his retirement and then Admiral John S McCain Jr, the father of long time presidential aspirant Senator John S McCain III. With the Foreign Service rank of Minister, Bob's diplomatic career was flourishing and he was well placed to guide Joosik's paperwork through. All she had to do was sign.

But Bob and Shirley's aspirations for Joosik struck an unexpected obstacle.

It was that this completely unexpected prospect of becoming an American had brought on in Joosik a renewed rush of longing for her family in Korea. She had not seen them for five years and her yearning for them was undiminished. It didn't matter at all to her that the material trappings of life in America and with the Feareys were vastly superior to those in which she had been brought up in Korea, nor that there were very few indications that the basket-case which was the Korean economy would ever deliver a better quality of life to its people, let alone to her.

She knew only too well that she was falling into a gap between two cultures and that she had already missed important parts of her formal education. Yes, she realised, there was still time to deal with this and to better prepare herself for a life in America. But first she had to, she must, go home.

And so it was that in 1967, at the age of twenty and with the reluctant blessing of the Feareys, who would keep their home and their hearts open to her, she returned, completely unannounced, to Korea.

o O o

For a moment, the biting chill of a clear November day in the early winter of Korea took her breath away as she stepped out of the aircraft and headed down the stairway to the icy tarmac of Seoul's Kimpo airport. As there hadn't been any space left in her compact white Samsonite suitcase, she had been in two minds about bringing the mustardy coloured corduroy mid-length coat which she hadn't used since leaving Washington DC a few years earlier. But at Shirley's insistence she had decided to carry it. Now, she quickly put it on over her light summer clothes of Hawaii. The sandals on her bare feet would have to do.

The taxi driver had difficulty finding Joohee's place, buried deeply as it was in an old part of the city just east of the dominating Namsan mountain. Finally, Joosik recognised the turnoff and, beyond, the narrow cobblestoned road up the steep icy hill. The driver thought his little taxi wouldn't be able to make it and, so, thanking him with a good tip, she set off up the hill, her suitcase and her heart in her hand and her cold feet and sandals slipping all the way.

Turning to greet her beaming new customer who had burst through the door to the shop, Joohee let out a gasp of shock and delight, dropped what she was holding and rushed to embrace her little sister.

Her father happened to be visiting from Mungangmyon and was resting in the family quarters at the rear of the shop. He dismissed out of hand the highly excited declaration that this was Joosik, because he knew very well that *his* Joosik was of very fair complexion whereas this stranger was dark. But as the effect of the Hawaiian sun on outdoors girls such as Joosik was explained and sunk in and given that, like any properly raised daughter must, she had immediately honoured him with the appropriate ceremony of deep kneeling and bowing, he melted.

The news that she was back spread quickly and she soon took the bus to Mungangmyon – into the heart of her the family and the arms of her mother.

After a while, she returned to Seoul to do one final thing before trying to work out what she would next do with her life ... stay here or go back to Hawaii. It was that she had to go to the Australian Embassy to renew contact with and thank those who had helped her rejoin the family of the Australian diplomats in Washington DC five years ago.

She set off in the early morning of a crisply clear day for the Australian Embassy. It was still in that funny little rented house on quite a large block at the top of a hill not that far from the presidential mansion, and the taxi skidded its icy way up the narrow winding road before depositing her, through the large iron gate and down the rough gravel driveway, at the Embassy's perfectly unimposing little green front door.

She had called ahead to be sure that the chief clerk, Kim, Moon Il, who had been so helpful in organising her papers to go to Washington five years earlier, would be able to see her and found that the same receptionist from that time, Miss Noh, was expecting her.

Kim had got caught up with something for the moment and while she stood there chatting with Miss Noh, she noticed someone looking her way from a desk in an open sort of office across the small lobby from the reception cubicle. Their eyes met and they both smiled. He turned back to his work, but the attentive Miss Noh said, 'Oh, he's our new Attaché, just here from his first posting in India. Would you like to meet him?' Joosik said, 'Well, yes, OK.'

o O o

Miss Noh said to him, 'Mr Debenham, may I introduce Miss Cho?

She's been living in the USA for a few years and has come in to see some friends here.'

He stood, smiled, went around his desk and said, 'Hello Miss Cho, my name's Howard and I'm very pleased to meet you.'

She said, somewhat huskily for a Korean lady, he thought, 'Hello Howard, my name is Joosik and I'm pleased to meet you too'.

He invited her to sit and the good Miss Noh thought she should be getting back to her work. Soon, Kim, Moon Il appeared and whisked her away for a while. Howard went through the motions of busying himself at his desk until they returned and then chatted some more with Joosik on one of the comfy settees in the lobby. By the time her taxi arrived, he thought his voice had become a little huskier too.

Chemistry is a wonderful thing.

o O o

Some months later, Robert Fearey was dispatched by his anxious family to find out what had become of Joosik. Her occasional letters seemed to indicate that she was alright, but they couldn't be sure. There had been nothing to suggest that she wouldn't be returning to them, but they were getting nervous. They had just moved from Hawaii to Okinawa where Bob had been installed as the US High Commissioner to the Ryukus, charged with the formidable task of managing the USA's return to Japan of the Administration of the Ryuku, or Nansei, islands which stretch southwest of Kyushu towards Taiwan and of which Okinawa is the largest. Owing to its geostrategic importance and the scale of US military assets there, the Ryukus had, up to this point, remained in US hands long after the end of MacArthur's imperious rule of Japan following the end of World War II.

Bob had his hands full but, as always, family came first and Joosik was family.

He flew into Seoul in the late evening and they met at his downtown hotel first thing the next morning. When Joosik arrived, he was pacing up and down just inside the entrance. After the mutual rush of pleasure and relief at seeing each other, Bob took Joosik to the lobby café and ordered coffee and snacks.

The conversation went like this.

'Is there anything else you would like?', he asked, but for the moment all she wanted was answers to her eager questions about Shirley and the children.

With that out of the way, he said 'Why haven't you come back to us Joosik? You were only going to visit your family for a while, and we are all missing you so much! Is everything alright?'

Joosik said, 'Yes, and I have been missing all of you so much too. I think of you and Shirley and the children all the time. But I love my family here very much and, after having been away for so long, I know they would be very unhappy if I left them again; or at least if I left again too soon.'

She paused and said with some hesitation, as if with a father who might not approve, 'But there's something else.'

'What is it Joosik?', he asked, 'Can I help? Is it something I can do? Just tell me what it is.'

'Well, this is different', she said. 'I've met someone.'

'What does she mean 'I've *met* someone?'', he thought.

'Oh .... do you mean ... a young man?', he asked.

'Yes .... and I ... well ... I love him'.

Bob had come prepared to fix anything that needed fixing in order to get Joosik back with her *Fearey* family, but he had not expected this. He wondered why he had not expected it. She was not a girl anymore – she was an attractive, vibrant, young lady. But he felt as protective of her as any father who really didn't want his daughter to grow up and be taken away by some strange man. How was he going to deal with this? Where was he going to start? Shirley would know, but Shirley wasn't here.

He sat back in his chair, taking it in. Then, reaching for his coffee, taking a steadying sip or two, he asked, a little lamely, 'You *love* him Joosik? Did you say you *love* him?'

'Yes, I do.' And there was no doubting her.

'OK then, but … who *is* he Joosik and how does he feel about *you*?'

She took a deep breath and set off to do the best she could. She described how she had met him at the Australian Embassy, how they had begun seeing each other, regularly and for some time now, and how she had really fallen for him.

Bob listened carefully, but was doing his best to be unconvinced. She still looked so very young and so vulnerable. He reached out, gently took her hand across the table and asked, again, 'Yes Joosik, I understand, but how does *he* feel about *you*?'

'Well … we get along very well … we're very happy … together', she answered with a confident smile.

Bob's mission was to get Joosik to come 'home' and, as she hadn't really answered his question, he thought he detected an opening.

'But is the feeling between you – yours for him and his for you – enough to stop you coming back to us … to me and Shirley and the kids and the life we want to help you build in America … as an American, as one of us? You're still so young … shouldn't you wait? There'll be lots of eligible young men knocking on your door Joosik.'

'If it hadn't been for Howard', she said, 'it would have been easier, but I simply can't go … I can't … at least, not yet.'

Bob said, 'Well, of course I'm happy for you Joosik and I do hope this works out the way you want it to work out. But, so that I can understand it better, and so that I can make a better fist of explaining it to Shirley and the kids when I get home, can I meet him?'

While Bob waited, Joosik called Howard from the hotel lobby, hoping that he would be able to join them, now, at the hotel. The Australian embassy was not that far away and he had been waiting for her call, but at the time it came he found himself busy doing something for his Ambassador that couldn't wait. He asked if they could 'meet at, say, 12.00, and wouldn't it be better if we did so at my house in Itaewon?' Joosik said she thought that would be fine with Bob.

Howard already knew a lot from Joosik about the Feareys and the strength of her relationship with them. She had talked about them often and there were times, in his mind, when he wondered why she hadn't returned to them in Hawaii. As they had got to know each other, he was so pleased that she hadn't returned, but for him it was too early to be sure that he was ready to offer her something better. He had already come to see and to really admire in her a person who, in her relationships with others, was so sure of her instincts. When she gave, she gave wholeheartedly, whereas he, he knew, had learned to be more cautious. There had been other relationships in his life, but none even close to what he felt he had with Joosik. It was new, it was more than special, and there was a really good name for it. But he was still hanging on, however tenuously, to caution.

Joosik had a key to the house and when Howard arrived, the big black US Embassy car was already in the driveway and the driver was sitting on a retaining wall having a cigarette. Joosik was pouring Bob a cup of coffee when Howard walked in.

Things went as well as they could. Bob could see that they were, at the least, very fond of each other and that something lasting might well come of it. Which, though, meant that he was going to have both bad news and good news for the family. The bad being that Joosik would not be returning to them, at least not yet; the good, that Joosik did indeed seem to be in love and that this young Australian, though he may not yet fully comprehend it, was pretty clearly in love with her. Bob knew about love, as he and Shirley had been deeply in that condition for a long time now and were inseparable.

They parted on warm terms – Bob with mixed feelings and some misgivings back to Okinawa that evening, and, together, Joosik and Howard a little further on towards their destiny.

Joosik with her Father, soon aftrer her return to Korea from Hawaii in 1967.

Joosik with her Father and Mother in 1977.

The three structures of the shrine at Mungangmyon which honors an era of the Sunchang Jo (Cho) Clan dating from 1437 to 1661 CE. It was constructed by the provincial government of Chungcheongbuk-do in 1975. Clan status was bestowed, evidently by royal decree, towards the end of the 11th century, to honor Jajang Cho for his service as Governor of Sunchang County in Jeollabuk-do Province.

Next
Early 1970 to early 1971

The first year of our marriage, 1970, was spent on temporary assignment to our Embassy in Tokyo where we lived – blissfully enough not to be bothered too much by what was going on around us in this vast and busy city – in a little one bedroomed half western, half Japanese style apartment on the fifth floor of a shaky building in the Takanawa district of Shinagawa. As it had not been built to any particular earthquake-proofed standard, the building rattled and creaked and groaned through even the mildest of the soft Kanto Plain's myriad shakes – one of which was strong enough in the pre-dawn of one morning to tip us out of our very cozy single bed.

Later in the year, only a month or two before leaving Tokyo for Australia, we honeymooned high up in the Japanese Alps, near Karuizawa, on the snowy slopes of the beautiful volcano, Mount Asama.

We expected to return to Australia for at least a year or two and I was keen to acquaint Joosik with her new family and her new country, of which she was one of its newest citizens.

Arriving in Australia, I was pretty clueless about how to get started with housing for us as I had previously been happy enough to use the single rooms available in government hostels. So until we could figure something out, we moved in with my brother Dennis and his wife Mary who had married at about the same time as us. By the standards of that time, they were in a flat of a reasonable size above Stumbles' news agency on the main street of my home town, Queanbeyan – only a few buildings up from where we had lived out our early childhood years above the shops next to the old post office.

While I was still on leave and before we had even started looking around for our own place, I received a message from the Department to call one of the staffing officers, John Hutchinson, as soon as possible. Dennis and Mary hadn't yet had a telephone installed in their flat, so I called John from a public telephone the next day expecting to be told where I would be placed upon my return to the Department. Instead he said, to my great surprise, 'Howard, due to unforeseen circumstances, David Mackie has to had leave Tel Aviv a bit early and it would be a big help to the Department if you could get there as soon as possible please'.

It was a small, though important, embassy for Australia in those days with only about seven Australians, and as Second Secretary and Consul responsible to the Ambassador for the consular and administrative functions of the Embassy, the idea of it was not unappealing. But while I was digesting this I said, 'John, we have only just received our stuff from Tokyo and all the cartons (well, there weren't that many) are in fact still unpacked and stacked down the living room wall of my brother's flat in Queanbeyan!'. What I was meaning to convey was the idea that it was a bit unfair to put this pressure on us when our feet had barely touched the ground.

'Well, Howard, that's perfect then, isn't it?', he said. 'Why with a bit of luck, we can have the removalists bring back the very same lift-van your stuff was in, reload the cartons and get them on their way to Tel Aviv without any of the usual fuss!' He was on a roll and added, 'Let's see … your leave is over at the end of this week, so you can come into the Department for a week to get a bit of briefing done while we organize your travel and you'll be in Tel Aviv by the end of the month.'

'Hell John, and with our heads still spinning?'

'Well, yes, I suppose so Howard', he said, 'and, by the way, how is you new wife?'

'She's fine thanks John, and she's really looking forward to getting to know her new country and her new family.'

'Yes, of course Howard, and we do quite understand, but we're really pressed here. Look, it's a good move for you. The Ambassador, Marshall Johnson, is a good bloke, and you are in fact readier than anyone else.' And so forth.

'Not to mention, John', I said, 'that the Department also regards me as being really well qualified, eh?'

'Of course Howard. Goes without saying.'

Right.

Anyhow, getting caught up in the moment and already excited by the wholly unexpected prospect of Israel, which had only in recent times been refreshed in everyone's minds through the so-called Six Day War of 1967, I said, 'John, I'll talk this over with Joosik and come in to see you tomorrow … OK? Oh, and in the meantime you might like to see if that lift van is still around.' Which really gave the game away.

'Thanks Howard, you won't regret it', he said.

I had time in my walk back to the flat to think about how Joosik would receive this news, but I knew she would be OK with it. We were both adventurers and this had the prospect of being a good one.

The sturdy little wooden lift van, with the Japanese shipping markings already blacked out, turned up two days later and, once reloaded with our untouched cartons, was on its way again in no time.

As were we.

We would find out, soon enough, just what kind of a different world there was out there waiting for us in the Middle East. A world which, though already fractured enough at this time through the very creation of the State of Israel, was, in its unrelenting turmoil, to become a major and enduring obstacle to world peace and security.

A lighter moment in Tel Aviv

Tel Aviv
1972

Eli Cohen was the faded name on the weathered timber board alongside the gate to the pathway which wended its way up to the somewhat decrepit little old two-bedroomed cottage which was to be our home in Herziliya B – then a very modest suburb north of Tel Aviv and suitably inland from fashionable beachside Herziliya Pituach.

Could this have been the Eli Cohen who, as Kamel Amin Thaabet, had been one of Israel's most effective spies until he was caught and publicly hung in Damascus in May 1965 – not that long ago? Hard to discover then, but our grumpy little old landlady who lived alone next door through a boundary of thick bushes did withdraw into a morose kind of silence when I ventured to ask during one of her surprise appearances.

This little place was to live long in our hearts as the first home for our first-born, Andrew, following his delivery at the Tel HaShomer (Hill of the Guardsman) hospital in nearby Ramat Gan by a remarkable Australian/Israeli dual national, our friend, Dr Laurie Jacks.

Later, we moved to a newer suburb, Kfar Shmayahu, which was closer to downtown Tel Aviv and where services were more reliable. Which was not surprising given that much of the land there had originally been assigned to former members of the Palmach – the elite fighting force of the Jewish underground's (Haganah's) resistance to Britain's much conflicted Mandate for Palestine. A Mandate which had been provided by the League of Nations, the forerunner of the United Nations, way back in 1922 when the British had persuaded most of those outside the Arab world that they knew best how to run it.

Anyway, in our only meeting with him, our new landlord, gave us quite a graphic account of his role as a Lieutenant Colonel in the storming of the Golan Heights during the Six Day War of 1967. Now, he said, he had been posted on very short notice to Amsterdam, which at that time was at the center of a sudden wave of letter-bombing of Israeli and Jewish interests in Europe. Interesting, we thought.

Over the road from us, in a much grander house, we got to know Menahem Golan and his family. My first encounter with him was about seeing if he wanted any help with some work he was doing high up on the roof of his house, because he was making pretty heavy weather of getting up and down a long ladder. Not surprisingly, in an enclave of this kind, it turned out that both of his legs were prosthetic. For the first time, I was shown over a car which had all of its operational devices on the steering column. Golan went on to become a very significant Hollywood film producer.

o O o

Although I was not quite 28, Tel Aviv was my fourth posting and our second together since marrying in 1970.

We stayed in the Dan Hotel down on the waterfront in the heart of Tel Aviv longer than usual, as housing had been hard to find. In some ways this suited us as it gave us time to get a good handle on the interesting downtown area, spreading as it did along the eastern shore of the Mediterranean and radiating inland from the heart of its business centre, nearby Dizengoff Street. The ancient trading port of Jaffa, already impressively restored, was a pleasant stroll south along a broad esplanade behind the beach, and the bustling open Souq Ha'Carmel or Carmel Market was nearby with fresh produce in abundance. The embassy was within walking distance north along Hayarkon street and just around the corner from the waterfront where outings on the beach had to be followed by scrubbing squashed globules of tar, the swill of tanker bilges, off bare feet with the turpentine conveniently provided in tins at the foot of each staircase leading back up to the esplanade.

The friendly staff of the Dan had probably realized before we did, from her sudden passion for fresh pickled gherkins and juicy Jaffa oranges, that Joosik was pregnant. They took it upon themselves to keep her well supplied.

My management role as Second Secretary was routine, but my other role as Consul was varied and at times challenging.

The most common cause of bemusement for some young Australians visiting Israel at that time, and alarm for their parents at home, was their discovery upon arrival that they were not only eligible for service in Israel's military, but could be detained until they did it. Two year's worth. Back then, under Israel's Law of Return, Jews, including those from interfaith parentage whose mothers were Jewish, acquired Israeli citizenship by virtue of the simple act of their first arrival in Israel. In time, we contributed to having this amended to allow a period of stay before the military service requirement kicked in. So that the hallowed kibbutz experience, without military service, could thus still be on the cards for visiting Jewish youth.

In the consular business though, having to deal with some sort of nasty incident is never far away – such as in the case of a young Australian, Helen Pinkus, who like so many before her had come to spend some time soaking up the Israel aspect of her heritage. Following some time out with friends one evening – not late – she had been followed back to her small rented apartment in downtown Tel Aviv by a bad type who, as it turned out, had only recently been released from an Israeli prison for a crime involving physical violence. She made it to her apartment with him hot on her heels and managed to lock the door behind her. But, to her horror, he set about forcing it open. Frightened out of her wits, she went out the window and started clambering down the outside wall using a drainage pipe. She was several floors up, the pipe came away from the wall and she fell back to her death. He was caught by the police, but it was too late for Helen.

As Jewish custom requires that burial be arranged as quickly as possible following a death, her distraught parents requested our assistance. On the Mount of Olives in Jerusalem, I witnessed her committal in the traditional white winding sheet to a tight plot in the rocky ground. Other than in her death, I didn't know Helen, but this did not make my role and the eulogy, which I delivered for her family at her grave side, any easier.

o O o

Israel was easy to get around and we soon became familiar with wonderfully historic places such as Nazareth, Caesarea, Haifa, Tiberius, the Galilee and the Negev. At that time we were able to drive down south past Eilat, which was cheek by jowl with ancient Aqaba at the top of the Red Sea, more or less along the scorched western shore of the Gulf of Aqaba to Sharm el Sheikh – which Israel had captured from Egypt during the Six Day War of 1967. Just south of Eilat, with our baby Andrew sound asleep in a basket on the back seat of our VW beetle, we snorkeled among the coral in an isolated inlet – with the barren rocky ridges of the Saudi shore opposite so dreamily painted in their pastel mauves.

At the Dead Sea, 1972. The sign says 'World's Lowest Point, 394 metres Below Sea level'.

Among our friends was a family of Palestinians who sold carpets out of an ancient store just off the square in front of Jerusalem's Church Of The Holy Sepulchre. Memorable indeed were their feasts of lamb poured steaming from unadorned earthenware containers over huge platters of nutty rice in the middle of their rolling orange grove on the outskirts of Jericho.

By the early part of 1972 we had been in Israel for about a year and were soaking it up. The one-sided outcome of the Six Day War, in which Israel's pre-emptive strikes had so devastated the opposing Arab forces, had instilled an outward sense of security in the country and the threat of conflict of any comparative significance seemed a long way off. Yom Kippurs had come and gone peacefully.

At the embassy, we nevertheless kept our plans for dealing with an emergency of this kind well up to date, keeping tabs on Australian residents and visitors and fixing channels of evacuation for Australians from the country should this become necessary. These included arrangements with Qantas and BOAC (now British Airways) for uplift from Tel Aviv or, should the airport be under attack, by sea from beachfronts and, as a last and more desperate option, convoying away from the fighting, probably south into the Negev desert above and beyond Masada, until some other form of rescue or refuge could be worked out. Such arrangements were required of very few of our diplomatic and consular missions back then, but have become common today.

The Sabena Hijack

The air of comparative safety took a turn for the worse when, on Monday 8 May 1972, four armed terrorists, two men and two women, hijacked Belgium's Sabena flight 571 just out of Vienna on its way to Tel Aviv.

Upon landing at Tel Aviv's Lod International Airport, they demanded the release of 351 convicted Palestinian terrorists being held in Israeli prisons. The aircraft and all on board were promptly towed to a distant part of the airport while Security Minister, Moshe Dayan, Israel's hero of the Six Day War, got negotiations underway. Ominous was the revelation that all Jewish passengers had been put together at the back of the aircraft.

As the Israelis had their reasons for keeping the names and nationalities of passengers close to their chests, I thought I would have a better chance of seeing if there were Australians among them by being on the spot at Lod. I went there with my Consular Assistant, Haya Pinkoffs, and we eventually found that there were no Australians on board.

Anyway, sometime on the following day, 9 May, the hijackers agreed to an external inspection of the aircraft, believing this was needed to validate it for onward flight. Sixteen Israeli commandos, dressed in the white overalls of airport technical staff, brazenly stormed the aircraft, killing the two male hijackers and capturing the two women. Three passengers were injured, one of whom died the next day. We were told that these three had, unwittingly, stood up as the storming began, making themselves indistinguishable from the terrorists and thus mandatory targets for the commandos. The commandos were led by Ehud Barak and one of their number, Benjamin Netanyahu, was wounded, apparently by friendly fire. Much later, Netanyahu would be the first of the two to become Prime Minister of Israel.

Although at that time the hijacking of aircraft was not new, the perpetrators and their purposes had until then been diverse. Its frequency had favored Cuba and Cubans, but Japan, Algeria, Ethiopia, Mexico, Nicaragua, India, Jordan and Yugoslavia had all experienced their own problems of this kind.

But the Sabena hijack heralded a new tactic by Palestinian terrorists against Israel. A tactic which would change the quality and security of international travel for everyone for a long time in ways which would, though, benefit sympathy for the State of Israel at least as much as it would raise awareness of the plight of the Palestinian diaspora.

Initially, the new terrorists of the skies belonged to the Black September Organization, which was founded in 1970 in response to King Hussein's ruthlessly uncompromising destruction of the Jordanian arm of the Palestinian Fedayeen following its attempt to take-over

Jordan. Their example, with the Sabena hijack, was very soon to be taken up by George Habash's Popular Front for the Liberation of Palestine (PFLP) which, from its founding following the Six Day War in 1967, became the second largest faction of Yasser Arafat's Palestine Liberation Organization (PLO).

Massacre at Lod

The arrivals hall at Lod International Airport was eerily calm. The dead and wounded had been taken away and the cleanup was in progress. Numbly, mechanically. The shocked official at my side was telling me as much as he knew of what had happened, but it was hard for us both to get our heads around the enormity of the atrocity as we trod carefully around the wretched blotches of darkening blood and tissue stains where the innocents had fallen.

o O o

It was a bare three weeks after the Sabena hijack – 30 May 1972. News of the attack on passengers who had disembarked from their Air France flight from Rome came to us very quickly – in the early afternoon – but all we learned was that many had been killed inside the terminal by automatic gunfire. That was it and we would just have to wait for more information, including the possibility of any Australians being involved. So I decided to get out to Lod fast.

Today, airports go into immediate and deep lockdown at the slightest hint of a security problem. Then, at the dawn of Palestinian skyjacking, even Lod remained wide open. All I had to do, if anyone asked, was to flash my diplomatic ID card and then help myself.

Unable to find anyone in the airport's administrative offices, I made my way into the terminal building and took the stairs down into the airy and high-roofed arrivals hall. At the other end, maybe forty or fifty metres away, was the line of passport checking counters and, on my right, the baggage carousels. The hall was maybe twenty five metres wide. By the standards of that time, quite modern and spacious.

I had expected to have to deal with bedlam and clamor, but all was strangely calm. The storm had passed and there didn't seem to be that many people around. Some would have gone off with the dead and the wounded, others to escort survivors away to safe places, and still others may have just been off somewhere drawing breath. Or was it that, for me, everything other than the horror of the scene was just not in the picture.

The official who materialized at my side walked the length of the hall with me, explaining quietly, breathlessly, what he knew about this charnel scene. He couldn't tell me the exact numbers of the dead and wounded and where they were from, but thought this would be available soon.

As far as he knew, three Asian men had been among the first to exit the aircraft and enter the baggage collection hall. They had stripped off their jackets and shirts and, dressed only in their trousers and T-shirts, had recovered their bags, which had been among the first to appear on the carousels.

They quickly extracted and assembled their automatic weapons and, spreading out, had opened fire on other passengers as they entered the baggage collection hall just past the passport control counters. He thought one of the terrorists had been killed accidentally by another, who had swung his weapon around too far. Another had been shot by security guards and a third had escaped through the flap over the baggage entry point onto the runway apron. He thought this one had been captured. He pointed out that had they been able to control the hall for a while longer the carnage would have been even greater, as a number of full ammunition clips had been recovered.

Our stunned passage through the hall, weaving our way around those wretched splashes and blotches which still so awfully marked the places of the death of so many innocents, did eventually come to an end. It turned out that there had been no Australians on the flight.

This was just the beginning of yet another deadly era in the defining of the great gaps that separate the haves and the have-nots of the world. Of the great gaps between the moral, the religious and the political values of the powerful and the disempowered – not to mention all the poor innocent folk caught up in between.

o O o

The three terrorists were members of the fanatical Japanese Red Army who had been recruited by George Habash's Popular Front for the Liberation of Palestine. Aware that Israeli security was concentrating its attention on possible hijacks by Palestinians, the PFLP had trained the Japanese in Lebanon and succeeded, spectacularly, in getting them to their mark.

For the PFLP, this had been a huge success. Never mind that the random slaughter had included people of many nationalities and religious faiths. World attention had been transfixed by the cry of the PLFP, however primitively and, to most, mindlessly savage.

It was a game-changer – one which would encourage more of the same from the PFLP and one which would refine Israeli preparedness and drive its fierce campaigns of retribution. But, as well, one which would be embraced, either publicly or otherwise, by most of the Arab world. It did leave many around the world who cared for the plight of ordinary Palestinians in a quandary.

At the Embassy, it ratcheted up our preparedness for emergencies. And the next was not long in coming.

Munich

Just three months later, on 5 September 1972, Black September re-entered the scene with the capture by eight hooded gunmen of Israeli Olympians in the profoundly unguarded Olympic village at Munich. Two Israelis were killed during the initial storming of the athletes' quarters.

Abetted by the appalling stupidity and ignorance of German security forces, which even refused to utilize available Arab speaking Israeli negotiators, five of the gunmen and all of their nine manacled Israeli hostages died in hail of gunfire and explosions at Furstenfeldbruck airport.

A few days after the massacre, a minute's silence was to be observed all over Israel to remember and to honor the slain Israelis.

It was a bright sunny day In Tel Aviv as the dreadfully mournful wail of air raid sirens started on time at 9.00 am. I stood up and turned to the window behind the desk in my second floor office – from which I had a panoramic view of Hayarkon Street in its long sweep up past the Hilton and other coastal hotels towards the northern beach suburbs.

Without exception, everything and everyone along that busy road and its broad sidewalks stopped. Everyone got out of their buses and their cars and their trucks and off their bikes and stood bowed and silent as the sirens etched the grief of a nation on my psyche.

Within two months, the German Chancellor, Willy Brandt, without first consulting with the Israelis, quickly caved in to demands by the two Black September hijackers of a Lufthansa flight, releasing the three surviving Munich terrorists who were greeted as heroes upon their arrival in Libya. It would later be claimed that this hijack was staged – by Germany and Libya – to allay German fears of Black September retribution for the death of their heroes at Munich. Brandt's image suffered a serious setback.

As Prime Minister Golda Meir, Defence Minister Moshe Dayan and Mossad were developing their plans of retribution for Munich, Yasser Arafat's Palestine Liberation Organization (PLO) was blossoming in prominence and political influence.

Rome
1973

In January 1973, transferring directly from Tel Aviv, we took up a year-long assignment at our Embassy in Rome.

What a welcome change this shaped up to be from the tensions and emotions which had rolled over us in 1972. But how silly it was that, in contrast with the standards of decency and composure set so effortlessly by Ambassador Marshall Johnston in Tel Aviv, the staff of this Embassy, me included, had to deal with the petty behavior of a snappy, detached, Ambassador and his cranky deputy. I wondered what on earth they thought they had to be so shitty about in such a place – Bella Roma, The Eternal City.

But this did not distract us from embracing our share of *la dolce vita a Roma* – the sweet life in Rome.

Ushering in our enjoyment of Rome, the good doctor Terra, still attired in his dinner suit, had to rush in to deliver our Jamie at the Salvatore Mundi Hospital when he arrived unexpectedly a bare two weeks after our arrival from Tel Aviv. To us, Terra's method of delivery, prompted as it may have been by not wanting to miss too much of the party, involved pushing our little newcomer out – the fingers of both of his hands probing deeply into Joosik's upper abdomen. Although I was cross about what seemed to have been the unnecessary additional pain which this caused, Joosik was, astoundingly, on her feet within thirty minutes of the delivery. Just as astounding was that, as with little Andrew's birth in Tel Aviv, she didn't utter a peep.

Joosik at the Rialto Bridge, Venice – 1973

Then followed our extraordinary introduction to residential Rome, being put up as we were in an apartment in the so-called Venerable English College in Via di Monserrato. The College had been founded in 1362 and had been used as barracks by Napoleon's troops during their occupation of Rome in 1798.

More colorful still was the history of Piazza Farnese which was little more than a few steps away from the College. Its uses in earlier times had included various methods of dispatching enemies, such as the much favored burning at the stake or boiling in oil. Later, in the 16th century, one side of the piazza was taken up by the construction of an imposing palazzo (palace), for which extensions were designed by Michelangelo Buonarroti at the behest of Pope Paul III in 1534.

This was fantastic stuff for a young Aussie family, but we soon had to move because in many ways it seemed as though the dark and gloomy apartment, though spacious, had not had that much work done on it since Napoleon's troops left. Also, Joosik found herself being more than a little spooked when she was there by herself.

We found a cheaper, though much airier and brighter, apartment outside the old city just across the ancient Ponte (bridge) Milvio over the serenely meandering Tiber. And we soon discovered that we had substantially less ancient neighbors such as Audrey Hepburn, who owned a nice enough bungalow over a stout fence behind us, and Lee Marvin who, we were told, kept an apartment somewhere above us. Neither of them ever came knocking, however, and we never did hear Marvin off on any of his Paint-Your-Wagon benders. Our neighborly 'mind if we join you' fantasy just didn't eventuate.

However much anyone could be caught up with their work in Rome, time had to be made for the great adventure of exploring not only this wonderful city, but the fortified craggy hilltop towns out there in the countryside surrounding it. One of the many joys of our time there was the manner in which staff in the family type trattorias which we frequented in places like this would dote on children, naturally including our little boys.

o O o

During our time in Rome we kept up, naturally, with developments in Israel and we had been as shocked as everyone else when, on Judaism's holiest day, Yom Kippur, which fell that year on 6 October 1973, much of the Arab world launched what it expected to be an offensive of overwhelming force against Israel.

They miscalculated, but the enduring legacy of this war, not only for the combatants, was that it drove the politics of the region, with very little relief, even more profoundly to the right. Where it remains.

o O o

The only event of any real significance for the embassy that year took place on 16 December 1973 at Leonardo da Vinci-Fiumicino Airport – just half a day after we had gone through it at the completion of our posting.

Early in the afternoon, Palestinian terrorists, this time from the Abu Nidal Organisation (ANO), sprayed automatic gunfire down the long airport departure terminal where, the night before, Joosik and I had gathered up our two little boys, Jamie still in arms and Andrew still a toddler, to board our Qantas flight to Australia.

Killing two people in the long, foolishly straight, wing of the departure area and shattering windows, the terrorists attacked a Pan

Am flight into which they tossed incendiary grenades, killing twenty nine people. Other gunmen took hostages on the ground, hijacked a Lufthansa aircraft and were allowed to set off on an odyssey of landings and attempted landings around the region which finally terminated with a hero's welcome for them in Cairo.

o O o

On my first day back at work in Canberra in January 1974, I was summoned to see the head of the corporate management division, John Ryan – who, unbeknown to me, would be our next Ambassador to Italy.

I had been expecting such a summons because in my role as the Embassy's key management person I had not kept quiet about the asinine behavior of the Ambassador, Malcolm Booker, and his Deputy, Mary McPherson, towards Embassy staff.

Booker's impenetrable aloofness and McPherson's egocentricity had blunted the morale of the Embassy well before my arrival in Rome and I had in a way brought a lot of it to the surface by being seen – especially by our long serving local hire staff – to be *simpatico* and thus someone among their cowed Australian masters to whom they could turn. Valued members of the staff were taking more and more time off for stress, a condition which in turn was being regarded by those who were causing it as a weakness and even a tool for culling. Booker's own Secretary, the experienced Susie Windsor, who had been given this assignment as a reward for having served in some really awful places, had been driven to such distraction that she once threw at him the manuscript of a book he was writing and tried to follow this up with her weighty typewriter. At a time when the Whitlam Labor government was in full swing, those who perhaps showed a little too much enthusiasm for Gough's several visits to his much loved Rome, were being openly scorned. Marked for special treatment was a former staffer of Whitlam's, Irena Kuznik, who was widely liked in the embassy and whose health had, as a result, taken a tumble. I copped it on a number of fronts, including for being 'too young' for the job (the experience of three previous postings counting for nothing) and, in but one instance, for giving too much attention in my role as Consul to a highly distressed Australian mother, Maria Lostia, who had come to Italy looking for her abducted children.

Anyway, I had come to feel strongly enough about what had become the daily grind of this, that towards the end of my time there, when the Secretary of the Department, Sir Keith Waller, came through on an official visit, I asked if I could see him. He agreed, but this was kept to me handing him a formal note at his hotel and leaving me with no feel at all for what he would make of it. But I was satisfied with having found the nerve to approach the top guy and steeled myself for whatever the outcome would be – if anything. No more than a few days later, to my surprise, Waller's executive assistant, Bill Farmer, rang from their next stop, London, to say that the Secretary had asked him to tell me that he had found my note helpful and in fact confirming of other rumblings he had been hearing about unhappiness in the embassy. Also that Waller would pass this on to Ryan in Canberra and would I please leave it up to the Department to take it from there. Gladly, I thought.

So here I was in Ryan's office.

Like his mentor, Sir Arthur Tange, Ryan was a strong supporter of The-Game-They-Play-in-Heaven (rugby of course) and thus of promising character. My first encounters with him had been back in my rugby days, soon after I had joined Foreign Affairs, when he had made a point of coming over to congratulate me as I came off the field after a tough game or two for Queanbeyan. I didn't kid myself, however, that this would save me from a bollocking if he thought I deserved it. He occupied a supreme position of influence over careers, and to sharpen my awareness of this I had learned, belatedly, that McPherson was the godmother of one of his children. So on my way to Ryan's office trepidation was not that far out of the mix for me and I was wondering, now that I was out of Rome, whether I was about to feel the iron fist inside the Secretary's soothing glove. But having firmly shaken my hand and invited me to take a seat – though not on the comfy sofa – Ryan simply and pleasantly enough put it to me that I should now regard Rome as being behind me and would I kindly take a job at the next level up in his division.

I said, 'Yes, but …'

'We are dealing with the morale thing Howard – OK? It's not forgotten.'

There being no reason to disbelieve him, I said, 'Oh, fine, thanks very much Mr Ryan.'

So that was that I thought. But it wasn't – at least not quite.

I had barely spent a day or two in my new job at my humble desk out somewhere among all the others in the middle of a large open plan area, haphazardly carved up as it was by little banks of forlornly drooping pot plants, when David Irvine plonked himself down in his pally way on my rickety visitor's chair. David had been in Rome with me as a junior political officer on his first posting and was now working in the political division which looked after Europe. An amount of small talk ensued of the kind that colleagues who had shared a posting engaged in when they came across each other back in Canberra. But I could see what was coming. The conversation went something like this:

'So mate', he asked, 'have you seen the article by Des O'Grady?'

'Which one David.'

He said, 'The one about morale in Rome – a full-pager on the back of the *Fin Review.*'

'Oh, that one. Yes I have – what did you make of it?'

Still pally though perhaps now ever so slightly forced he said, 'Well … actually … Robin Ashwin [his division head] wants to know what *you* make of it.'

'Well', I said, 'I guess that as you were there you would be able to tell him as much about it as there is to tell.'

Come on David, I thought – out with it. Cosseted though you young political guys were in Rome, you knew damned well what was going on.

'Oh yes, I suppose I could and of *course* I have done so, but we just thought you might have something to add.'

'Nope – can't think of anything in particular.'

That was as far as David was prepared to go without giving away the pretty bloody obvious suspicion that I may have been behind the O'Grady article; that I was his embassy mole. He rose to leave – still of his natural enough good cheer, if a little deflated.

'And we will definitely have that cuppa soon Howard?'

'Yes David, you bet.' Unless Ashwin puts a flea in your ear and sends you back for another go.

Of course it was supposed that it would not occur to silly me that young David had been sent on a fishing expedition. Had it had been a John Ryan rather than a freshman agent on behalf of a Robin Ashwin, the question might have been put to me straight and I just might have answered it the same way, even though I had by this time learned quite a bit about the value of trust between colleagues in our hallowed foreign service. But nothing else was ever said to me about it by anyone.

Des O'Grady was and remains a respected Australian journalist and author who was living in Rome during our time there (and still is) and had got more than a strong whiff of the unhappiness in the Embassy. I had come across him a few times on the diplomatic and other circuits and liked him, but I had no knowledge of or particular interest in his work. People in the embassy business came across journalists all the time – the good, the bad and the ugly. Unlike many of my colleagues, I wasn't one to avoid them, but nor did I especially encourage them. Like us, they were after all in the news business and surely it was in our interest, where this was appropriate, to help them get it right.

Anyway, had the question been put to me straight, I may well have revealed that O'Grady had actually taken me aside at some function just a night or two before my departure from Rome to ask me to have a look at an article which he said he would be sending to Sydney – though I may not have given the full gist of our conversation which was along the following lines.

I asked, 'What's it about Des?'

'It's the morale thing at the Embassy Howard and it's too far out there to be ignored.'

'Oh. OK, let's have a look.'

It was good and it was obviously very well sourced – no doubt from within the embassy.

After I had read it, he said, 'What do you think Howard?'

'Are you going to show it to the Ambassador?'

With a wry smile he said, 'You *know* he doesn't talk to us [the press] Howard.'

I kidded him, 'McPherson?'

'Come on Howard. Look, I know that you and a few others have been trying to put things right in there, but I also know that you have been banging your head up against a brick wall and that it must be hurting.'

'That may be so Des, but there are other ways of trying to fix it and I haven't been overlooking them.'

'Yes, OK, I understand that – but is the article right?'

'Off the record Des – yes – it's pretty well right on the money.'

'Thanks Howard. Let's have a drink.'

Yes, I could have gone running to Booker or McPherson, but they would have derided me for having any kind of contact with O'Grady and it wouldn't have changed anything except, perhaps, lowering me in my own esteem to the level of toady.

As for David Irvine – well perhaps this very early foray of his into the cloak-and-dagger stuff may have helped set his path towards becoming in later years the Director-General of the Australian Security Intelligence Organisation (ASIO). Let's see if his parting (in September 2014) contributions to the enthusiasm of Australian politicians for overplaying threats to our security and our hallowed way of life work out better for him than did this little O'Grady 'incident'. Contributions such as seeking to allow ASIO to gather every kind of electronic communication sent or received by Australians (the so-called metadata) and to vastly increase its powers of arrest and detention, and who knows what else while people are held, secretly (?), for interrogation. (Will ASIO adopt interrogation techniques, such as the tried-and-true 'non-torture' American waterboarding, in its holding cells?) Not to mention, furthermore, the proposed penalties, including imprisonment, for anyone who might dare to question the conduct or the outcomes of these new powers.

The Rogue
Assam 1977

Suddenly, impressively, there he was, flowing from the deep forest like a dark shadow onto the narrow grassy clearing not more than fifty metres downhill to our left. Startled by our own sudden emergence from the forest on the rough serpentine track, he feinted crossly towards us before thinking better of it and lumbering off in a muscular, rolling gait down across the track toward the forest which was fairly close up on the other side.

The steady old hunter, Puri, brought his double barreled 450/470 Purdey elephant gun up to his shoulder, but Hacharan smoothly pushed the gun up. 'Not yet Puri sahib' he hissed, 'we can't be sure it's the one'. The elephant surged into the forest and quickly disappeared.

In the fear and confusion of the sudden encounter, our village guides had not been able to positively identify him as the officially declared rogue. With only his right side in clear view, they could not see what they were looking for – the broken left tusk. We set off to find a way in. But not directly behind him, as at this point the forest was too thick and too much to his advantage.

Down the track we went looking for a way to get around in front of him where we might meet on terms more favorable to us. Me sporting a .375 magnum, bolt action, Holland and Holland, Puri, Hacharan and the villagers.

In a dip a hundred metres or so on we came to an open swampy area on our right, beyond which, back towards his last trajectory, rose a high grassy knoll in front of the forest. The swamp was the only way to get to the knoll and so we descended into it and headed towards a broad and fairly deep boundary of high bamboo and elephant grass on the other side, thirty or so metres away. We would figure out how to get through it or around it when we got there.

Picking our way from clump to slippery clump of grass across the swamp, we were almost through when there arose a mighty crashing and stamping right in front of us. No one had to be told what it was or what was about to happen. Transfixed, primal instinct and adrenalin took an electrifying grip. He had not been trying to put distance between us. *He* was coming after *us*. On *his* terms.

We were completely at his mercy. He was going to burst through right on top of us and those of us with the guns knew that, at this impossible upward angle, with his vital organs deeply protected, no amount of fire could stop him having his way with us. Stumbling back into the bog, we awaited our wrenching, tearing, bloody fate.

But just as glimpses of his hide shimmered wildly through the last stands of cover, he turned and retreated. Loudly. Furiously. Thankfully.

Hearts pounding harder than seemed possible, we staggered back through the swamp. Breathlessly. Dignity in tatters. Not enough air even for an oath.

Clambering back up onto the path, boots full of slime and leaches, regrouping, hearts still pounding, we could see him off at the top of the grassy knoll. Waving his head and trunk defiantly, triumphantly, he turned to his left for a last disdainful glare before again powering away into his forest.

The villagers pointed excitedly in his direction. 'Look sahib, look, the tusk is broken' was the obvious translation.

Mightily glad to be still in one piece, I had suddenly lost even the

Across the river …

… and into the trees

little enthusiasm I had had for the hunt and I was filled with a fearful admiration of the grandeur and the tenacity of the rogue. For today, the hunt was over as he would now keep his distance. So we began the long trek out.

But this was not to be the end of it.

o O o

My second posting to New Delhi, ten years after the first, was a consolation prize for the cancellation of my appointment, in 1975, to open a new Embassy in Baghdad.

No one had been able to tell me why we had suddenly wanted to be pals with Iraq. It was a good job though and, from what we could tell, Baghdad sounded appealingly exotic, if bloody hot. Our preparations had got as far as the packers being booked and a real estate agent getting ready to rent out our little house at the bottom of Curtin.

Why had it been cancelled?

Well, it had a lot to do with that nice man Saddam Hussein's petro-dollars cashed-up Baathist Party, a dodgy Pakistani loans dealer by the name of Tirath Khemlani, Prime Minister Gough Whitlam's hesitation in reigning in his foolish Resources Minister, Rex Connor, and Malcolm Fraser's dummy spit over what he regarded as being a reprehensibly (his word) secretive and procedurally irregular attempt to secure a loans deal to finance Connor's ambitious resources and infrastructure programs.

Known as The Loans Affair, it was Fraser's catalyst for bringing down Whitlam's government and ushering in his. And for putting the plan for the new Embassy on hold.

Flitting as he did through this silly landscape, Governor General John Kerr, even sillier in the undersized black silk top hat perched precariously on his pom-pom silver locks, was but one of the more comical distractions in all of the attending side-shows.

As they all headed off to see what was waiting for them around their next bends, we skipped our Baghdad one and came across the old one to New Delhi.

You beauty!

o O o

Anyway, well into the second time around for me in New Delhi and the first for Joosik and our little boys, it was 1977 and we had come to Jorhat, in the middle of Assam, at the invitation of our new Sikh friends, Hacharan and Habans Singh.

Hacharan was the General Manager of several vast tea gardens (as they are known in India) in the region and we had been introduced to him and his charming wife, Habans, in New Delhi by a close friend of ours, Gurchuran Puri. Coincidentally, Hacharan's brother, Iqbal, was, at the time, the Indian Defence Attaché at their High Commission (Embassy) in Canberra. Iqbal had recently been stabbed in his home by a member of the fringe Ananda Marga religious sect whose leader, it was claimed, was being persecuted by the Indian government. The same sect, or members of it, would later pose enough of a threat to me as Australia's Consul-General in Bangkok for additional personal security precautions having to be taken.

Puri had been a well-connected colonel in the Indian army when, following the collapse of the British Raj in the late 1940s, he was appointed as the first Indian Commissioner for the North East Frontier Areas (NEFA) which borders the vast and distant state of Assam – all previous Commissioners having been British. Hacharan had been a junior officer under Puri and now that he was back in Assam he wanted Puri to visit. He especially wanted Puri to help him deal with a rogue elephant which had killed many people in his district and where Hacharan was in fact the chief wild life warden. In his younger days, before anyone had been thinking about conservation, Puri had been an experienced big game hunter.

We happily agreed to be included in the visit, although I had doubts about being included in the hunt.

Puri (which he preferred to his first name, Gurchuran), Joosik, our two young boys and I set out from New Delhi before dawn for the four day drive across parched northern India, over the top of Bangladesh and on to Jorhat. There had been serious misgivings among some of my High Commission colleagues about the advisability of driving, rather than flying, especially through chronically drought stricken Bihar where armed highway banditry had become rife. But with Puri's savvy and excellent contacts, we would be in good hands on the road and we would be hosted along the way by the commanding officers of the army garrisons at historic Lucknow and Patna. For the final night on the road, we were booked into the government Circuit House on the banks of an impressive sweep of the mighty Brahmaputra River at Gauhati, the capital of Assam.

It was a drive like only drives in India can be. At times, the roads being cluttered with all manner of mostly entertaining traffic – from simple pedestrians and whole families on one pushbike, to horse and camel drawn carts, dilapidated and misshapen buses with passengers clinging to the roofs and hanging out of the doors, Tata trucks shouldering their way through and the odd elephant plodding along with its heavy load or on its way, brightly decorated, to some exotically festooned celebration. At other times, the roads being eerily deserted or, in the very early mornings, simply threading together countless sleepily stirring villages through the haze ever pungently rising over a thousand years of humble, unchanging, rural life.

And then there was one of the more mesmerizing sections – with the sun, at first a rippling red, floating languidly up and out of the reluctant dawn to present an impressive stretch of Hindustan's river of life – the mighty, the imperious, Mother Ganga (Ganges).

o O o

Hacharan and Harbans greeted us warmly on arrival and made us feel as though we had been friends for years. They lived in a rambling, generously proportioned, planter's bungalow and over the next few days we toured the immaculately manicured tea gardens and were the guests of honor for an evening of food and robustly colorful song and dance provided by the tea workers in their village on the estate. Hacharan was an enlightened manager who interacted in a remarkably progressive and human manner with all of those in his charge, regardless of rank, religion or caste. Generally speaking, the single caste Sikhs were much better at this than the Hindus.

He showed us where an elephant had entered a part of the village only a day or two before our arrival and had taken a huge draft of sweet fermenting liquor from the village still before lumbering off in a tipsily destructive ramble. No one had been hurt and no one had been threatened by the elephant, but many had been frightened and a valuable product had been lost. They had not yet devised a way of stopping the sweetly seductive smell of the still penetrating the nearby forest.

Hacharan explained that the rogue was, however, a different story. It had been declared such by Assam's Ministry of Wild Life Preservation after proof had been provided of it having killed the minimum qualifying number of twelve people. In fact, he said, twenty seven deaths had been verified and the number was most likely much higher as the forest dwellers invariably preferred not to involve the police when the cause of death was so obvious and the official inquiry would be so tiresome. They lived peacefully enough with the elephants and knew that it was unusual for one to stay in a killer state for long.

In rare instances, however, one would develop an enduring belligerence towards humans. Maybe because their incessant encroachment just plain annoyed the hell out of him or, more likely, because he was mad at everything for not being allowed back into the herd until his manners improved. Which meant, to make matters worse, no access to the females.

Hacharan went on to explain that the common elephant way of killing people was to plant one leg on them and pull the body apart with its trunk. We later met a villager who gave us a heart-wrenching account of his wife being killed in this manner by the rogue. Hacharan was keenly sympathetic to the plight of both the elephants and the villagers. But he explained that as many villagers in his district were living in fear and the rogue was obviously staying rogue, he had to go. The government license had been issued and Hacharan had agreed to get the job done.

o O o

A day or two after our first encounter with the rogue, Puri set off on his own with Hacharan's Land Rover and driver to have another go at finding him.

We stayed behind to soak up a large weekend market near Jorhat. It was a stunningly colorful and lively affair at which tribal people from the nearby regions administered by the North East Frontier Agency came to barter their wares.

By late afternoon, we were relaxing at the Jorhat Tennis Club on a pleasantly grassed rise above the surrounding plain when we saw off in the distance Hacharan's Land Rover belting down the dirt road towards us. It pulled up in an impressive cloud of dust and the driver breathlessly conferred with Hacharan. Puri had killed the elephant. Yes, it was the rogue and Puri especially wanted me, the photographer, to come quickly.

Because he had other guests to look after, Hacharan couldn't go, but he urged me to do so. Swept up by the macho moment and my own bravado, I agreed – without having much of an idea of what I was in for. What I did know was that Puri was at least two hours away, half of which would be travelled in failing light by vehicle and the other by foot through deep forest at night with no English speaking person in sight.

Down the road we went.

After a few kilometres I thought that a quick equipment check would be in order. Just as well. I found only a few knockabout jackets for the cool of the forest night, but no guns and no torches. We doubled back to the bungalow where I picked up the Holland and Holland and a handful of bullets. By sign language, I was assured by Hacharan's driver that torches of some kind would be supplied by the villagers at the forest entry point.

We arrived at the village as last light was fading over the deeply brooding forest beyond. Ancient flaming oil torches on thick sticks were produced and a man who had been on the hunt with Puri and knew where he was waiting stepped up. A few more volunteers joined us. We crossed the fifty metres or so of the darkly turgid river in a few dugout canoes (fine pieces of ancient craftsmanship in themselves) and clambered up several metres of crumbling clay bank on the other side.

Then off we went along a narrow trodden path through the swirling waist-high grass to the forest about another one hundred metres or so on.

Like it or not, I was thrust into the lead.

As we came to the fringe of the forest, the path seemed to be disappearing, so I stopped to get someone in the know to take the lead or point out the way. But they were all so close on my heels that they concertinaed into me and we all nearly fell in a heap.

It was funny, but no one was laughing.

So it suddenly struck me that my foolish adventure was to be in the company of rightly terrified villagers who were only going into the great forest way out there in remote upper Assam at night because they believed that the bold and fearless young sahib with the big gun knew exactly what he was doing and would protect them. For some reason they found the grim look on my face and the gun jauntily balanced on my shoulder reassuring.

Could it be that they were even crazier than me?

Anyway, I sucked in some air and plunged on into the forest with the light of the crude flaming torches dancing around us, searching for cracks in the walls of darkness and awakening some really interesting sounds of the night. Sounds which were new to me and which I could have quite happily done without.

Now a walk in the Australian bush at night can be interesting enough, but it is very unlikely that anything is going to come at you with any kind of intent. A crazed kangaroo or a kung fu emu? Unlikely. But here I was about as far from any recognizable support base that could be imagined and on a simple track which was hemmed in on all sides by the utterly dominant kind of forest that is completely unknown to most Australians. A forest which was home to a variety of nocturnal big cats, the elephants of course and quite possibly even the odd nest of dacoits or bandits. All as completely in their element as I was out of mine.

The villagers remained in a tight knot behind me and the slightest rustle nearby sent a discernible shiver through them. We pressed on. Puri and his own little band were in there somewhere.

An hour or so in, we could hear a group coming the other way. Light from their lamps flickered and danced through the forest ahead. Dacoits or friends? Rounding a tight bend we were suddenly upon each other.

It was Puri and for the sake of the villagers we gave each other a very civilized greeting. I thought better of 'Puri I presume?', but we were as pleased to see each other as any friends would be in the middle of the merciless night way out in the bloody wilderness.

The villagers of both parties were more openly enthusiastic in their mutual greetings and, fortified by now being a larger group with *two*

'Pity the proud pachyderm …'

Sahibs and *two* guns, they happily joined up to head back to the elephant. Puri explained that he had decided to leave at 9.00 if we hadn't shown up. It was 9.10.

There he lay on the ground in a small clearing. Confident of his power over we puny humans, he hadn't strayed that far from where we had first seen him. I had been worried that Puri might have got the wrong one, which would have rightly incurred the very serious wrath of the Indian government. A British diplomat had been expelled from the country fairly recently for such a transgression – or so the story went. But it was him alright – down on his right side in a small grassy clearing with his broken left tusk protruding from his sadly misshapen mass. The tip of his trunk, a delicacy for the villagers, had already disappeared. Other parts would be taken soon enough as word got around and the rest would be left for the forest to reclaim.

The shouts of exhultation from our entourage as we emerged from the forest brought the whole village out to line the bank of the river and haul us up out of our stout little craft with great joy and hullaballoo.

Despite government sympathy for their plight, the elephants were abundantly at the mercy of the relentless march of the shifting cultivators – those who had been clearing patches of forest, cultivating it for a few years until the soil was exhausted and then repeating the process in a new patch further on. Over many many generations, these cultivators had come to belong to the forest as much as the great variety of animals that also used it and depended on it. But the cultivators had multiplied into a relentlessly and destructively disproportionate dominance.

Pity the proud pachyderm or the graceful big cat or the magnificent constrictor that occasionally struck back.

o O o

After a reluctant and leisurely departure from Jorhat, we spent our first night on the long road back to Delhi in Gauhati – in the same Government Circuit House where we had spent our last night on the way in.

We had often used both these and government Rest Houses in our travels around the country, with the latter being considerably more rustic than the Circuit Houses which, as the name implies, were there essentially for the use of government officials with district responsibilities. Foreign diplomats were allowed to use Circuit Houses on application, but anyone could just bowl up to the Rest Houses and, by comparison, rough it.

On this occasion and no doubt with a little encouragement from the well-connected Puri, we were given the suite which was to be used the next evening by the Prime Minister, Indira Gandhi. Nice, but so what.

Well, the 'so what' of it hit me hard when, on the next day, we were about a hundred kilometres west of Gauhati, well on our way to a much anticipated diversion up to mystical Dahjeeling. Located on a high ridge in the cool foothills of the Himalaya and surrounded by some of the best tea growing country in the world, we would, with luck, be able to see off in the furthest reaches of eastern Nepal the world's third highest peak, Kanchenjunga. Shades of John Masters' *Far Far the Mountain Peak* and other tales of the Himalaya which so captivated his continuing readership, including me.

Anyway, back down on the Deccan this pleasing prospect completely evaporated when it suddenly hit me that I had left my bloody pistol behind in Gauhati. Sure enough, a forlorn rummage through our luggage in the boot failed to turn it up.

Well, having left it behind was one thing, but having left it under the mattress that the Indian Prime Minister would be sleeping on that night conjured up the possibility of all sorts of outcomes for me – none of them good. I had a vision of it being found by her security minders who might be already after me. Especially as I had never got around to actually registering the damn thing in India.

I had gotten into the habit of taking along this weapon, a Ruger .22 long-rifle nine shot pistol, whenever we took to the deeper Indian countryside. I was careful to keep it out of sight and was very sure that it was only there to be used in some really bad worst-case scenario. We did often go to fairly out-of-the-way places and, realistically, trouble of a kind which would not respond to reason was never actually that far away in India. So, at the Circuit House, out of sight under the mattress it had furtively gone.

Arriving back on the scene, I was greatly relieved to see that the Prime Ministerial party had not yet arrived and that there did not seem to be any kind of reception committee waiting for me. So at the front desk I asked as blithely as I could if I could check the suite for something I had left behind.

What, like this assassin's pistol?! they would ask as the advance body guard pounced.

But they didn't. Instead, I was graciously given the key and found the pistol where I had left it, despite the bedding having been completely changed and the room thoroughly readied for the Prime Minister.

Phew!

Assam. Joosik with Hacharan Singh.
The trophy is, happily, from a bygone era.

Helping Australians Abroad

Up until the time, in 1984, when I was appointed as the first Director of the newly created Consular Policy unit in the Department of Foreign Affairs (which had not yet been merged with the Department of Trade), formal guidelines for the conduct of the Department's responsibility for the welfare of Australian citizens (and businesses) abroad – as defined by the *Vienna Convention on Consular Relations*, to which Australia is signatory – were well enough intentioned but really thin. Not that this all changed overnight with my appointment, but creation of the additional resource at this level was certainly a step in the right direction.

In the 1960s and 70s, the way this business was conducted on the ground in so many different, invariably challenging, environments and cultures, was left largely to the good sense of the relevant Australians and their locally-engaged staff at our overseas missions. A good sense which was not always, however, that well-conditioned by life in easy-going Australia. A good sense which for most had been rarely challenged by the unexpected or the vicious or the chronically corrupt.

The better consular appointees, not always that well supported by under-resourced Canberra, took their work seriously and more often than not to heart. With precious little preparation before taking up their assignments, they were simply expected to deal with many deeply moving, emotionally traumatic and sometimes threatening situations – not all of which had happy endings. They were expected to cope. They were expected to turn up the next day with their brave face on and their best foot forward. Even had it been available, the unspoken stigma of seeking counseling would very likely have been avoided. We will never know how many personal casualties there were of this neglect.

They were the trailblazers of a fledgling consular service who, on their voyages of discovery, both of themselves and their work, were building a corporate experience which contributed to that seminal appointment of mine and, beyond, to the highly developed and responsive consular service which is provided by today's Department of Foreign Affairs and Trade. A service whose social and political importance cannot now be overstated at any level of government.

From the mid 1960s, my own voyage in Australia's consular service included dealing with accidental deaths, murder, disappearances, terrorism and the imprisonment of Australians abroad. Here are but a few of the experiences which I encountered along the way.

A Cremation in Goa
1977

As First secretary and Consul in this most welcome career reincarnation in India, I had responsibility for the welfare of Australians travelling or living in the whole of India – valuable Consulates-General in both Bombay and Calcutta having been recently closed to save budget.

The world's most populace democracy was a magnet for the young and the adventurous, many of whom were doing it on a shoestring – roughing it with other youngsters and taking their chances. India: kaleidoscopically diverse, colorful, mysterious and welcoming. But also full of danger for the naïve and the foolish.

As my role at the High Commission also covered a demanding range of management responsibilities, the day-to-day array of consular cases was handled by a dedicated Vice-Consul and one locally-engaged person. They were very busy. In a bit of an exception to the rule in those days, my High Commissioner, Peter Curtis, made it clear to everyone at the High Commission that, when the chips were down, nothing mattered more to him than the welfare of Australian citizens.

With a relaxed view of life and his feet firmly on the ground, Vice-Consul, John Smith, was especially suited to consular work. At the time of my arrival he had his hands full, including with a case involving the infamous serial killer, Charles Sobraj, who had preyed on and murdered tourists across Nepal, India and probably Thailand. Mansonesque in his own way, Sobraj had no trouble attracting female followers. In India, these had included an Australian, Mary-Ellen Ether.

They had been caught in New Delhi in the aftermath of one of their signature acts of drugging the evening meals of a tour group in the dining room at the Ashoka Hotel, just across the road from our High Commission, preparatory to robbing them after they had been given time to collapse in their rooms. This time, Sobraj had been heavy-handed with the doses and the tourists had starting slumping into their meals. (In the early 1980s on posting to Bangkok as Consul-General, I discovered that Sobraj had, before his swing through India, lived for a while in a small apartment just across the road from our embassy.)

Following her sentencing, Mary-Ellen Ether found herself a friend in Delhi's Tihar jail – none other than Indira Gandi. Gandi had been put in there by the man she both preceded and succeeded (following a short stint by Charan Singh) as Prime Minister – the ascetic and devotee of starting his day with a glass of his own warm urine, Moraji Desai. Ether was quietly released soon after Gandhi's resumption of the Prime Ministership.

The Sobraj story attracted interest around the world. Richard Neville, a sometime Australian author, was in and out of New Delhi researching for a book which he was going to write about the case. After a while, he was complaining to me that he was being harassed by cronies of noted American investigative reporter and author, Tommy Thompson, who was also gathering material for his book on the business. Thompson's book became the best-selling *Serpentine*.

Anyway, other consular business ranged typically across enquiries about sick and missing Australians, Australians who were succumbing to the easy availability of drugs, and those who pushed their luck a bit too far with normally forgiving or seemingly meek Indians.

The case load could at times be too much for just John and his assistant, Rita Cooke, to handle and so we shared it as best we could and I had to be sure that I took my turn with the difficult ones, wherever they popped up.

One of these came about when we were notified by the relevant authorities in Goa, the former Portuguese colony on the south western coast which had only recently been annexed by India, that they had a body which they believed was that of an Australian. They had his passport, though it had been badly damaged by water, and his body was in their morgue. As they were not sure that the two matched, our assistance was requested and I flew to Goa.

On arrival, I was met by an official and went straight to the morgue. Checking in to the hotel could wait.

I didn't have high expectations of the conditions I would find at the morgue. Just as well. The body was only lightly refrigerated, though it was at least out of sight on the bottom level of a bank of drawers. The stench in the room was not new to me, but it was thickly memorable.

I was told that the body had been recovered from a river where, the estimate was, it had been for about two weeks. If that were so, given the warm weather, it appeared to be in remarkably good shape. Who would ever know what the real story was. He was partially clothed and seemed to be in one piece. Positive identification had its challenges, but there were enough recognizable features for me to confirm his identity. In death, faces normally hold together longer than other parts of the body.

Canberra had been in touch with his family who had confirmed that they had not heard from him for some time and had asked, should it prove to be him, that we arrange for him to be cremated and for his ashes to be returned to them. This proved to be much harder to arrange for a Christian dying in staunchly Catholic Goa than I had imagined.

Cremation for members of the Hindu faith is the norm and I was told that a cremation facility was available nearby. But it was for Hindus and there had never been, in the knowledge of the official, a Christian cremation in Goa. Yes, the Portuguese influence had brought about a large Christian population there, but they staunchly preferred burial – to the extent that the church would have to sanction a cremation of any Christian anywhere in Goa, including at a Hindu cremation site. The Hindu priests would accommodate the cremation, but not without the approval of no lesser personage than the Bishop of Goa.

My local official was very good and we were shortly ushered into the august presence of the bishop at his palace, which was not that far away. (Yes, the homes of reigning Catholic Bishops were known in many places around the world as palaces.) He was very accommodating and we left with his seal of approval.

At the cremation facility, further challenges were waiting. It was, as I should have known, an open air one behind an ordinary cyclone wire type fence attended, or so it seemed, by just a few laborers. Once shown the bishop's approval, they agreed to arrange the cremation for the next morning. They would lay on the wood and build the pyre and supervise the cremation for what seemed to be a reasonable price.

I handed over the rupees and we headed off to the hotel. But on the way, the official, who was Hindu, remembered that while Hindu dead were usually prepared for cremation in a simple cotton winding cloth, Christians would, regardless of cremation or burial, have to have a coffin. He knew where to get one and said we could pick it up on the way to collect the body in the morning.

We arrived at the morgue with the coffin early in the morning. It appeared to be of sound timber construction, the right size and shape and with a nice enough lid.

In the morgue, the coffin was placed alongside the ground level drawer where the body was and a few helpers started lifting it into the coffin.

Feeling bad enough about how such a young life had been ended – by bad luck, misadventure or otherwise – and knowing that neither we nor his family would ever know which, I was aghast at seeing the body coming apart as it was lifted. It was in more of an advanced state of decomposition than had been evident in the drawer in the darkened room. A few more hands were needed and we managed to get the poor young man into the coffin.

Placed as it was on the concrete floor and with the body obscuring the inside of the coffin by the time I came to their assistance, I did not notice a horrible flaw in its construction until the coffin was being lifted onto the top of the only transport available – the usual two-toned black and yellow Morris Oxford taxi. It turned out that cost had been saved on the otherwise sound looking coffin by having only a thin sheet of cloth stretched across a few horizontal planks on its base. The body started sagging through the gaps and everything had to be carefully put back onto the roadside.

Protecting the body as best we could from the gaze of curious passers-by, we rounded up a suitable length of cloth and with some difficulty bound the body as securely as possible before returning it to the coffin and the top of the taxi.

I had seen funeral pyres before, including on the banks of the Ganges River at the holy city of Benares, but was nevertheless surprised to be confronted on this occasion with an impressively oversized one. About five feet high, it had been carefully built of sizeable enough logs in a crisscrossed fashion and was ready to go. The attendants were very respectful of the body and the process. Urns of flammable oils, most likely ghee and paraffin, were produced and the cremation got underway with what soon became a fierce fire.

The ashes would not be available until late in the afternoon, as the fire had to burn right out and cool naturally before, as it was explained, an appropriate selection of ashes, from the top of the body to the bottom, could be recovered from the mound of wood ashes.

In a somber mood, I left late that evening for New Delhi with the wax-sealed earthenware jar which was duly sent on to the grieving family.

The Guy with the Pistol
Belgrade 1979

It was just another polluted sunny summer's day in about the middle of downtown Belgrade and I was getting on with the usual routine up in my fourth floor office at the Embassy.

Around mid-morning, the phone rang. It was one of our two

Kashmir 1977.
'If there is a paradise on earth, it is this ...

Australian Federal Police security guard/receptionists downstairs.

'Howard, there's a guy down here with a pistol.'

'With a pistol?'

'Yes.'

'Is he threatening anyone?'

'No.'

'OK, where are you and where is he?'

'Well … he's in the lobby and we're in our refuge.'

'Oh. What's he doing?'

'Just sitting there by himself with the pistol in his lap.'

'Are there any other visitors there with him?'

'Not any more.'

'I'll be right down.'

o O o

Our posting to Yugoslavia came about because of our love of India.

Fairly well into our New Delhi posting, we had driven the one thousand kilometres or so up to the fabled Vale (valley) of Kashmir where we stayed for a week on a delightfully decrepit house boat – one of several operated by the venerable Hajji Bhutt. 'Hajji' because, as his red hennaed beard also indicated, he had done his hajj, or pilgrimage, to Mecca.

Located on the western shore of an outer reach of Dal Lake and hugging a large grove of ancient Chenar trees, our houseboat was probably an hour's languid paddle south in one of the lake's distinctive shikara – a small, flat-bottomed boat – from the hectic jumble of Srinagar. Across the lake, out beyond its eastern shore, rose the most impressive of the mountain ranges encircling the Vale – the Karakorum, home of the soaring K2, the world's most challenging peak for mountaineers and second in height only to Everest. On the eastern shore itself were the remnants of the fabled Shalimar gardens – a more comfortable paddle of about twenty minutes. Shalimar had been commenced in 1619 by one of the greatest of the Mughal emperors, Jahangir, for his wife, Nur Jahan – 'Light of the World' On one of the pavilions in the gardens is inscribed, in Persian, a famous sentiment attributed to Jahangir – 'If there is a paradise on earth, it is this, it is this, it is this'.

Apart from our being paddled around the lake and feasting our eyes on the beautiful Shalimar and other gardens, our many adventures during the week included almost losing our little six years old adventurer, Andrew, when, having clambered up one side of a large boulder, he promptly slid off the other side into the edge of a fast flowing snow-fed headwater of the Jhelum River where we had been fishing in the early morning. Plunging frantically in, I managed to grab him and all was soon back to normal – assisted as it was by the old cook from the

'... produced a frying pan from thin air and cooked up our brown trout catch ... '

houseboat who had tagged along with us. In our moment of need, with two of us towelling off from our ducking in the icy water, he quickly got a campfire going, produced a frying pan from thin air and cooked up our brown trout catch for a delicious breakfast all round.

Towards the end of the week, we drove up to one of the further reaches of the valley, passing occasionally through flocks of sheep and goats and their extraordinarily weathered, though friendly, herders who brought lambs over for the boys to cuddle. We had to turn back at the point where the road began its more serious ascent through ragged snow-capped ridges to the beckoning Tibetan plateau.

To take that one on, as we thought we must, we would have to return. But this would require more time than a normal posting period of two years would allow.

So, soon after we got back to Delhi, I set about asking for an extension. My timing could not have been worse.

The response from Canberra was uncharacteristically fast and to the point. They had to get someone to Belgrade quickly – as a sudden illness had led to the occupant of the senior consular and management position there having to be withdrawn.

They wanted me to go. It was a promotion. I didn't have a choice.

We not only didn't get the extension, but were out of New Delhi six months early.

o O o

And so it was that in early 1978 we found ourselves 'round our next bend – in Belgrade.

Suffering as we were from withdrawal symptoms, it didn't start off that well.

Belgrade was drab and dreary in both appearance and culture, with a stiff East/West relationship – even though Tito's guns were pointing north – and with what seemed to be pretty limited opportunities for adventure. Kaleidoscopic India had spoiled us more than a bit, but we'd be bound to find things and places to enjoy. The prospect of which came to be sweetened by our good fortune in having on hand one of the finest Australian ambassadors we had come across – Barry Dexter. A career diplomat and activist in aboriginal affairs, Barry had been a force behind Gough Whitlam's creation of the Department of Aboriginal Affairs and became its first head. In Belgrade, back in the diplomatic fold, the quality of Barry's human impact and reach was greatly complimented by his gifted wife, Judith.

Anyway, Wikipedia reveals that Belgrade, settled in one fashion or another since the 6th millenium BC, had been 'battled over in 115 wars and razed to the ground 44 times'. When a coup by military officers in March 1941 replaced the Axis friendly Prince Paul on the throne of the Kingdom of Yugoslavia with the much less friendly Prince Peter II, Hitler spat the dummy and promptly had the city bombed intensively for four days. As if that wasn't enough, precisely three years later, in 1944, the other side used 600 aircraft in a massive carpet bombing sortie which virtually finished the city off. It had been rebuilt by the time we got there but, understandably enough, on a shoestring.

My work as First Secretary and Consul was busy enough for me to discover in the middle of our first winter there that the buses did not start running until 4.30 am. I had been stamping my feet in the snow just down the road from our house in Dedinje for about twenty minutes before clambering on board. Empty, but as warm as toast.

Those were the days.

o O o

Anyway, here I was heading down in the lift to see what could be done about the guy with the pistol.

My first stop was with our AFP guys in their bullet-proofed refuge – which doubled as a reception counter.

'What do you suggest fellas?'

'We're not sure.'

'OK, he's just sitting there by himself cradling the pistol and hasn't threatened anyone with it, right?'

'Right.'

'He's alone, but if other visitors appear it could get worse.'

'Right.'

'And who knows what he might get up to if we just leave him sitting there?'

'Er, Right.'

'Well, here's what we'll do. Kell, why don't you call the police and get them to come quickly. Be sure to tell them that he is not threatening anyone at the moment. See if you can maintain contact with them on the phone so you can keep them up with what is happening.'

'What is happening?'

'Yes, while I am out there talking with him.'

'Oh.'

'Fred, please take the back exit, go around to the front of the building and stop any visitors from coming in.'

'OK.'

Out I went. There is nothing quite like fronting up to a stranger with a pistol for focusing the mind and the memory.

A smallish man in drab enough clothing, he looked up, languidly and without apparent hostility, from his seat on the bench – still cradling the pistol in his lap. As far as I could see, his finger was not on the trigger.

'Dobordan gospodin' (hello sir).

'Dobordan.'

'Good morning', I tried.

'Good morning'. Ah, he spoke English.

'Are you Australian?'

'Yes, I think so.'

'Mind if I sit down?'

'No.'

'Can I help you with something?'

'I'm not sure.'

'Do you want to give it a try?'

'I'm unhappy.'

'What about?'

'I'm not sure.'

We had a bit of a think about this.

'Are you planning to do anything with the pistol?'

'I don't know.'

'Can I have a look at it?'

'Sure.' And he handed it over.

'Is it loaded?'

'I'm not sure.'

'Mind if I check?'

'No.'

It was a small pistol – most likely a .22 or 9 mm and looked like it had been around for awhile. I had no idea what the make was and didn't really care. Little guns can hurt just as easily as big ones, especially at close quarters. Ask the mafia.

He wasn't bothered about me turning it over in my hands for a bit, so I slipped out the magazine. Six shot capacity by the look of it, but it was empty.

He had a distracted air about him. Neither especially alert nor anxious.

'Is there one in the chamber?'

'I don't know, I don't think so.'

I checked. There wasn't.

'Do you have any bullets?'

'Yes.'

'Can I have a look at them?'

'Well, alright.'

He took them out of one of his trouser pockets and handed them over. Three only.

'Is that all of them?'

'Yes.'

'Do you have any other weapons?'

'No.'

I handed the pistol back to him, but kept the magazine and the bullets. It was a trust thing. If he had more bullets, any move to chamber one could not be done quickly.

'Are you sure you wouldn't like to discuss anything with me?'

He rubbed his eyes in a tired sort of way, but slowly shook his head.

'Can I get you a drink?'

'No thanks.'

'Do you remember why you came here?'

He smiled a little wanly. He wasn't sure.

'Do you remember why you brought the pistol with you?'

'No, not really.'

'Do you have any medicine with you?'

'No, but I think I might have some at home.'

We had a quiet think about this. I wasn't sure that trying to bring his troubles to the surface would be helpful.

'I hope you will understand that we have had to call the police.'

He glanced at me, perhaps a little hurt, but nodded yes.

'I'd like to sit here with you until they come. Please tell me if there is anything I can get you.'

'OK, thank you.'

And so they came.

Our AFP guys had done a good job on the phone and out on the footpath. The police did not storm the Embassy. One plain-clothed man came through the front door – calmly enough.

We exchanged looks – mine accompanied by a discreet show of the magazine and bullets, indicating that things were under control. He, thankfully, held back.

I reached over and gently took the empty pistol from where it was resting in our visitor's lap. 'Do you mind?'

'No.'

'This is a policeman.'

'Oh.'

I excused myself from our visitor and he remained seated, quite calmly, while I joined the policeman a step or two away. I gave him the bits and pieces of the pistol and explained where we were up to.

I said that while the pistol had caused alarm, our visitor had not threatened anyone in any way. I said that he was obviously going through some emotional crisis, that he appeared to be on medication, and that he obviously needed help. I asked that he not be manhandled.

The policeman could not have handled the situation better if it had all been scripted for him. He took it all in as smoothly as if he had been contemplating nothing more threatening than a chevapchichi sandwich and he assured me and our visitor that he would be treated well.

I asked if I could be informed of what they learned about him and he agreed.

He asked our visitor to go with him and he got up without demur. I went out with them.

They were joined on the footpath outside by two other plain-clothed policemen. Our AFP guy stepped back. I shook hands with our visitor and policeman 1. They put him between two of them on the back seat of their car, but did not otherwise restrain him.

Our visitor waved wanly to me as they drove off.

I went back inside.

'OK, it's over', I signaled to our AFP guys. 'You can come out now. Well done.'

Back to my sunny office, though in a more reflective mood.

Within a day or two, true to their word, the police let me know that the man had been in and out of psychiatric care in Yugoslavia and was not considered to be dangerous, though the pistol was a new development. He was being cared for by those who had previously treated him and would be kept under police observation for the time being. He was a dual Australian/Yugoslavian citizen who had been living back in Yugoslavia for some time.

o O o

We did find things to enjoy about Belgrade and Yugoslavia, but would nevertheless have not wanted to miss our flight out at the end of our posting. This had become a distinct possibility as the day of our departure, 8 May 1980, coincided with Tito's funeral and his passing cortege had held up our path to the airport for a long time.

As widely anticipated, the wheels started to come off Tito's Yugoslavia soon afterwards. He had been the engine which had given new, if in many ways forced and unnatural, unity to the single state for all southern Slavs – Yugoslavia – 'jug" (south) and 'slaveni' (Slavs). No one else possessed the authority which he had won for his role in leading the hugely effective Yugoslav resistance to the Axis powers during World War II. It simply wasn't something he could pass on.

Although the inter-ethnic and religious hatreds of the Slavs were never driven that far beneath the veneer of the Tito years, few would have believed that they could produce, in such a short space of time after his death, a successor as crazy as Slobodan Milosevic. Or that the UN and NATO would wait so long before putting a halt to his extraordinarily murderous campaign to impose Serbian dominance.

While the collection of new sovereign states which arose from the bitter Milosevic years may well deliver more durable solutions to the needs of their people and the region, we were fortunate to have been there and to have been able to range around freely and safely during less tumultuous times.

Australian Prisoners in Thailand 1981/83

For the Department of Foreign Affairs and for me as Australia's Consul-General in Bangkok, Thailand presented an array of serious consular challenges in the early 1980s.

Australians were flocking there to taste the kind of quality holidaying which 'the land of smiles' offered in an exotic culture of great variety and beauty. Squalor and crime too, though mostly unseen by the average tourist.

In their uniquely and almost universally friendly way, the Thais were and no doubt still are wonderful hosts to foreign tourists. To their surprise, however, some Australians, such as the more hairy chested stubbies and thongs brigade, could find out too late that Thais did not take at all kindly to being pushed around. And that robbery, often in broad daylight, didn't take more than the discreet show of a sharp little butterfly knife to melt the boldest heart.

But the biggest challenge upon taking up my appointment in 1981 was the growing number of Australians in Thai prisons for drug offences – most involving the trafficking of heroin.

The Thais were responding to pressure, primarily from Western countries, to do something about the flow of drugs through Thailand from the rich poppy fields of the so-called Golden Triangle in the north – a hilly area spanning parts of Myannmar, Vietnam, Laos and Thailand. That shipments through Thailand were quite evidently being facilitated by corrupt Thai officials, both civilian and military, seemed to matter less than having a program which would give the impression in the West that something was being done. Western governments, including ours, were sending their police and customs operatives in to work with the Thais and, cynically as it often turned out, to land as many of their own citizens as they could in a legal system whose penalties were much harsher than in their own. Penalties which routinely included death.

Shortly before my arrival, the Australian media had been galvanized into action by the incarceration of a favored rugby league and amateur welterweight boxing champion, Paul Hayward, in Bangkok's notorious

Me and my consular team, Alan Moore, Bob Nash and John Atkins, meeting with Australian prisoners in Bang Kwang maximum sercurity prison, 1982.

Inspecting a Bang Kwang cell block.

Bang Kwang maximum security prison. Hayward, brother in law of the Sydney criminal, Neddie Smith, had, along with his friend Warren Fellows, been convicted of the possession of 8.5 Kilograms of heroin and sentenced to thirty years. They implicated the Australian owner of a Bangkok bar, William Sinclair, and he joined them at Bang Kwang, though he was released on appeal less than two years later.

The Embassy had been uncertain about how to handle the media stampede, which by the time of my arrival had Australians at home railing about the mounting number of Australian prisoners in both Bang Kwang and Klong Prem prisons. Uninformed and often plain anti-Asian sensationalism was neither helping the prisoners nor their families and friends who were caught in the middle. The Thais, who had probably expected praise for moving against the traffickers, were annoyed. My Ambassador, Gordon Jockel, a quiet and somewhat introspective man who preferred to keep away from the media, left it to me.

I invited the throng – the Australian media reps on the ground there and jocks on the telephone from Australia – to give me time to read up on the cases, consult with the people responsible for running Bangkok's prisons and meet with the prisoners themselves. Only then, I said, would I be informed enough to properly respond to their questions. They were to understand as well, however, the rights of the prisoners and their families to privacy and, in relation to intervening in both the legal processes and issues regarding prison conditions, the legal limitations of our consular remit. I suggested that in the meantime they might want to do their own research into the court transcripts of the cases that interested them. Most agreed – some with more grace than others – but the headlines kept coming.

In order to get the Thais on side, I went to see the head of the Thai Corrections Department, Khun Thawee Choosup. I wanted to have regular and direct access to the prisoners in order to see for myself the conditions inside the prisons. I would naturally consult with him about any concerns I had and would not be provoking public foot stamping. What we did would, in other words, be properly and privately between us – the Australian and the Thai governments. Urbane and fluent in English, Choosup said that this was the first time he had received such a request from a foreign embassy. He welcomed my interest and gave me access to all the prisons with no restrictions.

Over the next couple of weeks, I met and spoke with all of the Australian prisoners, listening to their stories and their complaints, explaining to them the limitations of our engagement with their legal processes, and assuring them that genuine complaints related to physical conditions, treatment by prison staff, food and medical care would be taken up with the Thais as rigorously as possible.

I found that although the prisons were as clean as any facilities of this kind could be in the unrelentingly humid and polluted air of Bangkok, the cell blocks were dark and crowded. In one, which was two floors high with cells running down both sides and a full length, floor to roof, open area in the middle – typical of the American kind so often seen in Hollywood movies – the center floorspace was crowded with Thai prisoners painting glue onto the flaps of envelopes. There were open cans of glue everywhere and the smell was overpowering. I didn't think this was a very good idea and said so until the prison officials and Choosup listened.

Typically, cells were shared by up to nine or ten people with one open squat latrine and one tap and wash basin in a corner. Clean enough matting rolls were provided for bedding on the smooth cement floors. Washing was done in cemented yards outside the cellblocks using long open tin troughs fitted with taps which delivered ample though very muddy looking water.

No one complained about any kind of gratuitous violence from either the guards or other prisoners. The prison routines, though firm, were largely benign. Foreigners were not singled out and visiting rights for family, friends and the press were reasonably generous. And the prisoners were provided with quite presentable medical services, with the main hospital facility for the men located at Bang Kwang.

If prisoners had money, which they were at liberty to receive from family and friends, they could have food of their liking delivered by local street vendors or nearby shops. Most of the Australians were able to take advantage of this to supplement what for them was pretty basic, though evidently reasonably nutritious, Thai fare. Especially offensive to the sensitivities of some of them was the standard unpolished 'red' rice which they were given instead of polished white. For a time, the ordering of supplementary food from outside was suspended when it was discovered that some of the Australians were adding vegemite and its available yeast to other ingredients to help produce a strong enough alcoholic brew.

The most unsettling thing for prisoners at Bang Kwang was the rattle of machine-gun fire, almost every Friday morning, when executions were carried out. Death sentences for Thais convicted of crimes more or less equivalent to those of the foreign drug runners were routinely carried out, whereas the death sentences for foreigners were routinely commuted to long prison terms. Foreigners could, furthermore, expect to be released on one of the King's regular amnesties after serving about a third of their sentences.

Time went by and visits developed into a fairly regular routine. My consular colleagues and I at the Embassy had a productive dialogue going with the prisoners and the prison officials and my relationship with Director-General Choosup had got onto a reliably good footing.

Paul Hayward appeared for a meeting with me at Bang Kwang one day with a few bumps and scrapes on his face and he didn't really want to talk about it. He had obviously had a run in with someone, but he wasn't saying who. I was pretty sure that he and others would have been quick to tell me if it had been the prison officers. I asked around and the story which emerged was that Hayward, getting into a bit of a habit of putting the wood on some of the Thais, had picked the wrong one and been given a hiding. Most foreigners, not only in the prisons, just couldn't get it through their heads how tough the Thais could be.

In due course, while on a routine visit to Bang Kwang, I found myself being escorted to a separate compound which I found to be occupied only by foreigners. It was fenced off from the rest of the prison and had a single one level cell block. The cells were about the same as the ones in the other blocks, but there was a covered outside area with tables and chairs which the prisoners could use at their leisure more or less throughout the day. Apart from the water in the open air washing troughs still looking as though it was coming straight from the mightily polluted Chao Phraya river, it was, overall, a big improvement. As long as they could keep the peace among themselves.

The Australians seemed pleased enough with this, though some were coy about how it had come about. It turned out that both the prison authorities and the Thai prisoners had become fed up with trouble-making by foreign prisoners. Not that the Thai prisoners couldn't handle it – all evidence to the contrary. But the prison officials concluded that if this was the culture the foreigners wanted, they could keep it to themselves.

All up, this was all going along about as well as I could have expected. The Australian journos too were settling down. Their level of mostly confected hysteria about the Thai legal system and prison conditions was deflating. Briefed as well as the Department in Canberra could manage, Australian politicians were not shooting from the hip as much as they once did.

We had got our consular role in relation to prisoners onto fairly steady ground but, in terms of my interaction with Director-General Choosup, this was about to be rattled.

At the end of a regular visit of mine to Bang Kwang, a representative group of the foreign prisoners, including some Australians, was milling around near my normal exit from the inner part of the prison waiting to attend an appointment with officials to discuss prison conditions. It was typical of the prison that there were only a few, unarmed, prison officers in attendance. Spotting me, the group came over and set about rehearsing their grievances with me as the attending officers looked on.

They said that if their demands were not satisfied all the foreigners would go on a hunger strike. This seemed a bit thick, I said, given the substantial improvements which had gone their way in recent times. Wouldn't it be better, I suggested, if they continued with the moderate course, which I would continue supporting, rather than risk undermining what had been gained?

But they didn't get it. Dumb maybe, but more likely just bored witless. The hunger strike not only went ahead but, unbeknown to me, the guys and most likely the onlooking officers managed to convey the impression up the line that I had encouraged it.

Sometime after this, I tried to make an appointment for one of my periodic chats with Director-General Choosup. His office said that he didn't want to see me.

'Oh, why?'

'Because you provoked the prisoners into a hunger strike which brought bad press down on the D-G's head!'

Perfect.

My freedom of access and movement at the prisons was withdrawn and, like the consular representatives from other embassies, I would henceforth have to make do with interviews through the bars at the general visitor areas and at the prescribed visiting hours.

I wasted no time making my annoyance known to the Australian prisoners. They said they had now been subjected to some new restrictions, such as the time they could spend out of their cells. I told them they were bloody idiots for having brought this upon themselves, but that I would do what I could to get back to where we had been. I said that they should not, however, be holding their breaths as the Thais were really, I thought justifiably, pissed off.

My election as Chairman of Bangkok's large Consular Corps and some friendly representations by my counterpart Consuls-General at the American and British Embassies, eventually led to Thawee Choosup and I making up and the restrictions on the foreign prisoners, which had not in any case been much more than a slap on the wrist, being removed.

An enduring problem in these prisons, as in most others around the world, certainly including in Australia, was the availability of hard drugs. The exception during my time in Bangkok was that this did not appear to have been the case in the women's section of Klong Prem. There, if new prisoners were addicts, they were taken aside and removed from their addiction – cold turkey – before joining the other inmates. I knew that this could be a dangerous business but, according to the Australian women there at the time, it worked.

Among the male prisoners, as far as I could tell, some who had not been addicted when they went in were when they came out. Those who had got into the trafficking business through their addictions, many of whom had evidently been 'mules' for the bigger, less visible, wheels usually remained addicts. But there were instances of some who never were users before and never became users during their incarceration.

Two had been in some sort of business together in Australia and, desperately down on their luck, so they said, had decided to infuse some quick cash by way of a one-time freelance. They gave a good impression of copping it on the chin and resolving to keep themselves clean until they qualified for amnesty – usually at about seven or eight years – and could then try to pick up the pieces of their lives. With the time they had to reflect, these two did not doubt that, apart from the normal risks associated with running drugs, they had been particularly vulnerable to the interests of those who could use them (dob them in) to help deflect attention away from the big time traffickers and their cronies in the established supply chains. The immunity of these chains would continue to be serviced as well by the periodic sacrificing of this or that pitifully dependent, and thus inconsequential, mule.

o O o

A salutary, if not surprising, lesson which I learned was that to the public at large in Australia none of this – what we had done to get on top of the human and human rights issues of imprisonment in Thailand – really mattered much. The undercurrent of public opinion, widely shared in Foreign Affairs, was why on earth we had bothered. Why should anyone worry about what happens in prisons to those lowlifes who are convicted of such serious crimes? Why shouldn't they cop it … and then some? Come on, who cares!

The answer was then and is now that the determination of punishment for a crime – any crime – is strictly an issue for the judiciary. One in which the sole and most bitter penalty concerns deprivation of liberty. One which does not and should not countenance the imposition of extrajudicial – unlawful – punishments which could further prejudice the health and safety of prisoners and the possibility of their rehabilitation. One which mandates that anything else should not be tolerated by any society, least of all the ones such as ours which claim so rightly to cherish, universally, human rights. And which are given to so proudly holding up their example to others.

My own take on drug addiction was then and is now that it is a horribly devastating *illness* which, though normally contracted by awful chance, peer pressure and the foolishness of youth, has to be combatted in a wholly unwarranted atmosphere of fear and loathing.

On my own initiative, one of my first policy outputs upon assuming, after Bangkok, my new role as Director of Consular Policy in the Department was to produce a comprehensive policy guideline on the consular responsibility of the Department of Foreign Affairs towards Australian prisoners abroad. I wanted to be sure that what I had learned up front over the past few years was suitably canvassed and provided as an interim policy and operational guide for the Department's consular operatives overseas. Mr Justice Michael Kirby, then President of the New South Wales Court of Appeal, commented favorably on the paper and provided me with some helpful advice.

Did the new policy guideline make a difference?

Yes, I believe it did, though with residual background snickering.

Murder in Pattaya
Thailand 1981/83

He was young, he was in his mid-twenties, and he was dead. Murdered on the side of a quiet little road in a scenic part of the country.

In the morgue at Pattaya, I could identify him easily enough from his passport photo, but only because the shotgun blast which had killed him had evidently been of small gauge and shot size and directed upwards to the back of his head, not the front. In other words, his face was still intact.

o O o

The Thai Foreign Ministry had informed us that they had the body and the personal possessions of an Australian man who had been murdered in the countryside near Pattaya. We had cabled their sketchy information to Canberra and the sad task of interaction with the man's family was underway. We needed more information and I went to Pattaya with a Thai member of our consular staff to get it.

Close enough to the bustling, polluted, tangle that is Bangkok, replete with sandy shores, waving palms, accessible islands and an uninhibited nightlife, Pattaya was a favorite destination for foreign tourists – though it had been clear for some that its seedier side had become visible enough to be undermining its other attractions.

Not that long after our arrival on posting in Bangkok, we had been taking our first turn at using one of the Embassy's modest weekend rental cottages on the outskirts of Pattaya town when a daytime walk with my wife and our two young boys down the main café/bar street along the beach revealed in this or that open-fronted bar, this or that scantily clad hostess with her face in the lap of this or that boofy customer. On another visit and at a different beach location, several young toughs threatened me with knives when I had asked them, politely enough, if they would mind not roaring their jet skis through the swimmers – which included our boys. And in another, which sealed our decision to find a better place for these cottages, when the behavior of dogs with a mass that had been washed up in front of the cottage closest to the beach caused one member of our Australian staff, big Bill Cox, who was there with his wife and their three little daughters, to discover that it was a man's body and that it had a bullet hole behind the ear.

o O o

The police showed us on a map where the body of the young Australian had been recovered. No one had been arrested and few clues had been found about who had killed him. More of an unlikely target they thought than most single men visiting Pattaya, as he had been there several times before on his breaks as an oil rig engineer somewhere in China and was therefore less of a stranger to the Pattaya culture. Though not suspected, they said they were looking for a Thai girl, possibly a hostess at one of the bars, who they thought had been with him more or less from his arrival in Pattaya, but who had disappeared immediately after the killing. They thought she had been on a morning spin with him in the countryside on his rented motorbike when he had been killed.

Given the nastiness and the corruption which pervaded the Pattaya scene, meaning that the young man may have upset some kind of tough or another, it seemed to me quite possible that the crime would not be solved and that no one would pay the price. The young man's family deserved more than this and we needed to show them that we cared enough to make as much productive noise as we could about it.

As I had half expected, the police, though polite and superficially helpful, had very little to give us and showed little enthusiasm for having a crack. So, with their sketchy little mud map in hand, down the road and out into the countryside we went to have a go ourselves. Yes, it was a bit beyond the consular remit of foreign embassies, but the police were OK with it and we weren't exactly armed and dangerous.

It was a clear day, possibly much like the day the young man and his girlfriend had chosen for their spin. The fresh morning breeze in their faces, her dark hair streaming. Two carefree youngsters out for a day's fun in easy-going Thailand.

Five or six kilometres out of Pattaya into the typically lush countryside, heading up the less used, partially sealed, coastal road towards the naval base at Sattahip, we turned off onto a narrow dirt one. A perfect choice for a spin on a rod and a picnic lunch somewhere down on the shady bank of a quietly flowing stream. The police's X on the map marked the spot, less than a hundred metres along, where the body and the bike had lain. We stopped and got out of the car with no idea of what to do next other than to feel something for the victim.

Back at the turnoff, from a lone store of weathered timber construction, several Thais were gesturing casually in our direction. A middle-aged woman disengaged from them and headed towards us. The others stayed put. Chances were she had figured out why we had stopped right there – a farang (foreigner), a Thai and their official looking car.

We strolled back to meet her.

As friendly and accommodating as most Thais are, it was possible that we might be in for a bit of a serve about what we thought we were doing out here on what was surely police business. Had someone around here been involved? Had someone warned them we were coming? Had we bitten off more than we could chew?

No, not at all. She wanted to help.

The manner of her telling of the story, standing there on the side of the empty, lonely, road left no room for doubting her account of what she had seen.

Having happened only days earlier, the killing was still very fresh in her mind. Fresh enough and vicious enough for her to be visibly upset in her telling of it.

She and others at the store, she said, had seen them coming down the straight sealed stretch of road from Pattaya. Two motorbikes. One, with its young farang man and a Thai girl, being harassed by two men on the other – the pillion passenger waving a sawn-off shotgun at them. In Thailand everyone knows a sawn-off shotgun when they see one.

Around the corner on to the dirt road they went and the young couple pulled over and got off their bike. The bike fell over and the guys with the gun stopped four or five metres short of them. The young farang walked back, steadily enough so it seemed. After a brief exchange of words, he passed over what seemed to be his wallet and then turned to walk back to the girl and his bike.

He was almost there, our witness went on, when the one with the gun moved up quickly behind him, raised the gun to the back of his head and fired.

The killers clambered back on to their bike and scooted off back in the direction of Pattaya leaving the girl untouched. She ran to the store, incoherent with shock. Evidently not an accomplice. The lady called the police and the girl disappeared. She wasn't telling us anything else about the girl and made it pretty clear that she had not trusted the police enough to tell them much about her either. Prudence probably dictated that she had not noticed enough of anything else about the killers to have them identified by the police.

Apart from the forlorn business of arranging the return of the young man's remains to his family and having to deal with our own feelings about such a vicious ending to such a promising life, that was it for us. There was nothing else we could do other than return to Bangkok and wait to see if the police came up with something else.

They never did.

Hostages in Colombo
Sri Lanka 1994

This didn't look good. It didn't look good at all. In fact it looked pretty bloody bad.

From our vantage point about thirty metres from the barred front gate of the vast Ansell compound in Colombo's Biyagama Export Processing Zone (BEPZ), angry young militants who had taken over the compound were thrusting two or three Australian hostages up to the gate for us to see. Assembling behind us were riot police and para-militaries fully geared up for a direct assault on the compound. Apart from the small Australian management contingent, the Sri Lankan workforce on site, numbering around eleven hundred, was not being allowed to leave.

o O o

At about 2.00 pm that day, 21 July 1994, the quietly spoken John Gardner, General Manager of the biggest single foreign investment in Sri Lanka, the Australian owned, state of the art $100 million Ansell high tech latex gloves operation, had called from his site office to tell me, calmly enough, that the whole place had been taken over by militants and that he had not yet been able to negotiate a way out of it. His management team, predominantly Sri Lankan, though including five Australians, was being held in the main office and were now being threatened with an assortment of weapons, though no firearms were in evidence. He mentioned broken bottles, acid filled gloves and, even more alarmingly, placement around the building of drums of explosively flammable liquids which the militants were threatening to set off in the event of a rescue attempt or if their demands were not met.

A team from the Janet Holmes à Court owned Australian Construction Company, John Holland, had been doing plant extensions, but had left the site before the takeover.

Gardner was working on the demands of the militants insofar as these concerned pay and conditions within his remit but, with major national elections just around the corner, it seemed to me that some political moves might be in play.

Gardner said he was being allowed free access to the telephone and that he had already spoken with his Managing Director, Harry Boon, who, though based in New Jersey, happened to be in Melbourne with the Managing Director of Ansell's parent Pacific Dunlop Group, Philip Brass. Also that both he and the militants were in touch with the management of the BEPZ and that things were hotting up.

He said he didn't think there was much I could do, but that as long as he continued to have access to the phone, he would keep me informed.

The hell with that. I told him that I was on the way.

From the car, I spoke with the Sri Lankan Foreign Ministry and Canberra and I told the Director-General of the BEPZ, Rohita Bogolagama, that I would be going straight to his office when I got there.

Pulling into the Zone thirty minutes or so later, I was horrified to see police or paramilitaries piling out of buses – fully kitted up for battle.

I made a bee-line for Bogolagama's office. He was surrounded by suits and was putting on a Mr Suave and Confident air. He seemed glad enough to see me and provided a quick rundown of the situation as he saw it. It was about the same as Gardner's, but pretty alarmingly anted-up by the gathering of the troops outside. He assured me that they were waiting for his orders.

I spoke with Gardner to tell him I had arrived and to see how things were going in there. He said they were about the same as when we had last spoken, with no signs yet of a lessening of the tension. He was more ambivalent about the appearance of the troops than me so we chatted about how catastrophic their use could be for everyone inside the compound, but especially for those around him in the management building, including the militants. There was no way of telling, I said, how competent they were and how much restraint we could expect from them.

Not for the first time apparently, Bogolagama called the President, the kindly, though bumbling, Dingiri Banda Wijetunga who had succeeded strongman, Ranasinghe Premadasa following his assassination in May.

To my amazement, Wijetunga seemed to be agreeing with Bogolagama's proposition that the troops, or whatever they were, should in effect storm the barricades. He told the President I was there and handed me the phone, expecting no doubt that that I would go along with this.

I didn't.

I told Wijetunga that it was surely in everyone's interest – not only the Australians in there, but all the Sri Lankans as well – that every effort be made to negotiate a settlement and that the safety of everyone on the site should be the paramount consideration. That however foolishly militant the agitators were, this should for the time being at least be treated as an industrial, not a military, confrontation. That it looked to me as though we were dealing with no more than a bunch of young hotheads, not something like the LTTE or the JVP. I observed, as diplomatically as possible, that the kind of bloody outcome which could flow from an aggressive invasion of the site might be to no one's *political* advantage. To my relief, he rather meekly agreed.

I handed the phone back to Bogolagama, whose air of authority had waned a little as he listened on.

The troops were stood down.

I told Bogolagama that I thought we should go down to the entrance to the Ansell site straight away and have the best kind of face-to-face with the militants which could be mustered. But I made it clear to him that my appearance would relate solely to the welfare of the Australians and the rest would be up to him. I said I thought he might see value, however, in him telling the militants who I was so they could see that there was a bit more at stake – a wider interest in the matter – than they might have imagined. That they were now playing out whatever their aims were on an even bigger stage.

The militants agreed to meeting us at the gate, but made it clear that they would have some of the Australian hostages with them in case Bogolagama's men tried something. Away we went, Bogolagama and his escort not looking happy.

The entrance to the Ansell compound was about two hundred metres away. Bogolagama propped about thirty metres short of the front gate. Fair enough I thought, as no one could be sure what kind of reception we were going to get. A bunch of the militants were there on the other side of the closed gate – young, nervous, putting on a bold face. They had three foreigners with them, closely attended though not manacled in any way. Two were Australians – an old school mate of mine, Tony

Coplans, Paul Caccioli, and a Canadian, Steve Yaeger.

Bogolagama thought it looked too dangerous to go on, but I didn't want the militants to feel they had to make some sort of demonstration to get him to keep his appointment at the gate. So I kept going while he hung back there with his guys, fretting.

My mind was very clear about what I could and could not do. On the *could* side, my responsibility was to make it clear to the militants that the Australian government was going to do its utmost to ensure that that there were not any missteps between the parties to the problem which would cause harm to our citizens. On the *couldn't* side, conditions of employment were an industrial matter between employer and employee and, as long as they could be negotiated without fear of violence, none of my business.

I was hoping they would not do anything silly enough to provoke Bogolagama into letting his boys off the leash, but as it turned out I need not have worried.

The militants, all fairly wide-eyed and youthful, seemed bemused, perhaps even a little relieved at my unexpected and uncluttered appearance. It was unclear to me who their leaders were, but after a bit of initial heat they listened quietly enough to my point of view which was that doing anything that could lead to anyone being hurt, whether by them or others, would more likely than not damn whatever their claims were, right or wrong, and condemn each of them to pretty severe penalties. I said I thought there was still time for them to calm down and negotiate properly – and they took this pretty well.

I went back to Bogolagama and told him that they now seemed to be disposed to calmer negotiation. I asked him if he would please do the same. Perhaps a little chastened by my willingness to go down to the gate, he said he would do what he could and headed back at a good enough clip to his office. He couldn't bring himself to go down to the gate.

I called Gardner from Bogolagama's office to fill him in. He said that the guys had returned and seemed to be a little less agitated. As long as Bogolagama got the negotiators back together quickly and in an appropriate frame of mind, things might just work out.

Ansell could not have had a better, calmer, person in the hot seat than Gardner who, as I already knew from previous encounters and a recent tour of the site with him, was respected by the large workforce as an able, kind and progressive leader – attributes which at that time could not at all be taken for granted with many employers in the BEPZ or, for that matter, elsewhere in Sri Lanka.

It had by this time become clearer to me that there was more going on than just the claims of the young militants on site and that Ansell, as the biggest, the most enlightened and the most supportive employer among the host of those operating in the BEPZ, had been targeted more for their marquee profile than their work practices or conditions. It was quite possible, I thought, that the youngsters in the front line were being manipulated by hardnosed unseen political stirrers into an explosive outcome which would damage the government and for which the youngsters would take the rap.

After a while, with the flashpoints having apparently cooled down, I headed back to the High Commission to update and to advise as many of the stakeholders as possible, including the appropriate Sri Lankan leaders, Canberra and the bosses of Ansell and Pacific Dunlop.

As I was on pretty good terms, across party lines, with the country's key political leaders I was able to make contact with them quickly, tell them what was going on and exhort them to contribute what they could to hose things down. Emphasizing again though, that my prime interest was the welfare of the Australians. I also spoke with the Inspector-General of Police who most likely had overall command of the Special Forces at the site.

Early in the evening, I returned to Bogalagama's office and let Gardner know I was back.

At about 8.00 pm, I was talking with Gardner on the phone when he told me that militants were coming into his office with Molotov cocktails and threats that they were going to set fire to the building if their demands weren't met – now. He said he had no choice other than to agree to their demands. He got them to come to the front gate to see Bogolagama and me.

Some heated discussion – mostly in Singhalese – ensued between the militants and Bogolagama and his aides. Gardner was there and made it clear that he would not put his name to an agreement without the militants guaranteeing in writing, simultaneously, the immediate release of all hostages and immediate evacuation of the site by the militants. Away they went and after further discussion between Gardner and the militants in the site office, the agreements were exchanged.

Gardner rang me in Bogolagama's office at about 11.00 pm to say that the gates had been opened and the militants had left.

I went down into the compound and stood with Gardener outside his main office block while he saw his staff safely off. No one had been hurt and, all things considered, Gardner and his staff were in pretty good shape.

I had some further contact with Phillip Brass and Harry Boon the next morning. Both were very relieved with the outcome. I also did quite a bit more interacting with the key political and police players.

o O o

Throughout this business, Bogolagama was hard to read as he always seemed to be waiting for someone else out there, apart from me, to show him the way. Which might have partly explained his performance years later as undoubtedly the most inept and inarticulate Foreign Minister the country has ever known. In fact, in the slavishness to (President Mahinda) Rajapaksa stakes at that time, he and one Palitha Kohona were very much alike. Theatrically hawke-eyed Kohona was, unfortunately as it turned out, head of Sri Lanka's Secretariat for Co-ordinating the Peace Process while, in 2006, I spent a lot of time with a group of dedicated Americans trying hard to push that process in the right direction. As a dual Australian/Sri Lankan citizen, Kohona remains under scrutiny for his alleged involvement in the commission of war crimes.

o O o

Anyway, quite a bit more occurred before Ansell could get back into production.

Harassment of Ansell workers attempting to enter the site, action against two other businesses in the Zone and some strike action elsewhere added to the impression that the Ansell incident was more a part of a wider political campaign than one aimed purely at growing conditions for workers. Sri Lankan workers had in fact been breaking their necks to get into the Zone, where the conditions and pay offered by foreign investors were generally so much better than they could expect from Sri Lankan employers outside. To me, it was pretty clear that the young militants really believed that their action was only about winning even better conditions – that they did not in fact know that the intention of their backers may have been to provoke a bloody battle which would be used to damage the government's chances of reelection.

In order to help Ansell's recovery, including getting its anxious workforce back to earning their incomes, and to have the new government (elected on 16 August) properly informed about Ansell's industrial policies, I arranged and attended meetings for Gardner with the new Prime Minister, Chandrika Bandaranaike Kumaratunga and some of her key Ministers, including Mahinda Rajapaksa, who would eventually succeed Kumaratunga as President. I don't recall Rajapaksa contributing anything to this discussion other than his ever toothy smile.

One of Kumaratunga's first acts as Prime Minister had been to put government onto a better footing with the country's union movement, including by declaring its intention to allow trade unions to operate in the Biyagama Export Processing Zone – something to which few of the foreign investors of Ansell's caliber had ever been opposed. Happily, this allowed Kumaratunga's Peoples Alliance to assume a more positive stance with unions and their members.

Enter Martin Quixote

At this point, I thought it was over. It had had its moments, but surely it was over.

Not quite.

I hadn't counted on Martin Ferguson who, completely out of the blue, came in swinging.

Or was it tilting – of the Don Quixote kind? Given Bob Hawke's tour d'force as President of the Australian Council of Trade Unions, had not his successors been left, after all, with little more than the spin of Australia's industrial relations windmills to deal with?

Whether windmills or giants, Ferguson, who was to become

an accomplished Cabinet Minister in Rudd and Gillard Labour governments, could have handled himself much better before spurring his charger in my direction armed only with his shabby view of my handling of the Ansell incident.

In fact his first sally, in the form of a letter to Foreign Minister, Gareth Evans, dated 18 August 1994, was fair enough in the sense that it amounted to an enquiry, however poorly informed, which was between himself and Evans. An enquiry which had the aim of eliciting a full account of what had actually happened. But while Evans was having the facts properly assembled, Ferguson couldn't resist a second sally, converting a scurrilous whinge to him by the General Secretary of the Ceylon Federation of Trade Unions (CFTU) into his own *assertion* that I had acted improperly. He included passages such as: 'I believe that such action of a High Commissioner is highly irregular and would be strongly rejected by Australian Government, as being most improper' and 'The actions of the High Commissioner, are widely known by both the union involved, the workforce generally and the Sri Lankan government.'

How true this last observation was, but how foolishly wrong-footed.

In a cop-this follow up, his assertions were released to the Australian press. Why bother waiting for Evans? Silver-tailed High Commissioner? Easy meat.

In his gratifyingly no-nonsense response, Evans pointed out to Ferguson that:

> Mr Debenham's presence at the site was solely because of his concern about the safety of the Australians involved in the incident. That concern was legitimate and Mr Debenham assisted in cooling matters down and persuading the authorities not to seek to resolve

> the lock-in by resorting to force which might have had disastrous consequences for both the Australians and the Sri Lankans involved'

He concluded his two page letter in these terms:

> Let me say that I am concerned that your letters conveyed these serious allegations as facts rather than simply as reports that would justifiably be matters of concern if true. I am disappointed too that no steps seem to have been taken to assess the veracity of the allegations prior to simply passing them on or to provide more substantive evidence to support them. Indeed the allegations in your letter of 31 August are unsourced. Naturally, I have considered them seriously as I would any criticism of the actions of an Australian diplomatic official overseas. I am concerned at the damage that may have been done to Mr Debenham's personal and professional reputation by these allegations, particularly as they appeared in the national press on 31 August. In the circumstances, you may wish to consider whether a retraction of the allegations is appropriate.

As thinly gallant as any such knight-errant, though in his own good time, Ferguson retreated from the windmill with a missive to Evans dated 3 November. Lame as his rickety Rocinante (to continue the Don Quixote analogy), he concluded in these terms:

> I regret that you feel disappointed in my approaches on this matter, but trust that you both understand the position I was in, the limited resources I have at my disposal to verify allegations, and that I acted in what I believed were the best interest of the Sri Lankan unions and the Australian Government in this case.

And who did he leave out of this 'acting in best interest' jazz? Why, his main target – the Australian High Commissioner.

There's never a Sancho Panza around when you need one.

Ferguson did not have the grace to acknowledge, with me, the error of his ways. He did not contact me and the retraction which Evans had pressed him to make did not materialize. Preoccupied and worn down as I was at that time by the viciousness of the civil war around me, sometimes at a very personal level, I could not be bothered pursuing him.

Former Attorney-General Gareth Evans had in any case already done him over pretty well.

o O o

By contrast, I did receive warm thanks from people such as Philip Brass, General Manager of Pacific Dunlop (who told me that he went to see Ferguson personally – to disabuse him of his errant take on the facts – as soon as he heard about it), Harry Boon, General Manager of Ansell, and Sri Lanka's Minister for External Trade, Justice and Constitutional Affairs, Professor G. L. Peiris.

In a letter to Sri Lanka's Prime Minister, Chandrika Bandaranaike Kumaratunga, Boon observed that:

> In our view, Mr Debenham has striven to be scrupulously fair and appropriately low key.

He elaborated on this theme in a letter to Evans dated 31 August.

Peiris left nothing out. In a personal letter to me dated 8 November, he included the following passage:

> I should like to make particular reference to the imaginative and constructive role you played in the problems which arose in Ansell Lanka (Pvt) Ltd immediately prior to, and soon after, the Parliamentary election which was held on 16 August. Manifestations of labour unrest which occurred in an environment pervaded by a high degree of political tension and anxiety were contained, and the new government was able to defuse a potentially explosive situation and to establish a framework for the achievement of industrial peace, largely because of the understanding and sympathetic attitude which you adopted, despite considerable provocation. I am deeply appreciative of the combination of principle, propriety and a firm grasp of all the elements of a complex situation which represented the core of your approach. Had you reacted otherwise, not only the relationship between Australia and Sri Lanka, but the political stability of our country at the present time could well have been gravely jeopardized.

Phew!

Though the incident was handled very well at the desk level in DFAT, the Department's somewhat boofy leadership at that time had nothing to say other than to lamely excuse itself (to me) for the mindless inclusion in its widely circulated daily news summaries of Ferguson's offending press release. Evans's rebuke of Ferguson was not similarly circulated.

A Haunting
New Delhi 1977

Despite the usual kind of ghost stories that did the rounds when I was a kid, I did not grow up either believing in the supernatural or having any particular fear of the dark. While not dismissing, as the years went by, the sincerity of seriously personal stories of close encounters of the ghostly kind, none of them made much of an impression on me.

Due to a very close encounter of my own in New Delhi in 1977, however, this changed.

o O o

As First Secretary and Consul, this was my second incarnation in New Delhi and I was very happy to be back. Though she had not been anywhere like it before, Joosik took to Delhi and India like a duck to water. We had a pretty little bungalow on the High Commission's twelve acre compound in the heart of Delhi's diplomatic enclave and had inherited a lovely ayah (nanny) Lilly, and a good cook, Daniel. With kaleidoscopic India at our doorstep and with me already having a pretty good idea of how to get around, our prospects for an enjoyable posting could not have been brighter.

I don't know when it first started, but bits and pieces of stories about a haunting in the office of the High Commission, the Chancery, were coming up from time to time in social get-togethers – from both Australian and Indian staff. Strange things, so it seemed, were going on there in the dead of night.

I had dismissed the oddity of a few occasions when, while doing some catch-up in my office at night, there had been footsteps along the hard terrazoed floor outside my office – which had culminated in the banging of a door down the corridor. When I had got up to check, a light, which had not been on when I came in, was shining from the Vice-Consul's office – but no one was there. And the night watchman in the front lobby couldn't remember letting anyone in. Well, he was getting on a bit and staff entry after hours did not have to be registered for my side of the Chancery. Ho hum.

In time, I had come to knock around a bit with our Vice-Consul, John Smith, and our Communicator, Ross Whiteside. During the winter duck season, we used to wade out into the vast post-monsoonal gheels (shallow seasonal lakes) beyond Delhi to wait for the ducks that would rise in great waves with the early dawn and, later, settle a few of their plump, gamey little bodies very nicely on to our dinner plates.

Idle time out there in the sometimes spooky dark before the shooting started could freshen up the latest chatter about the so-called haunting. It was good for a warming laugh. Must get some waders if we are going to keep doing this – up to our bloody hocks in freezing water.

As time went by, Ross, who had been in Delhi a bit longer than John and me and whose job often called him in to the bowels of the Chancery in the middle of the night to take out an urgent cable from Canberra, developed a noticeable change of attitude towards this haunting lark. He didn't like to talk about it anymore, apart from expressing some feeling for one of our Indian night-watchmen, Clifton, whose job it was to base himself in the lobby of the Chancery and periodically patrol the perimeter of the building and those internal parts of the Chancery to which he was permitted access.

Clifton (who was only ever known by this family name) was an older man, getting close to retirement. He had been a driver during my first posting in Delhi ten years earlier, but his pale blue Anglo-Indian eyes were failing and he could no longer handle the challenges of Delhi traffic. It had been a smooth enough transition for him and he was liked by everyone for his quiet and attentive manner. But a change was coming over him.

He came to my office one morning and closed the door behind him. In a clearly distressed state, he explained that he had become very frightened of strange happenings in the Chancery. This or that office light going on and off in the dead of night, doors opening and closing, sharp footsteps along those terrazoed corridors and so on. Fearing ridicule, he had tried to keep it to himself, but couldn't bear it any longer. I asked, but he said that it was not for him to say whether others who sometimes did his night shift had had similar experiences.

Such a level of distress and belief could not be dismissed as readily as I had dismissed my own 'encounters'. So I said I would see if I could move him to another job. Not as a daytime guard as this could be challenging and required a stronger, younger man. But give me a little time and I would come up with something.

Within days of this, John Smith, Ross Whiteside and I were strolling down the Panchsheel Marg (road) side of the Chancery a few hours after it had closed, but still in the broad daylight of Delhi's long hot summer days, when we saw a wild-eyed Clifton scrabbling at the armoured-glass side door. We rushed up the few steps to the landing in front of the door and were shocked to see that some of his fingers were bloodied by trying, evidently, to force the door open. He only had a key to the front door. John and I stayed there to comfort him while Ross took off for the service area behind the Chancery where spare keys to this and other doors were kept for emergencies in a combination safe. Ross sped back, the door was opened and poor old Clifton practically fainted into our arms.

We took him down the back for a nice hot cup of tea and, as he regained some composure, he explained that he had most unexpectedly found himself locked into a part of the Chancery which had previously been open to him to enter and exit as part of his after-hours rounds. It hit me that while he had been away on a period of leave, some new doors and locks had been provided in passageways in order to control the flow of visa applicants to the Immigration Office. These applicants waited in a shelter near that side glass door and, once they were inside, coded press button (Simplex) locks on the new corridor doors kept them from strolling into other parts of the Chancery. On the other side of these doors, staff could access the visa area by simply turning a handle.

So Clifton, just back from leave, had entered this area without having been told about the coded locks on the other side. To his horror, he found himself locked in. Locked in with what he believed to be his very own poltergeist. Locked in in a way which had otherwise never occurred because, whenever his poltergeist had played up he could use his key to leave by the front door and stay outside until the damned thing took a hike. Finding himself trapped by the new arrangements, he folded.

He took some more leave. When he returned, I had found another job for him, but asked if he would hang on as a night-watchman until the available position was vacated. Now that he had the combinations to the new locks and would not be trapped, he agreed in tolerably good heart to do it.

Well, it was during this time that an urgent classified cable came in in the middle of one night and, as Ross was out somewhere for dinner, Canberra's notification defaulted to me to assign the task to someone else. There was an ample roster of people to choose from, but I decided to do it myself. A bit of practice wouldn't do me any harm and the office was just a short stroll away through the compound.

Clifton let me in. He was relieved to see someone and we chatted for a while before I left him on his perch in the main lobby to tackle the first point of entry to the Australians-only part of the Chancery. Here, in sight of Clifton, our immutable security arrangements required an entry in an after-hours register. Name, time in, time out, signature. Then, entry at this point by way of another one of those Simplex locks. Next, down a long, broad corridor with the offices of the High Commissioner and others on the right and the pretty, moonlit central courtyard through full-length armoured-glass on the left. I hadn't bothered to turn the lights on.

Uncharacteristically, I felt a little uneasy as I got to the next set of doors at the end of the corridor which was alongside another corridor off to the left and the entrance just a little way down there, on the right, to the small toilet block for this wing of the Chancery. Beyond the toilet block was a full scale locked and bolted steel grille which blocked access to this Classified wing from the Unclassified wing on the other side. Much gloomier than the moonlit corridor I was in.

The Simplex on this door worked and I was then in the more deeply secured area. Out of the moonlight into the dark, I switched on the corridor lights. This strong door, with its thick steel plate insert and its heavy closer mechanism banged solidly in its usual fashion behind me. If you weren't quick, it would take your bloody arm off.

On my left was our communications and registry center, physically secured to the best standards known to us at that time. Twisted steel tang bars in the high density concrete walls of the vault.

Now I had to open a Chubb tumbler combination lock on a little safe set into the wall outside this center to get the key for the lock on the first, reinforced steel, door. This operated in tandem with another Chubb combination lock on the door itself.

But there was more.

Beyond the little lobby on the other side of this door was one more door with but a Simplex lock on it. The purpose of this was that during the normal working day, the steel door would be left open so that Australian staff could interact with the communicator and the registry clerk over what converted into a 'stable' door and counter.

All of which is to say, however tediously, that it was hard enough for a person of this world to get into the bloody place, let alone some damned (well, not necessarily I suppose) entity from another. But I'm getting ahead of myself.

So, leaving the steel door open and the stable door closed, I was in, but still had to open the door to the big walk-in vault in order to get the code stuff for the communications gear. Then, and only then, was I able to set about 'taking the cable out'. In those days of technical antiquity, the procedure for this was not easy. Harder still to recall now, so I wont. But it was time-consuming and those who, like me, only did it occasionally, had to concentrate.

Anyway, I was sitting at a desk fumbling my way through it all when I heard the heavy corridor door out alongside the toilet block bang closed. No mistaking it. No, footsteps could not be heard as this corridor was carpeted. But it wasn't long before someone started trying to punch the numbers in for the Simplex on the stable door. Good, I thought, help has arrived.

But the numbers didn't work and whoever it was tried again. Still nothing. Yet again.

In full flow with the cable business, I couldn't get up immediately to let whoever it was in. But when I did, maybe thirty seconds later, there was no one there. Funny, I thought.

I took the few steps across the little lobby to get to the corridor and looked up and down, but no one was there. Even funnier though, the corridor lights which I had left on when I came in had been turned off and there was no light coming from any of the offices down the corridor. It was pitch black and that heavy corridor door hadn't banged shut when whoever it was had left.

I called out, but no one was there.

I went back in and resumed work on the cable. Then I heard, by way of a little window high up on the back wall of my work place which was adjacent to the toilet block, a toilet flushing. OK then, whoever it is will no doubt be back for another try soon and I will be ready to let them in.

But it didn't happen.

I finished the cable, found it did not have the priority required to get anyone out of bed, locked everything up and left.

Once through that heavy corridor door alongside the toilet block, arms and fingers still intact, I noticed that the lights in the toilet block were on, so I paddled down that way, stuck my head through the outer door and asked if anyone was there. There was no response, so I turned the lights off.

It had all taken only about half an hour and I was happy to be on my way out.

Back down the darkly moonlit corridor alongside the High Commissioner's office I went, through the last secure door and over to record my exit time in the after-hours register.

Hmmm … whoever had come in after me had not recorded it in the register. As the guy who was also responsible for the overall security of the Chancery, I was a bit annoyed that the required procedure had not been observed. What's the use of a good security system if it isn't properly observed?

Clifton was there in the lobby and I asked him who it had been. He said that no one had come in after me. I asked him to think again. Maybe he had gone to the toilet or gone around the corner outside for a cigarette. He was adamant. He hadn't moved, he hadn't let anyone in and there was, as I already knew, no other way for anyone to get in after hours.

If Clifton had once had a sense of humor, he had lost it long ago. He was not kidding.

I gave him a brief account of what I had heard and seen. He said that this was just the sort of thing he had been telling me about and that my story was upsetting him to the point that, with his poltergeist obviously on the loose again, he wasn't going to stay inside the Chancery a minute longer.

I tried to calm him down, but he wouldn't be in it.

OK, as it was too late for him to go home, I suggested that he bunk down in the drivers' room in the outside service area down the back of the Chancery – and most likely not on the poltergeist's beat. It was well set up, catering as it did for our drivers when they could not get home after a late night duty. And I arranged for one of the compound guards to include the perimeter of the Chancery in his rounds that night.

I was feeling a bit spooked on my walk back home.

I had a pow-wow next morning with my only confidants on this strange-goings-on-in-the-middle-of-the-night business, John and Ross. Having done my show- and-tell, it transpired that they had had experiences of their own in the Chancery at night, but had not let on. Why would they? Who believes in ghosts and don't we know what people think about those who do?

John said he had a pet theory about who it might be. We were all ears.

Well, he said, a fairly recent occupant of his position had died from a heart attack while he was on the job in the Chancery and, as far as John had been able to gather, there had been no stories of this kind before he died. For reasons which I can't remember, John thought that this person – older, well experienced in consular business and very well liked in both Delhi and the Department in Canberra – had been put to rest in a local cemetery, but in a pretty perfunctory manner.

'OK', I thought, 'is there a way for us to see if it is him?' Challenging, because no image had ever been seen or utterance heard. Just noises and lights going on and sometimes off in the middle of the night.

'What about', I said, 'if good old Ross goes back on the locks file and gets the combination setting of that Simplex lock, on that inner stable door, which was in use at the time our colleague passed away?'

Ross's expression took a darkish turn.

'Yes, and what then?' he asked.

'Why', I said, 'you and I will go in on one suitably dark and stormy night and reset the Simplex to that very same combination. And wait. If it is him and if he does show up, the combination will work, the door will open and in he will come – transmogrified from poltergeist into a smiling apparition of our former colleague.'

'With whom we might then be able to reason about his scaring the pants off some people.'

John managed a grin, but Ross, the one member of the Australian staff who spent more time in the empty Chancery at night than any other, was unmoved.

'OK, so it's not such a good idea' I said, 'but wouldn't this be better than it getting set to that combination again, unwittingly? In which case, who do you think would be the first to find out?'

The humor of this was not that warmly appreciated.

In a thoughtful frame of mind, Ross got up and left. Probably, I guessed, to check the file for that combination in order to make sure that, at least during his remaining time in Delhi, the unwitting did not happen.

John organized a tasteful, if melancholy, grave-side memorial service to our departed colleague which he and Ross and I and a few of the Indian staff who remembered him attended. After this there were never, to the best of my knowledge, any more reports, whispered or otherwise, of such strange goings-on at that Chancery.

Not that I ever went in again in the middle of the night to check for myself. And certainly not after Ross had left after finishing his posting.

Clifton recovered his composure and to the best of my knowledge made it more or less happily to his retirement.

The Great Tokyo Land Sale 1988

The good sense of acquiring suitable property for our diplomatic missions abroad had been recognized by Australian governments from the beginnings of our foreign service back in the 1940s. London and Washington were the initial targets, but other opportunities emerged which, in the immediate aftermath of World War II, included a prime site in an inner part of Tokyo.

Japan was then under the administration of General Douglas McArthur and the Americans wanted their allies to resume their full diplomatic presence in Japan.

For Australia, the way was sweetened by the offer of an exceptionally attractive estate of 18,000 square metres in a coveted location.

Part of the attraction was that it had not directly suffered from Major General Curtis LeMay's horrific systematic firebombing, in March 1945, of Tokyo's more densely populated nearby areas with magnesium, white phosphorous and napalm. The same LeMay who, years later, as segregationist George Wallace's Vice Presidential running mate, reputedly indicated that, should he be given the chance, he would bomb North Vietnam back to the stone age. The same LeMay who was long celebrated as a true American hero.

o O o

In the process of easing out of our dependence on Britain in the conduct of our international relations, Australia's other start-up property acquisitions for its fledgling Foreign Service included a fine twelve acre site in New Delhi's diplomatic enclave, Chanakyapuri, and the impressive Georgian style residence of General George Patton in Bethesda, Washington DC. Legend has it that 'Ol' Blood and Guts' had used a basement room there to exercise his obsolete trademark Colt Single Action Army .45. The very one which in 1916 had accompanied him as a personal aide to General John 'Black Jack' Pershing on his abortive foray into Mexico to capture Pancho Villa.

These and other acquisitions were made on an ad hoc basis and it was not until Gough Whitlam, in the early 1970s, took the image of our foreign policy by the scruff of the neck that budget and resources were applied to a strategic development of our physical presence overseas, particularly in Asia. In a very short space of time, some of the finer Australian architects and builders were put to work in Beijing, Bangkok, Singapore, Kuala Lumpur, Jakarta, Manila and Paris, producing unmistakable physical monuments to Australia's commitment in these places.

For a time back then, I was close enough to this activity to have been the Department's contact person with Australia's pre-eminent architect, Harry Seidler, in his creation of our new Embassy building in Paris. This was to be on a magnificent clear site which had been purchased from the French National Railway Company for a mere $7 million. Given its proximity to the Seine and the Eiffel Tower, it was by any standards an extraordinarily good buy. It did not bother Whitlam for one moment that this purchase attracted about as much controversy as the purchase of Jackson Pollock's magnificent *Blue Poles* – which he had also inspired.

o O o

Anyway, the 18,000 square metre purchase in Tokyo went ahead. Even back then, it was a steal at around $90,000, as would have been, even more so, the alternative of the much larger adjacent site of the Mitsui Club for around $150,000 – the grand Mitsui Club building and all.

What we settled on came with a fine enough old mansion, dating from the 1920s, which the property's owner, the Marquis Hachiska, had modeled on baronial mansions in England – arising from time which he had spent there in his younger days. It included some secret passageways for the movement in and out of mistresses and an underground emergency escape route, not only for the mistresses, to a nearby canal.

A fairly handsome Chancery was built on the site in the 1960s as well as a small block of apartments for junior staff and three pretty ordinary bungalows for more senior ones. The embassy's growth had taken off, but most staff lived in the increasingly expensive suburbs.

In fact, during my first posting there in 1970, Canberra's projections for growth of the Embassy had been such that the Ambassador, Gordon Freeth (a former Foreign Minister and amateur boxing champion) and I arranged to have a look at the sizeable property next door which was owned by Japan's Ministry of Finance. We had got to the point of a price of around $3 million being mooted when an election in Japan brought in a new Finance Minister who scotched the idea. As things turned out less than twenty years later, this would have been a very fortuitous buy indeed.

Anyway, although the Embassy did continue to grow, Canberra's projections proved to be wildly overstated.

With the massive growth of its economy and influence, Tokyo had become a magnet to both Japanese and international business and the property market boomed and boomed. By the 1980s, accommodating our staff in the suburbs had become enormously expensive and the acquisition of a small nearby block of land and construction of some staff apartments on it had done little to relieve this. The large compound was obviously underutilized and something had to be done about it.

The real motivation for doing so, however, came about in 1988 when the Hawke/Keating government was desperately scouting for an infusion of funds. Keating's next budget had to have a better bottom line.

Anyone could see that in what was by then perhaps the most expensive real estate market in the world, doing more with less of our piece of land in Tokyo made sense. Prospects were high for good outcomes all round. A better office building, better and more residential accommodation and facilities for staff, and a better budget outcome for Keating.

The Overseas Property Office (OPO) of the Department of Finance in Canberra bounded out of the blocks and user departments – primarily Foreign Affairs, led as it was then by the academic, Stuart Harris – just got out of the way.

Typical of some of those who are given a bit of real authority, the OPO's up-yours approach set the stage for an awkward interaction with the Embassy.

Options carefully developed by the Ambassador and the Embassy community which would have delivered similar bottom lines to those being imposed by the OPO, but with more elegant overall outcomes, were brushed aside and the Embassy's role got assigned to the margins.

When the boys from Canberra delivered the phenomenal sale outcome of around $110,000 per square metre – for 6000 square metres – they believed that it was entirely of their own making. Enhanced as this was by the attending sale of the Embassy staff apartments block over the road from the Chancery, and net of the cost of providing a new Chancery and extensive staff residential accommodation, Keating's budget got a very handsome infusion indeed.

The OPO's role in the subsequent redevelopment of our remaining 12,000 square metres delivered a brutishly cluttered design and functional outcome and the landmark Hachiska mansion hit the dust.

o O o

The real story about how the sale outcome far exceeded all initial expectations did not in fact have much at all to do with the boys from Canberra.

Instead, it had to do with how rivalry among some of the biggest businesses in Japan was conducted. The bushido of Japan's corporate samurai.

Big property business in Tokyo had long been dominated by big Japanese conglomerates, their associates and their friends – the same ones which, with particular reference to their contributions to wartime Japan, Douglas McArthur had tried to emasculate during his post-war reign.

While the Embassy did not have a formal role in the sale process, it was to maintain a toothless diplomatic point of contact with representatives of interested parties. As Counsellor and Consul-General, this responsibility was assigned to me. I sat in on some of the key meetings and held the fort in between the visits of our geniuses from Canberra.

Although remaining strictly at arms-length concerning the detail (very little of which had been divulged to us by Canberra anyway), I came to know some of these reps well enough – though oddly excluding anyone from the successful bidder, who evidently disdained such contact – for them to give me their version of what had brought about such an astonishingly good outcome for Australia. Not a word of it was uttered to me though until it was all over and what *was* uttered may well have been just the bravado of great corporate disappointment. But it did have a ring of self-satisfaction about it.

o O o

For those who know something about the way big business of this and no doubt other kinds operated in Japan in those days, the story they told me will not be entirely unfamiliar. In the big time property development business, so it went, the serious players were well known to each other and shared the spoils through what was known as the 'tea-housing' system.

It worked this way.

Out of sight, a discreetly quiet tea house venue would be used for the 'competitors' to gather and decide whose turn it was to get this or that piece of the pie. Once done, the others would apply what would have all the appearance of high diligence in the preparation and submission of their bids – in a way which would assure delivery to the anointed bidder. Some Japanese sellers of property and/or buyers of development may have suspected what was going on and may indeed have got their own bit of the pie in the process, but foreigners would not have had a clue. Very few foreign entities other than diplomatic missions were then allowed to own land in Japan anyway and would thus have acquired little corporate knowledge of the Japanese way.

In the late 1980s, this was, so my interlocutors said, the way the players set out to manage the Australian Embassy plum.

Until, that is, another Japanese property developer, doing very well with its business offshore and elsewhere in Japan, decided that it wanted a piece of the Tokyo action without becoming or even trying to become a member of the established, the one and only, tea house. It would steamroller the tea house.

Ballsy, confronting and no doubt overdue, but doomed to deep and dark failure.

The tea-house tea-housed on how to deal with the upstart outsider.

The strategy was for the tea-housers to go at their bidding with such enthusiasm that the interloper would be either pushed out of the bidding or pushed up to an unheard of price in order to secure its intended marquee entry into the Tokyo market. To such a price, in fact, that they would have to find a way to have the existing building covenants for the land changed in order to recoup their outlay and turn a profit.

The interloper delivered the unheard of price and Australia had a very big payday indeed. Keating was delighted.

The interloper was ecstatic.

But discovered soon enough that it had problems.

Its whole strategy had been premised, so the story continued, on a high expectation that it would be allowed to build on its new site a tower office and residential block of around 110 floors which would vie with Tokyo Tower (higher than Paris's Eiffel) for downtown prominence. In the pursuit of this goal through several layers of government they were not discouraged, though they did not obtain formal agreement.

In Japan, there was nothing new about this kind of understanding, but in a case such as this where the players and the traditions were so big and the financial outlays were so high, it should have been clear to the interloper that they might not have been the only guys talking quietly to those in charge of building covenants.

The tea-house prevailed.

The change of covenant did not materialize and the interloper was stuck with only being able to put a building of no more than four floors height on the land.

Which meant that they were thus down the gurgler by over $600 million. More than that in fact, because the four story corporate structure which they put on it for their own use amounted to another outlay which would not, of course, have returned anything other than a monument to their failure.

The pain on the one hand and the tea party’s joy on the other must have been very great indeed.

Some time after it was all over, our Ambassador, Geoff Miller, was contacted by a venerated executive of the company which had purchased the site. The very executive who, so it seemed, had guided their interests in this project. He wondered if, in the best of understated Japanese business style, Miller might join him for a round of golf – naturally at one of the harder corporate courses for foreigners to get onto. He brought along an assistant and Miller took me. It was a most enjoyable round which, whether by our host’s design or not, we won.

In the Japanese way, not a word of business was spoken on the course, but at the post-game pleasantries over impeccably warm sake, a polite ‘kampai’, and an array of exquisitely restrained Japanese canapés, the poor man, though perfectly composed on the outside, was probably in hara kiri territory.

Good diplomatic practice had guided the appropriateness of the Ambassador not declining the hospitality of such a senior executive of such a large and influential Japanese enterprise. Equally though, it guided his quiet deflection of anything our host might have wanted to raise – which could only have been out of line – about the sale and its aftermath for his company. An aftermath which by this time had become excruciatingly apparent in the marketplace.

This did not, correctly, leave any space for the executive to say anything other than that he was headed into early retirement. But he was clearly gratified that he had been treated with such respect by an Ambassador who not only understood and had responded gently to his own, if unspoken, anguish, but was pretty handy with a golf club.

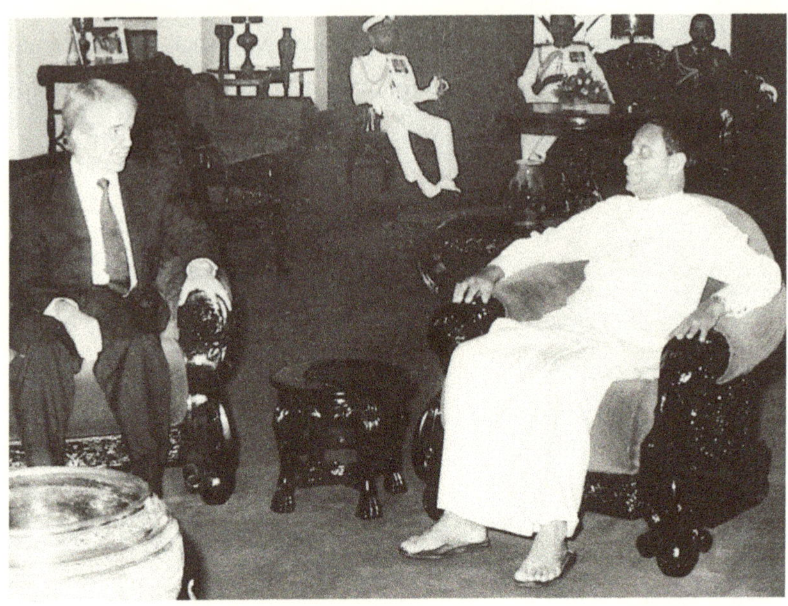

With President Premadasa at Sucharita, the Presidential Mansion.

With Premadasa at Annuradapura.

Knowing Premadasa
Third President of Sri Lanka 1992/93

He was a delusional tyrant who was damaging the good name of Sri Lanka. Sure, he had out-terrorized the terrorist Singhalese Marxist Janatha Vimukthi Peramuna (JVP), but he was using this and the fight with the powerful separatist Liberation Tigers of Tamil Eelam (LTTE) to excuse mounting human rights abuses and harsh methods of dealing with opposition to his rule. The judiciary had been cowed and economic change was being used as a tool to enrich himself and his political cronies.

So said many of the upper crust of Sri Lanka who, before Ranasinghe Premadasa shouldered his way into the Presidency in 1989 upon the retirement of the deceptively urbane J R Jayawardene, had been very comfortable with the self-serving performances of those who had led the country since the smooth transfer of power from the British in the late 1940s.

Back then, Sri Lanka's prospects had been more highly regarded than those of Japan, which had just been defeated in war for the first time – apart, that is, from 16th century defeats of its invading naval fleets by the turtle ships of Korea's Admiral Yi Sun Shin. Far better too than those of Korea, which had just been freed from its bitter colonial servitude to Japan, but would soon be at war with Kim Il Sung's Stalinist north. Both overcame huge obstacles to become progressive economic and democratic dynamos while Sri Lanka, barely challenged in comparison, languished in an adolescent culture of self and an enduringly vicious civil war entirely of its own making.

Back then too, Sri Lankans enjoyed a high rate of literacy, the economy had been almost everyone's cup of tea and the Westminster system of government had been embraced. Ethnic and religious harmony, though shaken from time to time, had never really come apart. With his curious mixture of trans-cultural names, Solomon West Ridgeway Dias (who not surprisingly preferred SWRD) Bandaranaike would soon change all of this. Husband of the world's soon-to-be first woman Prime Minister, Sirimavo Bandaranaike, and father of a future President, Chandrika Kumaratunga, he would be the first post-colonial leader to play the majority Singhalese political card against the minority Tamil and Muslim communities. Stupidly. Perhaps irreversibly.

The nervousness which the old elite felt about Premadasa was not entirely unreasonable. Apart from being from the other side of the track and with a father who had been in what they regarded as the unseemly business of running a fleet of rickshaws in the old port area, Premadasa and some of his closest cronies had been implicated in a series of extrajudicial killings which had included more than the odd political adversary. Some of these cronies, it was believed, had prospered from a corruption gravy train by way of their roles in Premadasa's ambitious infrastructure development programs.

But the same elite had also failed to discourage excesses of their own which had opened the door for a Premadasa style leadership. A door which had been fashioned by SWRD Bandaranaike and was kicked down by Junius Richard (who preferred JR) Jayawardene's response to an early and comparatively isolated act of terrorism in 1983 by one of several increasingly militant Tamil groups – the ambush killing of 13 soldiers in Jaffna by the fledgling Liberation Tigers of Tamil Eelam (LTTE).

In his viciously imperious way, Jayawardene stood back for several bloody days while the Singhalese mob vented its barbarous rage on the innocent minority Tamils of Colombo and while others, reputedly including Premadasa, orchestrated attacks on Tamil leaders and their property. The Tamil communities were, as Jayawardene had expected and many had applauded, cowed. But not for long. His vengeance played right into the hands of the militants, leading eventually to the ascendance of the LTTE, under the gifted though vicious leadership of Vellupilai Prabakharan, over more moderate Tamil militants. But also, crucially, into the hands of India's blooming clandestine support of Sri Lanka's Tamils.

o O o

Years later, in 1992, after he had relinquished the Presidency and the LTTE was firmly in control of a vast tract of the northern and eastern parts of the country, I called on 'The Old Man' shortly after arriving in Sri Lanka as Australia's High Commissioner. When the conversation turned to the LTTE, Jayawardene wondered why it was that 'you Europeans still don't understand what had to be done to rid Sri Lanka of this problem'.

'You have only to remember', he lectured, 'how the British dealt with the Germans in the Second World War'.

'But Your Excellency', I said in the diplomatic-speak used between Sri Lankan Presidents and Ambassadors, 'surely there is an important difference'.

'And what would that be Your Excellency?' he responded archly.

'Why, that the warring sides here are both Sri Lankan Your Excellency'.

He answered with his idea of a witheringly dismissive look and changed the subject. He was not accustomed to this key plank of the reverence which most Sri Lankans had for him being rebuffed, however politely.

o O o

Anyway, whatever people felt about or had suffered under Premadasa, and however valued and instructive were their points of view, my job was to get to know him and those members of his government who were in a position to influence the friendly relations which our two nations had long enjoyed.

In time, I was able to get sufficiently close to and trusted by Premadasa and his ministers and senior officials to have them listen to Australia's views on issues affecting the relationship. Issues of human rights, of trade and investment, of aid, and of multilateral ones such as those regarding the control of chemical weapons and nuclear non-proliferation. But in the beginning I was warned by the usual 'friendlies' in Colombo's diplomatic circle that he was hard to get along with and to remember that he had only recently expelled the British High Commissioner.

One on one, I liked him from the start. While we chatted in an ante-room of Sucharita, the Presidential Mansion, after the formal presentation to him of my Credentials, I told him that my father had been in Sri Lanka for four or five months in 1942 with the Sixth Division of the AIF. I said that he was in a photograph of four soldiers on the cover of an excellent book about relations between Sri Lanka and Australia which a former Sri Lankan High Commissioner to Australia, Dr Wickrema Weerasooriya, had compiled to mark Australia's Bi-centenary. I was taking a chance, because I knew that Premadasa seriously disliked Weerasooriya who, though by then a valued resident of Australia, had been a highly influential and vocal campaigner for his brother in law,

Gamini Dissanayake. The same Dissanayake who had recently failed in an attempt to impeach Premadasa and who Premadasa had run out the United National Party for his trouble. Gamini and I later became friends and I quietly participated in his political rehabilitation after Premadasa's death, but that is another story.

Premadasa didn't bat an eyelid. He said he had thumbed through the book preparatory to our meeting and that I should look closely at the photograph to see if the timber on the rickshaws in which my father and his mates had been pictured, in front of the old Hindu temple in C Street at Colombo Port, was polished or lacquered. For a person who was supposed to be uncomfortable with his roots, Premadasa said with some pride that if they were of polished timber they were from the biggest fleet of rickshaws in the Port at that time. A fleet which belonged to his father. I later checked and, sure enough, they were of polished timber.

We had got off to a good start. He spoke warmly of Sri Lanka's relationship with Australia and said he would be pleased to see me whenever he could. That I should not be a stranger.

There was no doubting that Premadasa was a hard man and that he had not flinched from doing whatever it took to get to the top. Not even the powerful Jayawardene, who had been grooming Gamini Dissanayake and Lalith Athulathmatduli to succeed him or to overwhelm Premadasa, could stand in his way.

He had become even harder after he assumed the Presidency in 1988, emerging from a brutal fight with the bloody Singhalese insurrectionist Janatha Vimukthi Peramuna (JVP), which had brought a frightened country to his knees, with greater power and greater resources and a new resolve to turn the country around. He wanted to break out of the old ways of doing things and he instinctively courted the support of the more impoverished majority of Sri Lankans, including the minority Hindus (Tamils) and Muslims (mostly of Tamil origin), who until now had enjoyed little effective political representation.

Unencumbered by the conceit and presumption of the old elite, Premadasa was cleverer than Jayawardene in dealing with the LTTE and in neutralizing the destabilizing covert work of India's CIA – the Research and Analysis Wing (RAW). As Prime Minister under Jayawardene's executive Presidency, he had not shrunk from publicly opposing Jayawardene's agreement, in 1987, to allow an Indian Peace Keeping Force (IPKF) into the north to bring the LTTE to heel. Nor, after he had assumed the presidency, from covertly boosting the military capacity of the LTTE to a point where the IPKF had to leave Sri Lanka with its tail between its legs. This also put the lid back on Tamil India's aspirations for a greater Tamil homeland, Dravida Desam. A homeland which would have incorporated the Tamil areas of southern India and north-eastern Sri Lanka.

Once the IPKF and its local proxies, most notably the Tamil National Army (TNA), were out of the way, Premadasa thought the way would be open for peace and he worked tirelessly to achieve it. He brought a contingent of ranking LTTE leaders to Colombo for secret peace talks, Prabhakaran's political strategist Anton Balasingham and his Australian wife, Adele, included.

This was followed by a series of discussions which included a face to face meeting in Jaffna between the Foreign Minister, ACS Hameed, and Prabhakaran. Premadasa was keen to meet with Prabhakaran himself, but Prabhakaran wouldn't be in it, remaining implacably suspicious of Premadasa's intentions. When the Chief Minister of the North East Province stupidly announced a Unilateral Declaration of Independence, the LTTE slaughtered 774 captive policemen and the war moved onto a different footing.

Lighter Moments, 1993

With Australian cricketing greats David Boon, Bobby Simpson and Alan Border …

… and the emerging Indian great, Sachin Tendulkar

Premadasa's extraordinary attempt at reaching out to the LTTE had failed, but he remained doggedly committed to getting them to the conference table. India, for a variety of reasons – not least being its abiding dislike of Premadasa and for that matter every neighbor in the sub-continent that disagreed with it – persisted in its clandestine determination to frustrate the process and to undermine Premadasa.

o O o

By now, the old Singhalese elite feared Premadasa and the swagger of some of his key ministers and cronies. In turn, Premadasa, believing that the country needed a dose of stern leadership, distrusted them and fed their fear. The UNP outcasts, Gamini Dissanayake and Lalith Athulathmaduli, who had put together their own political party, the Democratic United National Front (DUNF), told me with great clarity over lunch at my place soon after my arrival in Colombo that Premadasa intended to have them done away with. Internationally, serious unease about an increased incidence of torture, disappearances and extrajudicial killings – and increasing timidity on the part of the county's judiciary – was damaging him.

Although he had been accustomed to keeping his cards close to his chest, Premadasa wanted to start building some bridges.

He acquired the services of the widely respected Bradman Weerakoon to advise him on Foreign Affairs, he persuaded Sri Lanka's pre-eminent academic and Vice-Chancellor of the Colombo University, G L Peiris, to chair a committee to advise him on the disappearances issues, and he engaged a highly respected moderate member of Parliament in the opposition Sri Lanka Freedom Party, Mangale Moonesinghe, to examine the broader human rights issues.

These were not people who were going to sweep the issues under the table. I worked very closely with each of them. Slowly and with Premadasa's unassailability becoming more assured, changes for the better started happening.

o O o

Early on in my posting, I made it my business to attend his Gam Udawas or regional ministerial meetings. In a break with the Colombcenric practices of his predecessors, he took his Ministers out of Colombo to participate in and deal directly with issues arising out of a farsighted housing and village awakening program. Other western Ambassadors, many of whom were more comfortable with the smooth old Colombo elite, frowned on these functions as political stunts. But they were abundantly popular with the people and I was to see for myself how hard Premadasa pressed his Ministers to solve as many problems as they could on the spot.

My first Gam Udawa was at the ancient templed city of Annuradapura where the Mahiyangama Thupa (or Stupa) contained hair and collarbone relics of the Buddha – who had been fond of Sri Lanka and had visited several times. I was the only High Commissioner or Ambassador there. He had me sit alongside him at a simple desk in a simple school classroom while he interacted with petitioners who were crowding enthusiastically around us. Then he gathered up Mrs Premadasa and they showed me around the various places where services were being offered to the people – such as gifts of donated spectacles which she had organized. I was impressed and went subsequently to other Gam Udawas in embattled Tricomalee and Batticaloa on the east coast, both in areas which were controlled by the LTTE at night – and this sometimes required military escort.

o O o

Premadasa authorized me, as did the LTTE, to visit the large refugee camp at Madhu Church, deep inside LTTE held Mannar District, with the Country Director of the UNHCR, Dr Hasim Uttkarn. Later, he also facilitated me going to the beleaguered Army base at Palaly in the far north of the LTTE controlled Jaffna peninsula.

On my way into Madhu Church, Premadasa wanted me to meet the Officer Commanding the Northern Division at his forward base in Vavuniya, the charismatic and mercurial Major-General Denzil Kobbekaduwa.

From a good starting point of our mutual enthusiasm for rugby, Kobbekaduwa and I got along well.

He briefed me as best he could on what I might encounter. He was confident that the LTTE would leave me alone, but advised me to be as benign as I possibly could if I was confronted. I assured him that I had no intention of being otherwise. He knew that I was in good hands with Uttkarn who had been in several times before and that the LTTE would be unlikely to do anything to jeopardise the extraordinarily good work being done there by UNHCR and Médecins Sans Frontières – under what I found to be very challenging conditions. Most of the buildings associated with the church and its compound had at some time been heavily shelled and shot up.

I agreed to have a chat with Kobbekaduwa when I returned that evening but, as it turned out, he had been called away to some crisis or other by the time I got back. We had committed to seeing more of each other and I was looking forward to it, but the LTTE got him first with a pressure bomb up there somewhere along an unsealed back road.

o O o

I was the only western Ambassador or High Commissioner to accept Premadasa's invitation to attend a morning function on May Day 1992 at which, out in the back streets of Colombo, from a modest raised platform, he and Mrs Premadasa greeted Sri Lankans arriving from out of town for the major May Day function on the Galle Face Green which he would address that afternoon. The Premadasas personally served us and the others who were on the platform simple cardboard lunch boxes which contained a few sandwiches, a piece of fruit and juice.

I was starting to make some headway with him on issues of common interest between our countries – especially those concerning human rights which to Australia and others remained worrying and pressing.

On the occasion of making direct representations to him about Telstra's interest in bidding for a license for the fourth mobile telephone license in Sri Lanka (which they subsequently won), I discussed with him the value of fair competition for infrastructure projects and he confided in me a vision he had for major infrastructure development in the east. He saw this being focused on the beautiful deep water harbor at Trincomalee (which is remarkably similar in scale and shape to Sydney Harbor), but gathering in the enticing tourist areas and potentially rich farmlands of nearby Pollonaruwa. The kick-off project would be a conversion of the old British wartime airstrip at nearby Hingurakgoda into an international tourist and freight hub.

He was excited about the prospect which this held for breaking Sri Lanka's economic potential out of the stifling Colombo hub and bringing massive new opportunity to the people of the east – specifically to include the large concentrations there of Hindus and Muslims. He thought that this would do more to weaken the grip of the LTTE in the east than any amount of military activity. He wanted me to help secure Australian expertise to get the airport project fast-tracked and he saw much potential for Australian involvement in the development of the agricultural export sector.

I wasted no time flying over to have a look at the airport and then getting the preliminary studies for its development underway using the airports arm of our government's Australian Construction Services. They jumped at the chance – and soon had a team on the ground in Colombo.

Things were still not good on many fronts, but change was in the air. And Premadasa too was changing. His populist jobs and value adding export creation programs were gaining traction and ordinary Sri Lankans were warming to him. Infrastructure was definitely on the improve, though still hampered by corruption.

The spanner in the works was the ongoing conflict with the LTTE.

The unfathomable assassination of India's Prime Minister, Rajiv Ghandi, at Sriperumbudur, Tamil Nadu, in May 1991 by the LTTE's female suicide belt bomber, Dhanu, had turned India against the LTTE, but it still didn't want to do business with Premadasa. The LTTE continued on as strong as ever – keeping the more or less captive remnants of the Tamil population in the north and east under its control and the Sri Lankan military wrong-footed.

The LTTE's tactics were classically terrorist, with well-equipped and drilled fighters conducting hit-and-runs against isolated communities as well as police and military outposts. Against Sri Lanka's well-armed, though poorly motivated, forces they struck hard and disappeared quickly. In both the cities and the countryside, they bombed and disrupted, keeping the populace nervous and causing the streets of the major centers to be patrolled at night by heavily armed and often nervous soldiers. In the remoter villages, the LTTE occasionally and deliberately massacred simple folk – men, women and children, including both Hindus and Muslims – passing these off as government atrocities aimed at discrediting the LTTE. The government's position was not helped by incidents of its soldiers and police taking bloody revenge on the same innocent communities.

o O o

Hindus and Muslims in the vulnerable target farming communities of the East lived, invariably, cheek by jowl – because it had been sections of the coastal Tamil Hindus of the east who had been converted to Islam by the Arab traders of antiquity and thus both communities still had language and some aspects of ethnicity in common. The LTTE leader, Prabakharan, was uncomfortable with politicians who displayed ability in promoting unity with the country's Tamils as his take on this was that it detracted from his influence. They were thus marked for assassination, as were the best generals such as Kobbekaduwa.

Government accounts of these LTTE activities were commonly taken with a grain of salt by foreign ambassadors in Colombo, quite a few of whom wanted to believe all the dark stories they were told about Premadasa by the old Colombo elite. Few bothered to see what they could find out for themselves. For me, their chorus began to grate.

In 1992, I took matters into my own hands by obtaining Premadasa's permission to visit the site of a massacre which had occurred at a small village in the east by the name of Alinchipotana. I got there three days after it happened, but when many of the survivors had already found refuge elsewhere and the bodies of the slain had been removed. Some survivors were under the protection of the military in the local school and I was able to speak with them there and with others who were using their simple village homes during the day. They told a horrible story which, while it pointed the finger at the LTTE, was guarded because in this instance the Tamil speaking Muslims had been attacked and had then turned on the Tamil Hindus, with whom they had been farming for centuries, suspecting their complicity with the LTTE. The LTTE claimed the government had done it to discredit the LTTE.

A few months later, on 15 October 1992, another massacre was perpetrated in an exclusively Tamil speaking Muslim community, again in the east, centering on the simple farming village of Palliyagodella. This time I was able to quickly get permission, ostensibly from the Secretary of Defence, General Cyril Ranatunga, to fly in on the morning of the day following the attack with a government minister and the President's one man investigatory commissioner – a retired Rear Admiral. It was a harrowing experience in which I was allowed to wander around the village unattended while the Commissioner, for the purpose of conducting his enquiry, set up a rickety desk and a few chairs under an ancient tree just outside the village square.

I saw many bodies laid out in the square. On the outskirts of the village, two soldiers turned me away from a place at which they indicated I was exposed to sniper fire, but where the real issue was that they were burning the bodies of two LTTE fighters.

A little way down the rough dirt road that led out of the village, I squatted alongside a distraught and disheveled farmer outside what remained of his pitifully primitive pole and thatch hut which had been torched. He was gazing mutely at the congealed patches of blood in the middle of the road where he indicated quite graphically enough that his wife and children had had their throats cut. This had evidently been the preferred LTTE method of slaughter – in order to maximize killing opportunities by not frightening people away with gunfire. On this occasion it had all begun at about four am and LTTE women and children had been used to entice people out of their huts.

I felt angry and helpless. Wild-eyed and weeping villagers passed by with small bundles of possessions over their shoulders or in their little carts seeking refuge elsewhere.

I learned that, towards dawn, the village PA system had been used by the LTTE to reassure those who had managed to flee into the woods and ask them to assemble in the village square. The Sri Lankan military was arriving, so they said, and they would therefore be safe. Usually in family groups, they were ambushed and slaughtered on their way in.

o O o

That did it for me. I persuaded Canberra that the LTTE had in fact been the perpetrators of these two atrocities and that they should be publicly denounced as the terrorists they were. The origins of their savagery may well have been provoked by stupid Sri Lankan leadership, but this had gone far enough. Our Foreign Minister, Gareth Evans, so denounced them in the House of Representatives in November 1992.

Soon after, I was informed courtesy of both Sri Lankan and British intelligence, that I had been placed on an LTTE hit list.

A month or so later, I was in turn surreptitiously informed by someone who sidled up to me at a large social gathering that this had been a mistake on the part of the local LTTE commander and that my name had been removed from the list.

The two heavily armed military guards who had been placed at the gates to our residence and who used to so cheerfully wave me goodbye in the morning (as I tried to figure out alternate routes to the High Commission or wherever else I was going) were removed. We never found out who had been the intended target of a person who had been flushed out and killed himself with a grenade in the street just behind our place a few minutes before Joosik returned home one afternoon during the threat period.

o O o

On 23 April 1993, Lalith Athulathmudali, joint leader with Gamini Dissanayake of the increasingly confident DUNF, was shot dead at a rally by a gunman who was caught and killed – some said conveniently – by police. Though Premadasa denied involvement, there were plenty of influential people who believed otherwise.

Athulathmudali's funeral a few days later, which I had been tempted to attend, quickly deteriorated into a wild riot and a heavy-handed police response. It had reached its worst late in the afternoon as Joosik and I were approaching our home, which was not that far from the cemetery, in our car. A frenzied and wailing mob had crossed the road in front of us and it was covered with rocks and other debris. A large policeman strode up to us angrily waving his pistol over his head, but helped us through when he realized who we were. When we got home, we had to close up the house to keep the rolling tear gas out.

o O o

A few days later, the President's fiercely loyal Secretary, K H J Wijayadassa called to say that the President would like me to again join him in the streets of Colombo on the morning of Saturday 1 May 1993, preparatory to his usual May Day address to the nation on the Galle Face Green in the afternoon.

This was alright with me until Wijayadassa said that this time I would be the only foreign Head of Mission there and that Premadasa wanted me by his side as he moved around among the UNP party faithful. Though I was flattered and saw value in this for Australia's influence with Premadasa, Canberra's guidelines were clear – that Heads of Mission could not participate in such overtly political activity.

It was awkward, but I explained this to Wijayadassa and said I would still of course be among the other guests at the President's address on the Galle Face Green in the afternoon. He said he would put this to the President in the best possible light, but that he would be disappointed. I also spoke with Premadasa's influential Foreign Affairs Advisor, Brad Weerakoon, and the Secretary of the Ministry of Foreign Affairs, Bernard Tilakaratna.

Wijayadassa rang back to say it was OK – the President quite understood.

Around mid-day on Saturday 1 May I heard the distant explosion when I was nearing the end of a respite on the golf course. My partners thought it was fireworks, but experience strongly suggested otherwise. I suspected the LTTE and got home quickly to see what they had been up to.

Sure enough. A suicide bomber had made an attempt on Premadasa's life, but he was, reportedly, safe. Some members of his entourage and some bystanders had been killed.

A few hours later, the information was that Premadasa had been whisked away and that we would hear from him shortly. By night time, I suspected the worst and now the reports were, oddly, that they didn't know where he was. But in a front page newspaper photograph on Sunday morning, there he was, battered and misshapen, but to me still recognizable. The newspaper claimed subsequently that it had not been

The Sunday Times *(Sri Lanka) May 2 1993*

Minutes before the explosion

President Premadasa, centre, wearing a cap

Minutes after the explosion Pix by Alexander Balasooriya

At left, Premadasa's body

able to establish the identity of the person before the paper went to print, but it was pretty clear to me that the newspaper's blue bloods were most likely exulting over it.

What we later discovered was that the bomber was an LTTE operative who had been squirreled into the President's personal staff several years before to await instructions. He had pedalled up to the President's entourage that morning, left his bike nearby, said he had a message for the President and was allowed through. If I had accepted Premadasa's invitation, I would have been close to him. Maybe he wouldn't have been killed on this occasion if I had been there, because the LTTE had always been careful to leave foreigners out of it. But the decision to get him had obviously been taken and he would no doubt have provided them, eventually, with another opportunity.

o O o

Rumours abounded about who did it and why, especially so soon after the slaying of the popular Athulathmudali. Even India's CIA, the Research and Analysis Wing (RAW), long at odds with Premadasa, was suspected. But I did not doubt that it was the LTTE – believing that Premadasa had become entirely too popular, including with Tamil communities, that he probably thought he had the LTTE where he wanted it, and that the killing could in any case be blamed on a spontaneous Sinhalese payback for Athulathmudali's death.

o O o

The kindly but wholly ineffective Prime Minister, B J Wijetunga, was sworn in as President to see out the last year of Premadasa's term. His chumminess towards me, which included a one-on-one private dinner at the Presidential Residence, Sucharita, and a late Sunday afternoon drop in to our place with five minutes notice, wore a bit thin when on each occasion he would ask if there was anything I thought I could do for this or that visa applicant. However unspoken, we both knew that there was more in this for him than just helping out a friend or a constituent, but he took the rebuffs well and kept trying.

Anyway, Premadasa's grand vision for development of the east and the creation of real opportunity for its minorities and sidelining of the LTTE collapsed and disappeared. Completely. Without a trace.

o O o

Chandrika Bandaranaike Kumaratunga, who had recently returned to Sri Lanka, won a stunning landslide victory in the race for the Chief Ministership of the Western Province, which included Colombo, and set about acquiring the nomination of the People's Alliance party for the Presidency. Gamini Dissanayake, who had thought he was next on the hit list after Lalith Athulathmudali, started to believe in the possibility of his resurrection and even a run of his own at the Presidency for his old party (and Premadasa's) – the United National Party.

If they had both made it to the ballot box, the battle between them for the Presidency would have held much promise for Sri Lanka as both were, at that time, charismatic, energetic, and supportive of the ideals of Parliamentary democracy. And, whether they cared to admit it or not, both had the real gains which Premadasa had forged to build on.

In the meantime, we would have to muddle through the bilateral relationship with good old Wijetunga while the LTTE and the shattered remnants of Premadasa's people circled.

June 1994. With (L to R) President Wijetunge, Gamini Dissanayake and Bradman Weerakoon.

o O o

Gamini Dissanayake, who had become a good friend of mine, was assassinated just after midnight on 24 October 1994 while campaigning as the UNP's candidate for the 1994 presidential election. It had been his last event of a long day.

A female LTTE suicide bomber had stood up in the second or third row of seats in front of an open air stage and detonated a belt bomb as Gamini was bidding good night to the party faithful. Fifty or so others were killed and the bomber's head was later found in the gutter of a nearby rooftop.

I had spoken with him on the telephone a few hours before this meeting to confirm our breakfast at his house the next morning. I wondered if he might be too tired for this after what had been a grueling campaigning foray into the countryside, but he was buoyed up and said we had a lot to talk about.

A day or two later, we went to Gamini's house shortly after his prepared body had been brought in so that, in the customary way, the public could pay their respects and bid him farewell. We looked and looked for Gamini's wife, Srima, but could not find her. We came across her devastated brother, Wickrema Weerasooriya, who took us to Srima. She had been sitting in a short row of chairs in front of Gamini all along, but was so distraught that we had not recognized her.

Srima forlornly took Gamini's place as the UNP's presidential candidate, but was soundly defeated by the PA's hugely popular Chandrika Kumaratunga.

Chandrika had also become a friend, but that too is another story. Suffice it to say that when she did win the Presidential race, she invited Joosik and me to her inauguration ceremony. Afterwards when I got to her through the throng outside and gave her a congratulatory peck on the cheek, she said, happily, 'Just like an Australian'.

A day or two before our departure from Colombo upon the completion of my appointment, President Chandrika invited us over for a farewell lunch for which, despite all the staff at her disposal, she had prepared a few dishes and brought them out from the kitchen herself.

The Trouble with Sri Lanka

A version of this was published as an Op Ed piece in Melbourne's The Age *on 16 March 2009.*

What must not be overlooked in commentary on the armed conflict in Sri Lanka is the extent to which Tamil militarism was, in the first place, spawned by the deliberate demonization of Tamils over the early years of Sri Lanka's independence from Britain. WRD Bandaranaike was the first prominent leader to openly fan the flames of majority Sinhalese hatred of the Tamils (both Hindu and Muslim) in the 1950s for political gain, and successive Sinhalese dominated governments have followed his lead, repeatedly and shamelessly spurning opportunities to make amends.

The situation took a significant turn for the worse when, following the failure of the JR Jayawardene government to promptly intervene in the deliberate and cowardly slaughter of thousands of innocent Tamils throughout Sri Lanka in 1983, the Liberation Tigers of Tamil Eelam (LTTE) emerged as a force which was prepared to use the same tactics. To fight terror with terror.

In his retirement, an unrepentant Jayawardene explained to me at his residence in Colombo in 1992, where he liked to hold court as the grand old man of the United National Party, that, following a tit-for-tat killing of policemen by Tamil militants, 1983 had been about giving them (the Tamils) a lesson – a 'bloody nose' – to put them in their place. He likened the conflict in Sri Lanka to the struggle between 'you Europeans' during the Second World War and scoffed at the notion, at the obvious difference, that the Tamils of Sri Lanka were surely as Sri Lankan as the Sinhalese. Jayawardene was not alone in this view then and nor is he now.

Both sides to the conflict have committed atrocities of a kind which to most Australians is almost unimaginable.

President Ranasinghe Premadasa permitted me in 1992 to see some of the handiwork of the LTTE. To see the carnage for myself before the bodies were cleared away and to speak with some of the shattered survivors (in one instance crouching with a wild-eyed farm laborer alongside the drying pools of blood where his family had died) in the immediate aftermath of the carefully planned slaughters of simple farming folk – old and young, men, women and children – in the pitifully poor eastern farming villages of Pallyagodella and Alinchipotana.

But neither he then nor his successors since have been by any means as accommodating when it came to checking out the handiwork of government forces which was then and is still well reputed to have been of equal savagery. By the time of his assassination in 1993, Premadasa was, however, coming around and did among other things facilitate a limited review by a small group of Ambassadors, which included me, of the widespread and abundantly terrorist practice of extrajudicial killings and disappearances of many Tamils at the hands of government forces. At his personal invitation, I was to have been at his side on the back streets of Colombo on the day he was bombed to death in 1993, but the conventions of diplomacy had not permitted it.

While most ordinary Sri Lankans – Buddhist, Hindu, Muslim and Christian alike – recoil from the horror and bloodshed, it is not surprising that many Tamils feel that it is only the spectre of the Tigers and their ability to strike back which prevents further pogroms against their people. The answer for many has been to flee their country to either the refugee camps in southern India or, for the more fortunate, a new start in other countries.

Twenty five years on from Jayewardene's 1983 and over sixty five thousand deaths of mostly innocent non-combatants later, in a small country with few resources which others find worth coveting, this nasty ethnic war of mutual terrorism and culpability continues unabated. As do the nasty and sometimes deadly little intrigues between political personalities and parties, whose essential interest in the struggle with the LTTE cannot get past how to use it to maintain power in Colombo.

Successive governments have more or less dressed up their intention to negotiate a peace settlement in order to assuage the feelings of the UN and donor countries, including Australia, but not nearly enough to fool anyone, least of all the LTTE. What has become a reliably ineffective response to this has obviously emboldened the government of President Mahinda Rajapaksa.

It is now clearer than ever that there is little hope of progress until Sri Lanka produces the kind of courageous and visionary leadership that can admit to the errors of the past and reach out in a sustained and material way to all Sri Lankans, thus providing a sound basis for drawing the LTTE into the political process. They did it with the murderous JVP back in the late eighties when it had almost brought the country to its knees, but that was different: the JVP were Sinhalese. Unhappily, such a leadership, more or less free of the political and other kinds of corruption which have plagued Sri Lanka for so long, is nowhere in sight and the safety of Sri Lanka's minority communities remains as precarious as ever – perhaps more so.

The current leadership of the country, like most before it,

ploughs aimlessly on in the quest of maintaining power at all costs with scant knowledge of or regard for what it takes to forge community and nation. Greed and payback remain the dominant motives of Sri Lanka's political leadership. Ordinary Sri Lankans, disempowered and cowed through decades of dominance by the business and political elite and effective denial of access to the rule of law, are still easily duped into believing that they will be better off when the Tamils have been crushed. As the leadership of the country well knows, this does not necessarily only refer to the LTTE. And this is where, in its abandonment of the peace process and its declared aim to defeat the LTTE militarily, it has to be very careful if a new bloodbath of the proportions of the one inspired by the Sinhalese leadership in 1983 is to be avoided.

It is at least doubtful that the highly disciplined and motivated force of Velupillai Prabakharan's LTTE can be wiped out by President Mahinda Rajapaksa's salaried soldiers who are largely in it for the pay that they cannot earn at home. Sure, government forces should be able to outgun the LTTE in anything approaching military set pieces, but it is most unlikely that they will ever be able to match them in guerrilla warfare. And not only in the jungles of the north.

Without the measure of restraint and independent monitoring and mediation which a true peace process can provide, the Rajapaksa government is quite evidently committed to throwing whatever resources are required into the fray and to further deluding itself and many Sri Lankans into believing that the days of the LTTE are numbered. Though this might well continue to be backed up by claims of higher body counts and more incursions into LTTE territory, the consequence of pushing the military arm of the LTTE to the wall could be a dramatic upsurge in urban terrorism by the

> LTTE. An option for which, after all the years of its existence, it could be well prepared.
>
> Should infrastructure, transport and even tourism become systematic bombing targets, Sri Lanka could be brought to its knees. Rajapaksa, or whoever is in power, would then have to think again about a peace process, but this time from a position much weaker than the one which applied back in 2006 when a small group of uniquely qualified Americans (see www.publicinternationallaw.org) and one Australian Advisor, tried quietly, at the highest levels of the Sri Lankan government, to show them the way. As it turned out, they only pretended to listen.

o O o

I was wrong about it being unlikely that the Sri Lankan military would be able to beat the LTTE.

As it turned out, Prabakharan had prepared for nothing beyond maintaining the status quo. He did not expect annihilation and thus did not have a plan to thwart it. Like me and many others, he had not countenanced the possibility of a huge player like China coming in over the top of the West's long standing goal of forcing a negotiated peace agreement between the parties to the conflict.

At the time of writing my article for *The Age*, western influence over Sri Lanka and control over its supply of armaments remained such that it could not arm itself sufficiently to be able to abandon the peace process and win the war militarily. Having forced a stalemate on the battlefield, such as it was, this strategy seemed to be working, though at the cost of continuing viciousness on both sides to the conflict and an unending death toll.

Working, that is, until the Chinese, bigger on business opportunity than on Western type morality, turned up.

Well they had in fact always been around, patiently building rapport with generous donations of facilities starting with the quite lavish Bandaranaike Memorial International Conference Hall back in the 1970s. Working on the foundations of a functionally pragmatic relationship. Doing the sort of things that others wanted to be paid for.

So when the time was ripe, when a Mahinda Rajapaksa came along, when the West's code of requiring supplicancy from the Third World no longer suited Sri Lanka's leadership, the Chinese option was solidly in place. An option which had and was willing to provide the military resources needed to defeat the LTTE. In return, that is, for awarding Chinese business vast development contracts. The West was out and China was in. Big time.

Rajapaksa went in boots and all against the LTTE and collateral Tamil communities in the north in ways which have been widely condemned and which are under ongoing, however apparently toothless, examination by the United Nations and the European Union.

Which did not, however, deter Australia from accepting the appointment, as Sri Lanka's High Commissioner to Australia, of Admiral Thisara Samarasinghe, despite the fact that his command responsibility for the reported shelling of Tamil civilians fleeing the conflict in the final months of the fighting in 2009 was then and remains under scrutiny as a war crime.

Also remaining under active scrutiny is the disappearance, during the final few years of the war, of a number of Sri Lankan journalists and political figures who had been openly critical of the Rajapaksa government's actions. As many of them had been described by government functionaries – including the Secretary of Defence, Rajapaksa's serially stupid and invariably incoherent brother, Gotabaya – as 'traitors', there is little doubt about who was behind these disappearances.

Not surprisingly, there has been widespread rejoicing in Sri Lanka over the defeat of the LTTE. For the time being at least, the stifling atmosphere of war and oppressively visible security measures on the streets have disappeared. But it remains to be seen whether the majority Buddhist attitude toward the minority Hindus and Muslims will change for the better – whether they can now be embraced as brothers and sisters. So far, the Rajapaksa government is showing no more signs of providing the kind of leadership required to inspire this than did the pathetically flawed governments, all those years ago, of SWRD Bandaranaike and JR Jayawardene.

As for China, its strategy to achieve a dominant role in Sri Lanka's future is well advanced with the construction, as only some examples, of a major new port facility in the south, which has been named the Magampura Mahinda Rajapaksa Port, the associated Mattala Rajapaksa International Airport, and the key extension of the A2 highway to link Colombo to these facilities – which does not yet have Rajapaksa in its name.

With the lion's share of funding and construction being provided by Chinese corporations and banks, and with none of the attending transparency formerly required by western investors to bother about, there are bound to be plenty of corrupt fingers – both Chinese and Sri Lankan – in these plump pies.

Yes, it can be said that the realpolitik approach of the Chinese has stopped the killing and given Sri Lankan business and infrastructure a big boost. But it cannot at all be claimed that this is going to influence a corrupt and vicious government to mend its ways or to attend to the huge wounds that separate Buddhist Singhalese Sri Lankans from the rest. Nor that it will have any effect at all on ordinary Sri Lankans coming to exert any more real influence over the way their country is run than they have in the past. The Chinese way should keep Rajapaksa type governments in power for a long time to come.

As for distant and, in this theatre, now even more inconsequential Australia, Sri Lanka's smarmy blandishments about the post war safety of its minorities and political dissidents receive only that level of scrutiny which serves Australia's damnably unconscionable bipartisan insistence on having a tough guy excuse to return desperate refugees, especially but not only Tamils, to the hands of their tormentors. The kind of tough guy approach which our politicians know will appeal, lamentably, to the majority of Australian voters.

o O o

Letter to the Editor of the *Sydney Morning Herald* dated 10 July 2014 – not published

> To me, it is profoundly sickening that our government is so brazenly conspiring with the deeply corrupt and murderous government of Sri Lanka in its ongoing repression of their country's minorities. A government which, through its terrorization of Tamils was directly responsible for the emergence of the equally terrorist Tamil Tigers. A government of continuing terrorist persuasion over the ensuing years which, following its victory over the Tigers has done little to foster reconciliation and inclusion. A government which is under determined investigation by the United Nations and other international agencies for apparent war crimes and crimes against humanity. A government which is, for these reasons, being shunned by some of our closest allies.

Our government's mealy-mouthed posturing about its tough actions saving lives being lost at sea conveniently, maddeningly, ignores the reasons why refugees risk fleeing their countries and getting on leaky boats in the first place. Do Abbot [*Prime Minister Tony Abbot*] or Morrison [*Minister for Immigration*] or Bishop [*Minister for Foreign Affairs*] and their mates have the slightest inkling of what terror, repression, hopelessness and the fear of torture and death or the sudden disappearance of a loved one in such circumstances is about? Do they care? Those of us who *do* know, who have actually *seen* what is happening on the ground, could be forgiven for concluding that they don't.

As troubling is the hesitation of the Labor Party in getting out there and campaigning against this outrageous activity in the strongest possible terms and, in so doing, contribute to informing the Australian public about what is really going on. About heartlessness and inhumanity. And about aiding repression. If nothing else will motivate the risk averse Shorten [*Bill Shorten, Leader of the opposition Labor Party*] and company, they should recall the cost to them of the craven Beazley [*Kim Beazley, then Leader of the opposition Labor Party*] led attitude towards the Tampa affair in the run up to the 2001 Federal election. A cost which was a direct outcome of underestimating the feelings of Australians about the plight of *those* refugees and the blatant lies that were being told about them by the desperate Howard government.

In stark contrast with the fear and loathing of our major political parties, Christine Milne [*Leader of the Australian Greens*] is to be congratulated for her keenly informed and vocal stance.

1992. With President Gayoom.

Up On The Reef
Maldives 1992

The almighty grinding and scraping of the metal hull on the reef brought the Ministry's powerful and commodious launch to a shuddering, fishtailing, halt. As we were picking ourselves up off the floor of the open area behind the cabin, an impressively strong spout of water burst open the aft engine cover and rose a good few metres above the wallowing deck. It seemed pretty damned clear that we wouldn't be afloat for long. And how long would it take, I thought, for ruptured petrol tanks to start spewing slick and fumes and sparks. The captain, such as he was, turned the coughing engine off as Joosik and I retreated to a point from which we could launch ourselves into the water.

o O o

It was early 1992.

Having taken up my appointment as Australia's High Commissioner to Sri Lanka and settled into Colombo, it was time for me to present my credentials to the President of the Republic of Maldives, Maumoon Abdul Gayoom, as Australia's new non-resident Ambassador.

So early one bright and typically sticky Colombo morning, Joosik and I boarded one of Air Lanka's aged and thirsty Lockheed L-1011 Tristar aircraft for the short flight out into the middle of the upper Indian Ocean, bound for the capital of the Maldives, Male. As perfectly comfortable as we were in business-class, the captain nevertheless came down to say hello and take us up to first class. The Sri Lankans were very kind to Australian High Commissioners in those days. On a later flight to Australia on one of these Tristars, the Captain invited me up to sit just behind and a step above him for a remarkable view of our landing in Sydney.

Closer to our destination, we tracked over some of the glorious palm-fringed islands and sparklingly pristine coral atolls dotting the deep blue of the ocean in my diplomatic bailiwick to be. Disembarking at Male's tight little airport, a warm and uncluttered official welcome culminated in our being put onto a stout motor launch for what was to be our digs for the next couple of days on the nearby, suitably modest, resort island of Kurumba.

As my meeting with the President was scheduled for the morning of the next day, we had the rest of this day to familiarize ourselves with Kurumba. The first little island there to be developed as a resort, it was just delightful. As time went by, it was to provide us with occasional welcome respites from our immersion in the troubles of Sri Lanka.

There, just outside our room, was the first coral beach either of us had been on. Dazzlingly white, the sand was a little coarser than the Australian versions, but just as doable in bare feet and providing of the perfect foreground for the outrageously colorful banks and varieties of double-flowering bougainvillea which lined the beaches.

We had come equipped to do some skin-diving and were soon into a hypnotic world of sun-bleached corals and wildly colorful little fish. Equipped with small pouches of breadcrumbs for the fish, Joosik settled into accommodating her own enthusiastic little clusters in the shallows as I continued in a languid pattern out towards the edge of the reef, some sixty or seventy metres away.

Pausing to feed my gathering entourage along the way, something induced me to have a look around.

Sure enough, cruising in at about three metres and at eyeball level was a reef – or white-tip – shark. Strange, I thought, how adept predators are at slipping up behind you but, equally, how naturally different species make eye contact. Having done so, the clear message from my new companion was one of curiosity rather than food chain. It did a graceful U-turn and moved away from both me and the direction in which I had left Joosik, occasionally peeking back to check my position and composure. I figured it was time to stop encouraging the excited little fish.

So … time to have a look over the edge of the reef which was about another twenty metres or so away. Joosik caught up and I left mention of the shark out of it for the moment.

As we drifted over and along the edge, we were very taken by how dramatically the ocean there sunk down and down to a bottomless black. We put off thinking about this as there was so much happening along the steep reef face. Fishes of all kinds and sizes were darting in and out or gliding along – until one, at probably five or six metres below became the victim of a very large grouper which darted out from some nook and sucked its sizeable enough prey whole into its great maw. But which then, following a few cross twitches, promptly spat it out through its big fleshy lips and returned with evident disgust to its place of ambush. The clever fish, having obviously produced some spike or excrement not to the grouper's liking, swam disdainfully away. The corals further down were putting their less-bleached colours on display.

A little spooked by the deep, Joosik decided to move back in. I told her about the shark and she said she would keep a look out for it. She had spent a lot of time skin-diving when she lived in Hawaii and was pretty comfortable with what goes on in the ocean. So we separated and on I went along the reef edge, but a little further out in order to see more of the reef face. Soon I noticed the pull of a current, but the effect of this could wait, I thought, as there was so much happening down there.

After a while, I bobbed up to see where I was in relation to the shore and Joosik. OK, I was still near enough, but in a very short space of time that current, now obviously stronger than its warm embrace had lulled me into believing, had taken me quite a distance. I realized with a bit of a jolt that I would have to make it back over the shelf before I was swept out into the ocean beyond an approaching sharp curve in the reef. Think of it as a rip Howard – easy does it.

I made it back over the edge and, though I was still a few metres off the bottom, I could get up just enough to make out Joosik a hundred metres or so away. We exchanged waves and I recommenced my snorkeling back across the wildly varied outcroppings of coral and the little canyons and valleys and the teeming life in and around them.

Which was when something again told me to check my tail. Sure enough, my old mate, the two metre reef shark, was coming in again, but this time with her big brother. Damn.

Oddly – because a few close encounters on Australian beaches in my youth had instilled in me an enduring fear of sharks – I wasn't that concerned. The difference here being that through my mask I could see them as well as they could see me – face to face. Which was very different to treading water off some Sydney beach waiting for the right wave while trying to suppress fear of the dreaded sandpaper-like scrape on the legs or worse. Stay calm Howard – snorkel on, but keep an eye on them and hope they are not joined by others for what could become an uncomfortable frolic.

Happily, curiosity remained the go as they did no more than keep pace with me, not bothering to get closer than a few metres. What developed more or less into an inquisitive escort terminated about half way back to the beach and I felt quite exhilarated about it all when I finally paddled out to meet Joosik who was toweling off. No, she hadn't had any encounters of her own and, no, she hadn't noticed any dorsal fins tailing me.

That evening we dined out on the beach between the palms and the lap-lapping of the coral shore, sand between our toes, pastel sky melting into indigos and violets as the stars came out. Soon, we had candlelight dancing across our handsomely gnarled lobster and twinkling through our wine – as the rhythm of the ocean met the edge of that busy reef out there.

o O o

The presentation of my Ambassadorial credentials to President Gayoom went ahead smoothly the next morning as did our ensuing chat.

Gayoom, who had assumed the Presidency in 1978 and was to last at the helm until he permitted a genuine election in 2008, had brought a degree of stability, development and freedom to the nation, though there was still much to be done. In this, still the earlier years of reawakening of and assertion by Islamic States, he was a genuine moderate. Well educated in respected universities in Colombo and Cairo, he fostered tolerance and humanity – including in relation to women's rights – and was tough on all forms of extremism. Corruption there may have been, though it was not overly apparent. Importantly, he defied the influence of those madrassas (Islamic seminaries) in Pakistan which actively recruited impressionable Islamic youth for the purpose of fostering jihad.

Australia had had an easy enough relationship with the Maldives and one which was currently benefitting from the emergence of a number senior bureaucrats and politicians who had very fond memories of their time in Australia, when they were youngsters, as Australian funded students of the Colombo Plan. As Australia's representative on the Colombo Plan Commission – headquartered, yes, in Colombo – I was eventually to join a few other country representatives in a failed advocacy of its retention. Although it is now, twenty years later, being revived, the influential foothold which it once enjoyed in emerging Asia has been lost.

Anyway, with the formalities over it was back to Kurumba for a quick change into seagoing gear before being picked up by a government launch and our Ministry guide for a whip around some of the closer islands to see the odd model resort, village and business. It was a straight out government VIP program to usher us through a sampling of the best they had to show. Fair enough. With what seemed to be an assured Captain and crew of three or four, we got underway.

As we gathered speed, it was just another perfect day in this little island nation out on a calm sea, with the clean salt air and the occasional, refreshing, bow spray in our faces.

The Ministry's information sheet reminded us that this nation of around 300,000 people comprised some 1192 islands and atolls, spread over 90,000 square kilometres, which were the remnants of the volcanic and other mountain tops of a mighty submarine mountain range out there in the great deep of the Indian Ocean, with the lowest natural high point of any country on earth – 2.4 metres. It would be the first nation to go under as the sea rose. Australia was providing the science to tell them just when they would have to get into their boats, but only time would tell whether, when it came to this, we would have developed sufficient humanity to offer them refuge. In the meantime, other countries were providing real-time relief through projects such as Japan's powerful seawalls of massive interlocking precast concrete pinwheels at key points along the Male shoreline.

We hopped from island to island, village to village, from simple subsistence living to small scale ventures, from the new Coca Cola plant (for goodness sake) to a newer still garment manufacturing business and so on. We did not overlook in relation to this latter enterprise that the factory was populated by a large number of young ladies who had obviously been shipped in from other islands and whose living quarters seemed to be crowded – with bars on all windows and heavy padlocks on the doors. For their protection of course, though we were not convinced.

o O o

Visits and satisfyingly modest hospitality over, and having crisscrossed a lot of ocean, our Captain set a course for Male. Dusk was not that far off, with those pastels again gathering high in the sky for their soft descent into the extraordinarily calm ocean. As calm in fact as, well, a mill pond. And as calm as we had all become in the lulling embrace of this wonderful moment out there in nature.

Which was why our Captain did not see the reef. The reef which would in normal conditions have had a different and defining surface play to the surrounding, deeper, water and would thus have signaled a clear warning of the reef below.

He gunned it. The bow rose and we would be back at Kurumba within the hour.

Which was when we came to that almightily crunching, gouging stop and Joosik and I had instinctively moved to a rapid disembarkation point of our own choosing – without any life jackets or suitable little emergency craft of any kind in sight.

Shock and horror abounded. The Captain turned off the coughing, spluttering, but not yet smoking engine and joined his crew to deal with the water spout. One of them got down into the engine compartment and, miraculously, plugged it. We were still testing the air for fumes and still wondering whether we might be jumping or getting blown off the craft.

After a while, the good Captain indicated that we were neither going to sink nor be blown to fiery smithereens. We were actually afloat, there were no gurgling sounds, and a quickly deployed anchor was holding us steady at about a metre clear of the reef. He assured us that the boat had not been badly holed – why, it was just that the whole propeller shaft had been ripped completely free of the craft. But it would soon be found. And what, I thought, were they going to do when they did find it – bung it back on and we'd be off? Let's see. Our nice young Ministry official was mortified.

While two of the Captain's men were stripping to go over the side, another began twiddling with the ship-to-shore radio up on the wall immediately inside the cabin. In the beginning, he raised a bit of faint static, but it died. The Captain had a go but, muttering something about the battery, gave up. We thought we might be in for a longish night.

Over the side went the two guys and swam out to what we could now see was the edge of the reef. The boat wallowed in the mill pond, straining gently against its anchor as those colours of the evening sky and the sea began coalescing. They returned soon enough lugging the propeller shaft with the propeller, astonishingly, still attached. It had been dangling, precariously, on the edge of the reef, presumably above one of those big drops to into the black deep. After a brief confab with the Captain and roping up the shaft for ease of lowering it, they actually went back over the side with an assortment of tools in the impossible belief that, skin-diving, they were going to attach the whole thing and we would soon be on our way. It wasn't long before they hoisted themselves and the shaft back onto the boat and sat down dejectedly to catch their breaths. We admired their pluck as fulsomely as we could, but could not raise their spirits.

Right. Time for a reality check. We huddled with the Captain and our Ministry guy.

Help won't be mustered, I suggested, until we have been missed and this might only begin to dawn over there in Male when we don't turn up for our dinner appointment with the Minister and the Secretary for Foreign Affairs at 8.00 pm. But then where will they start looking? Do they have a copy of our itinerary? Will they be able to tell from our last appointment what our trajectory back to Male might have been?

Two or three little lights had appeared through the palms of a small island about a kilometer away. So it was inhabited, but could we attract their attention? We were too far away for hailing to be any good and we didn't have any signal flares. Nor did we have some kind of inflatable that might be paddled over there for help. Was it too far to swim? Maybe, but none of the crew were good enough swimmers anyway. Would Howard be silly enough to attempt it, I thought? Maybe, but what about the sharks and the currents and the night?

But it was by no means all bad. The weather was holding and we weren't sinking. So – let's just settle back and wait.

Joosik said with a wistful smile, 'Maybe we could do a little fishing?' Cool as a cucumber. Everyone had a laugh but, sorry, no fishing gear.

Well, after the moonless night had enveloped us and a carpet of stars and the bright swathe of the Milky Way came out to brighten us up, we heard an outboard motor way out there out there somewhere, but couldn't see anything or tell if it was coming our way. The crew flashed torches and eventually a torch responded, at first faintly, some distance away. It eventually came alongside and turned out to be no more than a three metre tinny with three people aboard, one of whom was a government Minister. The relief on their faces at the sight of us all calmly and quite comfortably awaiting our rescue was touching.

They had in fact come all the way from Male, which turned out to be about forty minutes away. No other kind of craft had been available and they were desperate. We were bundled in along with our young Ministry guy, fitted up with life jackets, and off we went waving goodbye to our dejected crew. Of course, now that they had been located and were not in danger, a tow would be sent soon enough.

By the time we tied up at the Kurumba jetty and were greeted by the anxious Secretary of Foreign Affairs, we were ready for a hearty dinner. We were only a little late, but we assured him that we could do a quick change and be with him in a no time. We wouldn't miss it. Honest!

But, mightily concerned that we must be exhausted, both emotionally and physically, he would not be talked out of taking us to our hotel where he had arranged for us to be suitably pampered. Our protests were to no avail as to him they were, surely, just a manifestation of some hopefully transitory stressed-out dementia. Having seen us safely to our room, he went off to assure the President that we had survived. We asked if he would please ensure that everyone who mattered was told that our crew and our young official had behaved impeccably. Given the extraordinarily serene conditions out there, I surmised that the whole thing might even have been scripted for our entertainment! This did get a laugh, but he was not convinced.

Oh well, nothing for it but back down to the damned balmy beach for another splendid candlelit lobster supper under the starry, starry night.

Waiting to ensure that we had had a long enough night of recovery, President Gayoom telephoned the next morning to satisfy himself personally that we were fine.

We were of course not only fine, but couldn't wait for our next go at the Maldives.

With (L to R), Doug Anthony, Andrew Peacock and Gareth Evans.

The Gallery
Canberra 1995

Gareth Evans had a really good idea.

Yes he did.

Why not provide the new, as yet unnamed, Foreign Affairs and Trade building, just down the hill from Parliament House, with a portrait gallery?

Portraits? Portraits of whom?

Why, painted portraits of past Ministers for Foreign Affairs and Ministers for Trade.

Oh, of course.

Well, perhaps not *every* minister, but at least those who had been in office for significant periods of time or had made a distinctive mark or even, yes, in some cases, both.

Now who fitted nicely into both of these categories and who, at that time, happened to be in charge?

The idea was admirable enough, arising as it did from his own broad interest in the arts and culture and what he had seen for himself of the hallowed galleries of this kind in foreign ministries with longer and grander histories and traditions of diplomatic service than ours – in nations where diplomacy has at times been admired and respected. Nations unlike ours, that is, where Australians tend to regard diplomacy and culture as a bit of a put-on.

But it set the stage for what, in the course of just a few hours on one balmy and otherwise unremarkable Canberra afternoon in 1996, turned into a most satisfyingly comic interlude over in the hallowed halls of our Governor General's mansion and in the otherwise dour business of public administration.

o O o

Upon my return to Canberra from Sri Lanka in 1995, a chronic absence in the Department's Senior Executive of anyone with suitably broad management skills propelled me into the hot seat of running the Department's interests in the construction and fitout of its grand new headquarters building over on State Circle, just below Parliament House in its sprawling domination of Capital Hill. Like some vast gray skeleton, the superstructure of the building was already up, but the hard parts, such as cutting edge security, IT and international communications requirements, not to mention coordination of the gaggle of contractors, was just getting underway.

The project was owned, in the fullest possible sense, by Gareth Evans, who had been Australia's Foreign Minister since 1988 and who in the minds of many, including me, had been one of our best. He had steered it through a difficult Cabinet and budget (requiring some $175 million) process as well as the minefields of protracted public, media and parliamentary carping.

I knew as well as anyone else that when it came to projects which he held close to his heart, Evans could be a bit of a tyrant with the officials involved. And that, for this most visible of his projects, with all its deadlines and constraints, I would be on one of the sharpest points of his attention. But what did this matter, I thought, after the murder and mayhem that had so recently enveloped me in Sri Lanka?

When it came to the Department's tough-guy Secretary, Michael

Costello, and one of his deputies, the smugly self-assured Kim Jones, presenting me to Evans in his commodious office up on the Hill, both of them nudged me forward just as gingerly as they possibly could before meekly retreating out of range of what they assumed would happen when I gave Evans his chance to give me one of his legendary serves.

Well it didn't happen. And up to the completion of the building, on time and under budget (who had ever heard of such a thing, especially in Canberra!), Evans and I maintained a cordial relationship, the essence of which was that he pretty well left it all up to me – as long as I understood that he was never that far away.

o O o

After a while, Evans decided to leave open the qualifying criteria for his portraits gallery idea so that he could more readily co-opt into progressing his plan a few prominent people who were still alive and kicking and were not only from the ranks of Labor. Such as Bill Hayden (former Leader of the Australian Labor Party and, at this time, Governor-General), Doug Anthony (former Leader of the National Party, Deputy Prime Minister and Minister for Trade) and Andrew Peacock (former Leader of the Australian Liberal Party and Minister for Foreign Affairs).

Evans's sell was to include asking the very same Hayden, Anthony and Peacock to check out the new building with him, well advanced as it was, though still with enough time to get a few portraits together for the grand opening. I was to show them around.

Peacock flew up from Melbourne and was the first to arrive at the site – in a bit of a huff over something which, as I learned a few years later when I was sent to Washington (partly because of a flagging aspect of his Ambassadorship) to a specially bumped up position, was not that rare.

Evans arrived with Anthony, but he was also not in much of a good mood. There was nothing rare about that either. He was miffed about Hayden having just told him that he would not be joining us but would, instead, take tea with us at Government House afterwards. In the mood stakes, Citizen Anthony had the wood on both of them.

Anyway, off we went, Evans getting into the swing of showing off his big building project, of which he was amply and justifiably proud, and making the odd aside about his gallery idea.

Evans of course earlier worded all of them up a bit on this, averring that it should not be at any cost to the taxpayer. Private money would have to be raised and neither Anthony nor Peacock thought this would be a problem. Some portraits were already out there, including a good one of Evans by Greg Bridges which had won the Packing Room Prize in the Archibald competition of 1992, and an existing one of Anthony which could probably be secured on a loan basis. Others would have to be commissioned and would of course include portraits of former Ministers such as Peacock and Hayden. Some of the assumed greats from earlier times such as Menzies, Casey and McKewen would get guernseys.

From the time of our arrival at Government House, the plan, and Evans's demeanor, started unraveling.

Though probably not expecting a comradely embrace on the front steps of Government House, Evans seemed to be comfortable enough with the normal preliminaries for attending the august presence of a GG, including being asked to hang around in the foyer while Hayden was informed of our arrival. His composure did take on a slightly different texture, however, when the Aide came back to tell us that His Excellency would be delayed and that we might just cool our heels a bit longer.

Given that they were all old sparring partners, the feeling was that

Hayden was bunging it on a bit. Evans fumed that this was 'just like fucking Bill'.

With this much love in the air, it was hard to tell how things would work out.

In that earlier incarnation of mine as Australia's High Commissioner to Sri Lanka, I had been invited to Government House during my mid-term consultations to brief Hayden – essentially on the war with the Liberation Tigers of Tamil Eelam. The arrival formalities were about the same as the one his mates were now getting. Hayden had been affable, interested and not uninformed throughout our meeting in his study. Suddenly, there were three sharp, evenly spaced, raps on the door precisely upon completion of the assigned time – fifteen minutes if I remember correctly – for the audience, Hayden's loud enough 'come!' (so reminiscent of Walter Matthau bidding George Burns to 'Enter!' in *The Sunshine Boys*), the military Aide's march into the study, his discreet click of highly polished heels and his declaration that it was time for His Excellency's next appointment. Upon which Hayden rose, bade me farewell and the Aide escorted me out, though not by the scruff of my neck.

Anyway, here I now was with these old mates when Hayden ambled in and in his weary sort of way said hello and motioned us not to some cozy little nook, but to a large adjoining room where we all sat on a long bench-type sofa beneath a bank of windows which, had we been facing them, would have offered a nice view of the grounds. In another setting, it would have been a comfortable enough arrangement until the next train came in.

Me and Evans on His Excellency's left, Anthony and Peacock on his right.

Had H.E. seated us this way, I thought, or was it just by chance that the lefties were on his left and the righties were on his right?

And if it *had* been so arranged by H.E., who the hell had let on that I was a lefty?

Evans proceeded to put his best foot forward with a chummy enough outline of the gallery plan – warming to something which would surely not require much of a sell, especially to those present who were going to be in it. Who wouldn't want to be in it for Christ's sake?

Well, he had really only just got going, with a few helpful chip-ins from the others, though more enthusiastically from Peacock, when Hayden said, in effect and again in his weary (or was it worldly) way, 'But wouldn't a good set of photos do the job'?

Philistine Bill.

The silence was deafening.

Evans stiffened.

Knowing that he was anything but undemonstrative, I put a hand gently on his arm and, in order to give him time to suck in a bit of air, held forth with the best supportive sort of off-the-cuff summary of the position of the Department and its adoring staff that I could muster. Difficult, because the Department didn't really have a position. It had always been a Gareth thing.

But, visibly fuming, Evans had lost his place and just couldn't find his way back.

The game was over and he and the others knew it. They knew that although the idea was admirable enough in the context of Evans's world stage, Hayden's inferred instinct about its suitability for Australians was astute. He had sensed what the media might do with such adornments to what they had already dubbed 'Gareth's Gazebo' and he was in any case already assured of at least one painted portrait of himself in a more hallowed spot than the DFAT building: Governors-General clearly outweighing mere Foreign Affairs and Trade Ministers in this respect.

Or did he just want to rub Evans's nose in it?

Mates can be like that.

Especially when they are so entwined.

Intellectually.

(Hayden's brooding introspection was of course no match for Evans's sagacity.)

Anyway, we didn't stay for another cuppa.

Nothing more was said – ever – about the painted portraits gallery.

o O o

Alexander Downer, who was quite a different character to Evans, both in intellect and wit, succeeded Evans as Minister for Foreign Affairs just before the building was completed. He wanted little to do with Evans's baby, although he quite enjoyed taking over the baptismal and naming rights.

Anthony and Evans got rooms named after them in the new building. Peacock didn't.

Owing no doubt to some complex of his regarding Evans's public speaking ability, Downer got quite a giggle out of naming the building's lecture theatre after Evans. What a wit. Not as much of a giggle though as, later, Australians everywhere got out of Downer modelling a fishnet stocking for the media.

Downer settled on naming the new building after one of his heroes, Lord Richard Casey. To be precise, Baron Casey of Berwick, Victoria, and of Westminster – yes, that significant borough in the most intensely blue-blooded heart of London. Casey had a stellar career in service of both Britain and Australia. Controversially, he left Australia during World War II to take up appointments offered by Winston Churchill

– in 1942 as UK Minister of State in Cairo, and in 1943 as Governor of Bengal. Later though, he did serve as External Affairs Minister under Menzies and, finally, as Australia's 16th Governor-General.

I thought it was a bit of a shame that such a place should be named after someone who, like Menzies, had been reluctant to distinguish between 'the old country' and ours. Reluctant, that is, to set a course of our own in foreign policy. Theirs was of course a different time and they were by no means on their own, either then or later, in their fealty to Britain and especially to the Crown. Ask John Howard.

Downer named the street in front of the building after another of his heroes, the former long serving and hard-nosed protectionist Deputy Prime Minister and Trade Minister, Sir John 'Black Jack' McEwen. Upon the drowning of Harold Holt in a challenging surf at Cheviot beach in Victoria on 17 December 1967, McKewen had served briefly as Prime Minister for the time it took the Liberals to elect a new leader. In relation to Empire and crown, 'Black Jack' was, or so it seemed, more of a downright digger than the others.

The most humorous tongue-in-cheek suggestion about who the new street outside the front of the building might be named after came from John Bowen, a former highly ranked diplomat and Labour Party identity. It was Tony Street, Foreign Minister from 1980 to 1983, and the name would thus have been Street Street. Good one John.

Washington DC
11 September 2001

After coming home from our tenth posting, Sri Lanka, at the end of 1994, we had no intention of taking another. The war around us there and the pervading viciousness of the political scene had taken an emotional toll. Friends had been bumped off in the worst possible way and out in the villages I had had my fill of gross inhumanity, death and destruction. I had also had enough of the treacherous kind of games which a few supremos in Canberra were given to playing when they were safe from face-to-face encounters with their 'mates' – their colleagues out on the front lines.

Prominent in this kind of argey-bargey were the swaggering in-your-face Labor Party apparatchik Secretary of DFAT, Michael Costello, and his most favored (or so it seemed) Deputy, the durably devious Geoff Forester, who a little while later would be given a key role, remarkably, in an important enquiry into pedophilia in the Department – for which the result was doomed or, perhaps more so, preordained from the outset.

As far as I was concerned, Joosik and I had more than done our bit overseas and had taken our fair share of risks and knocks in bringing up a family out there. There were plenty of worthy jobs in Canberra, our sons had finished their high schooling and we would now be there to help them run their next courses.

Unlike at earlier times in our life with Foreign Affairs, a few years in Canberra did not change our resolve to stay. We had got our loved Georgian style home out in leafy Chapman back into order and things

Joosik at the Pentagon a few days after 9–11.

were chugging along quite nicely for the Debenhams.

But it came to pass that they were not chugging along that well in Washington DC. Former Foreign Minister Andrew Peacock was the Ambassador and although he and the Prime Minister, John Howard, had in the past battled over leadership of the Liberal Party, they were mates. Howard had appointed him to the job in 1997 and by about the end of 1998 Peacock was giving his ear a belting over management of the Embassy and his demand for a key staff and structural change to fix it. The flutter around the Department in Canberra was that morale at the Embassy was sinking fast and that Peacock himself, though highly effective on 'The Hill' in DC, was at least a part of the problem.

So what, I thought. Don't bother me with this stuff. I'm over it.

Anyway, the key consular and management job at the Embassy was substantially upgraded and so would soon be advertised in the usual way within the Department. Its new formal title would be Minister/Counsellor (Management) and Consul-General. Quite a mouthful, yes, but as the first of its kind in our foreign service it created a buzz. Aspirants began working the corridors to muster support and to get whatever fix they could on what was really going on in Washington and what they would have to deal with if they succeeded. But the advertisement was not emerging. Ho hum.

Ashton Calvert asked to see me. Ashton had been Deputy Head of Mission in Tokyo when I was there in the late 1980s as Counsellor and Consul-General and he was now Secretary of the Department. We got along well. It was not hard to like and admire him as, in addition to or perhaps despite of his doctorate in mathematics (of all things for a diplomat) following on from his Rhodes Scholarship at Oxford in the mid-1960s and a stellar career in the Department, he had a refreshingly open way about him and a quick-witted sense of generous humor.

He asked me if I would take the job and I could see that he wasn't kidding. I had told him before that Joosik and I had had our fill of overseas postings, but he was ready with the hard sell. The Prime Minister, he said, was concerned that morale at the Embassy was so low that he had heard of mutterings from journalists about it. He did not want this to surface as a media topic and a distraction from the important work of the Ambassador and the Embassy. He wanted Calvert's assurance that he could find the right person to arrest this so that he could confidently invite Peacock to withdraw from the day-to-day management of the Embassy. He said he thought that the clincher for the supremely pompous Peacock would be less about my extensive and varied career in the management and consular work of the Department than the fact that I had been a Head of Mission – a rare achievement for someone from not quite the right side of the Departmental track. Calvert said if I agreed to the appointment he was ready to assure the Prime Minister that I could achieve what he wanted. But he warned me that dealing with both Peacock and his Deputy, Meg McDonald, would be bound to have its moments and that he would be depending on me to keep my cool.

I was not that thrilled about the prospect of being hauled back into this game. A game which had long been understaffed, undervalued by an uninformed public, over stressed and vulnerable to long distance personality games in some of the dark little play spaces of senior management and ministerial offices in Canberra. It wasn't as though I had been asked to do a duet with Paul McCartney or to stand in as a centre against the All Blacks. But I could hardly reject Calvert's faith in me and Joosik had always wanted to return to the United States where she had spent some happy years before we met.

So it was that in mid-1999 off we went. To help ease us in to the new assignment and give us a preparatory feel for the U.S., we took two weeks leave en route for a rambling drive from Seattle to DC. Spending more time than we had planned in the Rockies, we got to Omaha, Nebraska with only a few days left for the final dash to DC via Kansas City, Louisville and Cincinnati. We arrived in good heart.

Tragically, in connection with an issue concerning the exchange of intelligence material with the Americans, a senior Australian Defence staffer in the Embassy committed suicide a day or two before I started there. This understandably attracted a great deal of attention from Canberra and the Australian media, and caused even more unhappiness within the Embassy.

After a while and a few little hissy tests, Peacock did more or less leave me to manage the embassy, but there were indeed times when I had to recall my undertaking to Calvert to maintain my cool with both him and his alter ego Deputy. In the process, it didn't take much time for me to figure that in their goading and bullying behavior towards those around them in the Embassy, both might have benefitted from having had some of the real-life, gut-wrenching, experiences of others in our foreign service in their otherwise impeccable resumes. As it turned out, Peacock came to the end of his appointment six months or so after my arrival and was succeeded by a career diplomat and confidante of John Howard's, Michael Thawley. Michael was cut from an entirely different cloth to Peacock and, was in fact not that unlike Ashton Calvert. In time, he helped add some fine touches to the gains which had been made in lifting the morale of the embassy.

o O o

11 September 2001 started off as just another day really.

With the color and the crisp chill of early Fall attending my usual early morning drive out of leafy Arlington across the Chain Bridge – that old relic of the Civil War – down Canal Road I went along the glistening Potomac, rounding past the brightening Kennedy Centre, wending my way along Georgetown's sleepy M Street and a little further on to the Embassy at 16th Street and Massachusetts Avenue – 16th and Mass Av. Just a block or two from the heart of DC – Dupont Circle.

I liked getting in before the rush and having a quiet coffee over the night's emails from the other side of the world as the day brightened over my vista of Scott Circle. So named in honor of 'Old Fuss and Feathers' brevet Lieutenant General Winfield Scott who, in 1866, was the first to achieve this rank since George Washington. Good old Winfield – forever to sit there atop his bronzed charger proudly reflecting on his litany of achievements. Such as his successful command of the 7000 troops used in 1838 to remove, in a merciless death march from their cherished homeland of antiquity in Tennessee to far away Oklahoma, the pitiful remnants of the once proud Cherokee Nation.

Thus it was off to my usual start of another day at the supremely secure center of Western power and wealth, freedom and justice for all and so on. Well, they were working on it.

It would be even busier than usual as the Howards were in town. Again.

Howard was getting along famously with George W, that paragon of wit and Republican virtue.

Who knows, there may yet be a George W Bush Circle somewhere in downtown DC.

Richly Alfred E Numanesque, the deeply bronzed shrine to repose therein would depict this figure of undaunted courage – Top Gun George Dubya – USAF jumpsuit 'n all, on a flight deck far far away, flippin' the bird to some deserving antichrist – other than the NRA that is. Incorporating as it might, at the Great Leader's feet, depictions of other leaders such as Blair and Howard dipping into the Freedom Fries. More tellingly still for the just completion of such a deserving tableau would be the further incorporation of those master puppeteers – this time darkly Vaderesque – Cheney and Rumsfeld.

This fitting shrine would be unveiled just after those famous chiselled-in-stone words over at the famous nearby Memorial were restored to what must surely have been Thomas Jefferson's original version of his contribution to the Declaration of Independence (July 4, 1776) – namely, in italics:

'We hold all these truths to be self-evident, that all *white Christian* men are created equal, that they are endowed by their creator with certain inalienable Rights, that among these are Life, Liberty and the pursuit of Happiness.'

Knowing as we do that the existing version did not at all reflect Jefferson's own appalling behaviour in relation to just about everyone who *wasn't* white and Christian. Ask the Indigenous and African Americans. And ask about Sally Hemings, the slave who Jefferson *inherited* through his wife, Martha.

Happily, other Americans of truer goodwill have, in the two hundred and fifty years since, worked hard, if not yet with complete success, to apply the version which made it into the Declaration.

o O o

Anyway, the well-oiled embassy machine had been humming over the first few days of the visit and the PM was to address a joint sitting of both Houses on The Hill the next day, 12 September. Along with others from the Embassy, I was going to be chirping along in his little Aussie cheer squad.

By the time the Embassy was coming to life, our Ambassador, Michael Thawley, was already with Howard at the elegant Willard Hotel, near the White House and not that far from the Embassy.

American style, the first communal pots of coffee were perking away around the office when my deputy stuck his head around the door and said I should turn on my TV. Some idiot, he thought, had accidentally crashed his little aircraft into one of the World Trade Centre towers in New York. I wandered over to have a look on his TV.

The fixed image from a weather camera perched on top of a building across the East River in Brooklyn revealed only part of the damage – a darkly smoldering slash high up on a far corner. Nothing too catastrophic it seemed, but I had an uneasy feeling. The TV commentators were bemused. No reports of any kind were in, but news teams were haulin' ass. You bet.

Suddenly, as we watched, a large aircraft, silhouetted darkly against the brightening early morning sky over Hoboken way, sliced silently, terribly, murderously across the screen and disappeared into the other tower in a ball of fire.

'That was not an accident', I said.

The TV commentators went ballistic.

I tried to get Thawley on his cell phone, but he wasn't picking up. I asked his personal assistant to get hold of him on their link and, if they hadn't already done it, have him and the PM get to the nearest television. Thawley called a few minutes later to say he was getting everyone over to the Embassy as quickly as possible. Mrs Howard had already left the Willard on her separate program, but was being gathered in and redirected to the Embassy.

Not knowing whether Washington would be next, and in the knowledge that our Embassy was close enough to big targets such as the White House and the Capitol building, we decided that we would put them in the sub-basement of the Embassy which had been built at the height of the Cold War and contained some specially reinforced areas. Now surrounded by building services, it wasn't flash, but it provided the strongest physical security we had as well as a couple of telephones. The rest of us would soldier on above ground.

I rang Joosik at home and told her what had happened. Worrying about whether there was more to come, I asked her to stay inside and watch the television. As our house was centrally air-conditioned, I asked her to be ready to turn it off (to eliminate outside air exchange) if she heard a loud explosion or there was a white flash. Melodramatic maybe, but the possibility of a 'dirty' bomb, using radioactive material, being deployed in Washington had been in prospect for some time and at this stage of the attack I was keeping my mind open.

Thawley and Howard were delivered to the Embassy in a flourish dramatically typical of the US Secret Service – which is responsible for the security of diplomats and visiting government dignitaries.

Guided by our waiting staff into our secure basement garage, each of the armored black and blacked-out Secret Service vehicles bottomed-out as they zipped over the dip at the roller door entrance just below my office.

I met Thawley and Howard at the lifts and took them to the sub-basement. Howard's entourage, which included the Head of his Department, Max Moore-Wilton, and the head of Foreign Affairs and Trade, Ashton Calvert, was close behind. Howard was perfectly calm and pleasant; Thawley, as usual, assured and unruffled. Thawley and Howard had worked closely together in Canberra before Howard appointed

Thawley to succeed Andrew Peacock in Washington – and they were a good team.

We received word that Mrs Howard was on the way in with her own Embassy and Secret Service escorts.

I left them with some Embassy hands to help them set up while I resumed dealing with the security of the Embassy, its staff and their families. On the way, I had to intervene between our own guards and the pretty hyped-up Secret Service agents to have the agents understand that we were perfectly capable of looking after our guys while they were on our turf. No buts fellas. They weren't happy, so they put on an impressive show of cooling their heels outside the Embassy.

Then on to bedding down the hot lines for the flood of calls that were already coming from the Australian community in and around DC, visitors and our various outposts around the country. Not the least of which was our Consulate-General at the center of the immediate storm in New York. I spoke with Canberra and we braced ourselves.

The Director of my consular team, Michael Corbitt, had no sooner set about his initial tasks than he rushed in to tell me that his partner had telephoned from his car heading out of DC on the other side of the Potomac's 14th street bridge, a couple of kilometres from the Embassy, when he had heard a roaring bang. He turned expecting to see a pile up on the road, but to his horror saw instead, off on his right, smoke rising from the nearby Pentagon building. He hadn't seen an aircraft, but I suspected the worst.

I went down to tell the boys in the basement. Howard was calmly chatting on the phone with someone in Canberra.

I left them to digest this news and returned to my own operations center where we were attempting to account for all staff of the Embassy and to contact their families. Two members of our large Defence

Joosik at left with some family members at the World Trade Centre, New York – not that long before 9/11.

contingent had had appointments at the Pentagon that morning and the embassy's Defence team was having difficulty contacting them. They were located in due course – unharmed.

Breathless unedited reports were now coming thick and fast over television and radio about a fourth aircraft which seemed to be headed for Washington. There were also reports of an explosion at the Capitol building and a fire at the State Department. People were being evacuated from both and it was being reported that many had been seen running from the Capitol building. The evacuations turned out to be correct, but the explosion and the fire not. I could see from that view of mine across Scott Circle that a stampede out of the city was underway. Not good I thought. And, sure enough, the roads were soon in complete gridlock.

We asked our people and Embassy families to stay put. If the situation became even worse, we didn't want to have to be looking for them all over Washington and having to tell anxious friends and relatives that we didn't know where they were.

o O o

We never knew what the exact target of the fourth aircraft had been because, clearly barrelling down a course set for DC, it crashed near Shanksville in rural Pennsylvania. The prime candidate targets were assumed to have been the White House and the Capitol Building – which were just down the road from the Embassy – and CIA headquarters at comparatively distant Langley.

The first two would have been the ones most easily found from the sky by nervous terrorists – being the standouts of the iconic buildings lining the highly visible Mall in central DC. Although the President was out of town, many of his top aides and the Vice President were there in the labyrinth of offices in and around the White House.

At the Capitol, both houses of Congress were in session. Had it struck there, the massed leadership of the country would have been devastated. Had it struck the next day, our Prime Minister and his party, including me, would have been among them.

In the absence down south of the President and in the rush by the Secret Service to get him airborne and out of harm's way, the Vice-President, Dick Cheney, hit the airwaves and did what he could to inform and reassure a deeply rattled nation.

Within a few hours of the crash, there were reports of debris strewn down several miles of the crash path – I recall it being first reported as *eight* miles. Observers and journalists were reporting that they were being kept well away from the crash site – apparently, some were surmising, because it had not taken the impact of a whole aircraft.

Months later, Cheney revealed that he had given the order to shoot the aircraft down, but had then been so relieved to hear that this had been overtaken by the heroic but ill-fated intervention of some of the passengers. This brazen spin, orchestrated as it so evidently was by one of America's most accomplished spin-masters, was widely and gratefully embraced by Americans as the story they *wanted* to believe.

To those who were following the rivetingly unadorned reports coming in from witnesses on the ground at and around the crash site, the painfully obvious truth of the matter was that United Airlines Flight 93 had been shot down by USAF aircraft.

Then both of the World Trade Centre towers in New York collapsed in front of a nation which had not been so glued to its news outlets since Vietnam.

o O o

As there was no point in proceeding with the Prime Minister's visit, plans were soon underway for his return to Australia. This was easier said than done as all civilian aircraft had been promptly, impressively, grounded after the attacks and there was no telling when they would fly again.

We were going to bunk the Howards at the Ambassador's nearby residence overnight, but the situation in Washington had stabilized sufficiently by late afternoon for them to be able to return to the Willard. The Pentagon was still burning and the news was in about Donald Rumsfeld's showy dash, cameras rolling, from his office on the other side of the Pentagon to do what he could at the crash site.

New York, like Washington DC, was in a state of emotional devastation and we at the embassy were seeing what we could do with our much more substantial resources to support the huge tasks confronting our modestly sized Consulate-General there. We realized that they would not be able to give much time to their own emotional and other needs until after they had cared for Australians within their sizeable consular district.

Our Consul-General there, Ken Allen, a banker on a one time appointment to the Foreign Service, had only taken up his appointment a few weeks earlier, but he quite angrily dismissed my offer, which had Ambassador Thawley's enthusiastic support, to go to New York and help him. Certainly he had an experienced career Consul in Mike Nash, but as this was going to get very big and stay that way for quite a while, Allen eventually agreed to me sending him some of my full-time consular operatives to lend a hand.

o O o

The streets of DC were eerily quiet when I went home late that evening. The gridlock was over and the military had come out in their Humvees and the odd Armed Personnel Carrier to direct traffic and to patrol the streets around hastily barricaded major sites. Fighter aircraft had been patrolling overhead since shortly after the attacks and would keep it up for weeks afterwards. For us, the high visibility of the military was reminiscent of our experiences in places like Seoul in the late 1960s, Bangkok in the early 1980s during shows of strength by the military, and Colombo in the mid 1990s.

The third world had come to DC. The Americans were seeing on their own streets what many in the rest of the world had been living with for a long long time.

It wasn't clear when the President was going to reappear. Bill Clinton, in the middle of a visit to Australia, was single-mindedly making his arrangements to get back to New York – where he reportedly arrived before the President. The American public cut Bush a fair bit of slack over his hesitation. Wasn't it just the Secret Service doing its job? Sure, but who was the Commander in Chief?

Early in the afternoon of 12 September, the PM and his entourage submitted to the final embrace of the Secret Service which swept their cavalcade of vehicles out of the Embassy, bottoming-out again as they swung out of our garage into Massachusetts Avenue, heading at a fair clip up to Dupont Circle. Then on to the special US military aircraft at Andrews, home of Air Force One, which would link them with a Qantas flight to Australia from Honolulu.

o O o

The challenges for the Embassy in the aftermath of 9/11 would be trying and would include a couple of full scale evacuations of the Chancery during a prolonged anthrax scare. But these were enveloped by the composure, energy and ability to improvise which had characterized its responses throughout this crisis.

Full-on enough as it was before 9/11, life in Washington had taken on a new intensity. But I didn't doubt that my early morning entries into DC through sleepy Georgetown would soon enough resume their soothing part of my routine for preparing for whatever was going to happen next in that paranoid little part of the world, Washington DC, inside the Beltway.

And although I knew that, for the Americans and much of the western world, the 9/11 atrocity would long outweigh anything of any scale in the history of terrorism anywhere, I hoped that it would in time have them better understand, and more evenly and compassionately respond to, what had long been the plight of others for whom the human costs of terrorism had invariably been on such an appallingly different scale.

But I wasn't holding my breath.

Beyond 9/11

'Compelling.'

'The major publishers are not much interested in the kinds of 'awful truths' that we are writing about.'

– Noam Chomsky

So where will 9/11, with its huge images and suffering and rage and calls for eternal retribution, come to rest in history?

In the West – that is among the powerful and successful and wealthy democracies – and in some of the more affluent dictatorships which are propped up by the West to suit its economic interests – the 9/11 attacks will long be remembered like the first death in the family. Like the first realization that awful things don't just happen to others and that they can even happen in the sanctuary of home. Even if every citizen is armed with a bible and a bazooka.

Within the family of comfortably advanced, essentially Christian, Western nations, there was, understandably enough, a great outpouring of shock and horror, compassion and outrage. A circling of the wagons against the forces of darkness out there in the other world, especially in the world of Islam – the other great bible bashing faith of the world.

An Islam which, if we are not careful, will come to be as deeply and stupidly despised by many in the Christian West as the Jews have been for condemning one of their own so long ago – the fundamentalist prophet of Judaism, not of Christianity. (That's right, Jesus was not a Christian.) The prophet so admired and respected by Muhammad.

The prophet who inspired a collection of New Testaments – a careful selection and construct of which made the Christian bible what powerful men *wanted* it to be. The bible on which Muhammed modeled *his* bible of Islam – the Koran – for his theocratically rudderless people. Both of whom – Jesus and Muhammed – though so much alike in their beliefs – have been so falsely and so relentlessly used to both inspire and excuse, over the millennia, extraordinarily vicious campaigns of conquest and subjugation.

Anyway, in that other world, where the substantial majority of the world's population lives and where most, including Muslims, Buddhists, Atheists, Taoists, Hindus, Christians, Sikhs, Pagans and many others – all human beings, all His creation if you like – crave their share of peace and freedom, or just a fair go, 9/11 was probably of passing interest only. Not much more than a brief spectacle. Unless, that is, 9/11 were to actually wake the US and the rest of the West up to the extraordinary scale of terror which has already been experienced so widely in that other world. Terror that has been prolonged, that is ongoing and that has, in recent history alone, cost tens of millions of lives. Realising, as if waking from a dream, that in that world, in that reality, a mere three thousand lives in an event which was over, mercifully, in a matter of hours was in fact just a drop in the bucket.

We in the West should be very careful about judging the condition of the world in relation only to what is done to us.

How different are the scales by which we and the rest of the world judge the outcomes of terror? Well, compare the cost of 9/11 with a few examples of what others have had to bear. Not once, but over and over. Not quickly, but invariably drawn out – painfully, horrifyingly and without pity.

Starting with America – the America once described, deservedly, by

Martin Luther King as being 'the greatest purveyor of violence in the world today'.

Sure, it is a great nation which has done great and positive things. Where, as but one example, would the world have been today had it not been for its massive intervention in World War II?

But both before and very often since then, its bullying and its deceit on the world stage has been of pathological proportions – often akin to the foot stamping and pouting of a wealthy and spoiled child accustomed to getting its way.

Such as in the concocted reasons given by Lyndon Johnson (the Tonking resolution) and George W Bush (weapons of mass destruction) for the invasions of Vietnam and Iraq. Such as in the doctrine promoted not only by Johnson of dealing with South American States solely on the basis the US's economic interests and thus its damnable propping up of murderous and corrupt right wing dictatorships. Standing up for the oppressors and the tyrants.

Such as in the extraordinary excesses of the Nixon/Kissinger years – starting with Republican candidate Nixon's sabotage of Democrat President Lyndon Johnson's Paris peace negotiations on Vietnam, in 1968, in order to help kill off the vaunted peace platform of Johnson's anointed successor and Nixon's rival for the presidency, Hubert Humphrey. Which led more or less directly to four more years of terror and bloodshed before Nixon and Kissinger were credited with securing peace on terms remarkably similar to those which had been proposed by Johnson in the first place. And for which Kissinger received, staggeringly, the Nobel Prize For Peace.

Such as in their enthusiastic continuation of Johnson's doctrine on South America which quite evidently included the orchestration of Pinochet's bloody coup against the democratically elected government of Salvatore Allende in Chile – with its aftermath of prolonged terror and repression.

Such as in their deception of the American people in justifying Nixon's bombing of North Vietnam and invasion of Cambodia – which provided such extraordinary impetus for Khmer Rouge recruitment and its slaughter of up to 2.5 million Cambodians. A slaughter which attracted little interest from the West other than in its criticism of post war Vietnam for intervening to stop it.

o O o

To provide one telling elaboration – in this instance in relation to Vietnam – tapes of discussions in the Nixon Oval Office which were made available in April 2002, thirty years after they occurred, provide a chillingly unequivocal record of the extent to which the deeply unbalanced Nixon had been able to so readily kow a close cohort of immensely powerful people around him into supporting his massive campaign of terror and inhumanity against North Vietnam, Laos and Cambodia and the extent to which this was either deliberately misrepresented to or concealed from the American people.

These extracts from those tapes are drawn from Daniel Ellsberg's '*Secrets: A Memoir of Vietnam and the Pentagon Papers*' published by Viking Penguin in 2002.

On 25 April 1972 –

> *President Nixon:* 'We've got to quit thinking in terms of a three day strike [in the Hanoi-Haiphong area]. We've got to be thinking in terms of an all-out bombing attack – which will continue until they – Now by all-out bombing attack, I am thinking about things

> that go far beyond … I'm thinking about dikes, I'm thinking of the railroad, I'm thinking, of course, the docks …'
>
> *Henry Kissinger* (then Nixon's National Security Advisor): '… I agree with you.'
>
> *President:* '… we've got to use Massive force …'

Later, at noon, they were joined by H R Haldeman, Nixon's much flawed Chief of Staff and Nixon's Press Secretary, Ron Ziegler.

> *President:* 'How many did we kill in Laos?'
>
> *Ziegler:* 'Maybe ten thousand – fifteen?'
>
> *Kissinger:* 'In the Laotian thing, we killed about ten, fifteen …'
>
> *President:* 'See, the attack in the north that we have in mind … power plants, whatever's left – POL [petroleum], the docks, … And, I still think we ought to take the dykes out now. Will that drown people?'
>
> *Kissinger:* 'About two hundred thousand people.'
>
> *President:* 'No, no, no … I'd rather use the nuclear bomb. Have you got that Henry?'
>
> *Kissinger:* 'That, I think, would just be too much.'
>
> *President:* 'The nuclear bomb, does that bother you? … I just want you to think big, Henry, for Christsakes.'

This, clearly, is the language of genocide – not of war between armed forces.

On 2 May 1972, in conversation with Kissinger and Alexander Haig (then Kissinger's military advisor at the NSC), Nixon said '… And I want this clearly understood. The surgical operation theory is all right, but I want that place [North Vietnam] bombed to smithereens. If we draw the sword, we're gonna bomb those bastards all over the place. Let it fly, let it fly.'

On 4 may 1972, he elaborated on this decision in discussion with Kissinger, Haig and John Connally (then Secretary of the Treasury), thumping perhaps an imaginary map on his desk.

> *President:* 'Vietnam: Here's those little cocksuckers right in there, here they are. (Thump) Here's the United States (thump). Here's Western (thump) Europe, that cocky little place that's caused so much devastation … Here's the Soviet Union (thump), here's the (thump) Mid-East … Here's the (thump) silly Africans … And (thump) the not quite so silly Latin Americans. Here we are. They're taking on the United States. Now, goddamit, we're gonna do it. We're going to cream them. This is not in anger or anything. This old business that I'm 'petulant,' that's all bullshit. I should have done it long ago. I just didn't follow my instincts.'
>
> ' … I'll see that the United States does not lose. I'm putting it quite bluntly. I'll be quite precise. South Vietnam might lose. But the United States cannot lose … Which means, basically, I have made the decision. Whatever happens to South Vietnam, we are going to cream North Vietnam.'
>
> '… For once, we've got to use the maximum power of this country … against this shit-ass little country: to win the war. We can't use the word 'win'. But others can.'

In a later exchange Nixon observed to Kissinger: 'The only place where you and I disagree … is with regard to the bombing. You're so goddamned concerned about the civilians and I don't give a damn. I don't care.'

Kissinger responded: 'I'm concerned about the civilians because I don't want the world to be mobilized against you as a butcher …'

It was obviously not the act of butchery that was of concern to Kissinger, but that its discovery might reflect badly on Nixon and thus, of course, on him.

The root of Kissinger's abject sycophancy in relation to his master, Nixon, can be adduced from another tape – on 6 July 1969 – when, in discussion with John Mitchell (Nixon's Attorney General), Haldeman and Ehrlichman (Nixon's Counsel and Assistant for Domestic Affairs) about the source of White House and National Security Council) leaks, Nixon said, 'Well, in any event, when you say Nixon papers – Are these papers – not apparently from me, or are they? … I don't see how they could be … because I, I've scared Henry within an inch of his life from the time he's been here. He's never going to get anything from me out on anything.'

How does the duration and the scale of the World Trade Centre atrocity in New York stack up against what this reveals about the ferocity of prejudice and criminality at the very top of American leadership which delivered such horrific outcomes to millions of Vietnamese over the years of their agony?

Of course when they became known there was a great outpouring of public outrage over revelations about the secret workings of the Nixon administration and Nixon was hounded out of office. Many of those closest to him served prison time and Nixon only escaped the indignity of this for himself by securing, no doubt as the shabby key for his deal to resign the presidency, a full and unconditional pardon from his successor, Gerald Ford.

What will never be known, however, but which can be readily imagined, is how differently Nixon and company might have fared in the court of American public opinion if agents of Ho Chi Minh had delivered at around the time of Nixon's greatest peril the kind of retaliatory act – however puny by the standards of what was being done by America in Vietnam at that time – that might have seen but one little screaming and naked American girl running down a street in, say, Manhattan with the deep napalm burns on her back still smoldering. Kim Phuc was but one Vietnamese girl who suffered such a fate (*'The Girl in the Picture'* authored by Denise Chong, published by Simon and Schuster, 1999). Tens of thousands of Vietnamese children suffered this and worse fates. The total death toll of Vietnamese numbered by some estimates up to 3.1 million and the great majority of these were civilians. The exact number will never be known as the Americans did not bother to distinguish between civilians and combatants in their body counts. Millions more suffered and died over the ensuing decades from the effects of the indiscriminate aerial spraying of 18.2 million gallons of the extraordinarily toxic defoliant Agent Orange (Dioxin).

As can be seen elsewhere in this chapter, Nixon was not the only US President to misbehave, often abominably, in office, but he is the only one about whom such a vast amount of material became available for public and judicial scrutiny. Material which could not be denied, but which in time could be and has been overlooked by most. How otherwise can, as but one example, the excesses of the Bush/Cheney administration be explained?

o O o

Mostly at the hands of the Americans, the devastation of Korea during the war of 1950–53 – of its towns and villages, its people, its livestock and produce and its infrastructure–was of an unimaginable scale. A scale which was largely and wilfully hidden from view and which quite evidently involved widespread war crimes and crimes against humanity. Unlike in the Vietnam War of not that many years later, there were fewer war correspondents and cine-camera men around and in any case little of their material made it through the military censors. There were no Pentagon Papers and no Daniel Ellsberg. President Harry Truman pretty well let the US military under Douglas MacArthur and his successor, Matthew Ridgway, have its head.

It was a hard and bitter war, often fought in appalling weather and over challenging terrain. Early on, the American and UN forces (which were commanded by the Americans) suffered crushing defeats and had to battle up and down the peninsular with both North Korean and Chinese forces. Any sense of whom they were fighting for and whether they could or should bother about distinguishing between friend and foe seemed to have almost completely disappeared by the time they started to make headway. All those of oriental appearance became 'gooks' and the gooks were the enemy.

A sense of the terror then inflicted on the Korean people at large can be gathered from the following few sample excerpts from the book *'The Bridge at No Gun Ri',* written by three Pulitzer Prize winning journalists, Charles J Hanley, Sang-Hun Choe and Martha Mendoza (published by Henry Holt and Company, LLC in 2001).

> We attacked every type of target. We did some major damage out there', the (American) Air Force General Emmett O'Donnell Jr. told U.S. Senate committees in 1951. 'I would say the entire; almost the entire Korean Peninsular is just a terrible mess. Everything is destroyed.' General Curtis E. LeMay, the U.S. bombing expert, came away from the three year war with this impression: 'We burned down every town in North Korea, and South Korea too.

As mentioned elsewhere in this book, LeMay was the one who in March 1945 directed the systematic carpet bombing of heavily populated areas of Tokyo with those materials which were most effective in the destruction of human beings – magnesium, white phosphorous and napalm – and who was later reputed to have said that given the chance he would bomb North Vietnam back to the stone age. What better person for Douglas McArthur to let loose on the hapless rural communities of Korea. And how well this evidently qualified him to be regarded by his countrymen as a true American hero.

And:

> The U.S. Far East Command defined 'war crimes' only as acts committed by the enemy. Col. Howard Levie, the army lawyer who oversaw war crimes investigations from MacArthur's headquarters in 1950, acknowledged years later that U.S. commanders in Korea and other wars worked with blinders on. 'I think we've done very badly on trying our own people on war crimes' Levie said. He said American brutalities were relatively rare in Europe during World War II but became more common in Korea "because American soldiers considered Orientals to be 'gooks', that's why. They considered them to be lesser beings."

And, in relation to media censorship:

> The celebrated CBS newsman Edward R Murrow, leaving the Naktong front in mid-August, sent a radio report to New York saying the U.S. military was creating 'dead valleys' in South Korea, and wondering whether the South Korean people would ever forgive America. His network, CBS, refused to broadcast it, infuriating

> Murrow. [In addition to military censorship] News organisations were operating under a self-censorship criticism of the U.S military; those who violated it could lose access to warfront coverage.

Given their suffering during the prolonged Japanese occupation, the Korean War and the vicious rule of the American sponsored Syngman Rhee, the Koreans know a lot about terror.

o O o

'There's always more to add. The official USAF's accounts of the bombing of dams in NK (North Korea) read like something out of the Nazi archives. Unrestrained glee about the massive destruction, particularly of rice fields, so important to "Asians". Or Kissinger's calm transmission of an order from his Master (Nixon) to General Haig: massive bombing campaign in Cambodia: Anything that flies against anything that moves. Mentioned in *NYT (New York Times)* without comment, elicited no reaction that I could find. Hard to match in the archives of genocidairies.'

From conversations with Noam Chomsky

o O o

In 1966, it was the USA's role in the overthrow of Indonesia's Sukarno which brought Suharto into power on the back of the slaughter of several hundred thousand ethnic Chinese – presumably because, as Chinese, they must have all been commies. As well, at other times during the late 1960s and the 1970s, American influence can be found in the delivery of a coarse and murderous military government in Greece; the bloody coup by junior military officers against the democratically elected government of Sheikh Mujibur Rahman in Bangladesh; and the excesses of Suharto in East Timor.

In all of these and other such scenarios, the terror and carnage suffered since the end of World War II monumentally outweigh what has been suffered by the USA over the 11 September 2001 attacks on New York and Washington DC.

o O o

The Americans have not of course been the only ones at it.

By most accounts, an average of not less than 8,000 people *a day* were slaughtered in Rwanda in 1994 over about one hundred days of well telegraphed government sponsored murder and mayhem. That is, at least 800,000 Tutsi slaughtered then and 200,000 Hutu slaughtered a few years before. Burundi followed – not on quite the same scale, but still at the cost of many thousands killed through almost unimaginably vicious and unrelenting terror.

Pleas for help from the killing fields of Rwanda were rejected. The UN's head of its peacekeeping operations at the time, the ambitious Kofi Annan, was evidently not only complicit in the refusal to allow intervention by the meager UN forces which were already on the ground there, but presided over scaling them down to a point where the remaining force could do no more than protect itself.

It took the touchingly liquid-of-eye Annan ten years to say, after all his ambitions had been realized, that 'I could and should have done much more to sound the alarm and rally support'. What a fake! Of course he didn't say what people like Bill Clinton and his Secretary of State at the time, Madeleine Albright, might have done about his prospects had he actually had the guts to promote a different line to theirs. What a guy and what handsome credentials this provided for him to trot out in his failed mission as a UN Special Envoy to the slaughter in Syria years later. How could those nasty Syrians have treated me so?

How could they – the Clintons, the Albrights, the Annans and so many other leaders of their ilk around the world – have turned their backs on the TV footage of Tutsi refugees begging departing UN forces to kill them mercifully rather than leave them to the butchers and the rapists? (How many would have preferred jumping from a tall building instead?) Could it have been because they saw black, because they saw non-Christian (even if many of them were), because they saw no economic value, because they saw cost and because they had seen Hollywood's ridiculous *Black Hawk Down*? We could ask about where their moral values were – but only if we assumed they ever had any beyond their ballot boxes.

How comforted the survivors and the families of the slaughtered must have been when Albright and Clinton apologized – years later and well after the feelings of their voters didn't matter a jot. Many others, such as the French under Francois Mitterand, who continued arming the Hutu throughout the slaughter, could and should have apologized, but didn't. Where was Australia's voice? Did it really have to be quite so muted and humbled by the big players?

But they not only did it again in another place far, far away, they were doing it at the same time as Rwanda.

Where?

Bosnia.

Oh yes.

But the Bosnians aren't black.

No, but a lot of them are Muslim. And what is there to care about over such a poor little place anyway.

How could these people and their Western cronies have stood around for so long watching Milosevic, Karadzic and Mladic run amok? What were they waiting for? Were they still watching reruns of *Black Hawk Down*? (Nixon's reaction time might have been different, but then with George C Scott playing George S Patton for him on a continuous film loop in his White House den he might have just whacked everyone.)

Has the appeal of these people diminished on the lucrative western lecture circuit? Have they become any more humble? Do they really give more of a damn now than they did then?

Did the UN and, for that matter, NATO, reform themselves, vowing never to just stand by should such terrible things ever happen again? Ask the Syrians.

Going back a little further we can reflect on the extraordinary campaigns of terror in China presided over by Chiang Kai Shek and Mao Zedong, which cost tens of millions of lives. About the same as in Stalin's USSR. Of course, the way our history is told, and embellished as it is by our own experience with the Japanese during the Second World war, we could be forgiven for thinking that the Japanese inflicted much greater pain and death on the Chinese than the Chinese inflicted on themselves. But they didn't. Not even close. Though they did certainly set a high bar for wanton brutality and savagery.

The horror stories told in the 1950s by the British about the rampaging Mau Mau in Kenya and that murderous Jomo Kenyatta were criminally concocted in order to protect British rule. The truth was revealed, however belatedly, in works such as Caroline Elkins' Pulitzer Prize winning *Imperial Reckoning*, in which she provided a harrowing account, forensically researched, of British terrorization of virtually the entire Kikuyu nation of Kenya. One and a half million people were detained in appalling and degrading conditions. ' ... tens of thousands, perhaps hundreds of thousands' died or were killed. By contrast, Elkins was only able to find indications that 'fewer than one hundred Europeans, including settlers, were killed and some eighteen hundred loyalists died at the hands of the Mau Mau'.

The British had not been obliged to learn anything in this respect from the outrageous deaths in their concentration camps of 27,000 women and children during the second Boer War of 1899–1902. A war in which Australia so willingly participated.

Confronted with complaints about the emergence of concentration camps in Germany before the start of World War II, the swaggering dandy, Goering, apparently pointed to the model provided for them by the British in their African colonies.

Way back when the British East India Company was gaining ground on the sub-continent, the Kashmiris actually outsmarted British designs on their territory by not permitting them to buy land. They have since, nevertheless, been terrorized into submission by both India and Pakistan – through the failure of the United Nations to bring about the act of self-determination which was to have taken place soon after Atlee withdrew Britain from India in the late 1940s and the Indians and the Pakistanis marched in.

Which, though, pales in comparison with the scale of terror and slaughter brought about by Britain's hit and run in the creation of the State of Pakistan. In effect, those good old Brits drew the new frontiers overnight and left the next day, without having either provided or put in place any kind of protection at all for the inevitable flight of Hindus from Pakistan, Muslims from India and Sikhs from the Punjab.

Sure, blame Jinnah and Nehru or even Gandhi, but how many in the halls of power at Whitehall, mightily miffed as they were by the loss of their wondrous Raj, thought that those ungrateful natives probably only got what they deserved? Did either side of British politics, so exquisitely represented as they were in this horror by socialist Prime Minister Clement Attlee and Lord Louis Mountbatten, darling of the royal right, really give a damn?

After all old chap, what could have we done to stop it?

Plenty.

Germany's slaughter of millions of Jews, Gypsies, Slavs and the disabled or disfigured might have been moderated had Western leaders (Winston Churchill being a standout exception) and influential church leaders such as Eugenio Pacelli (Pope Pius X), spoken up early on, before World War II started, about the Nazi's plans. Plans which had been much more visible to everyone at that time than has ever been adequately admitted since.

Why is it that since then it has been mostly up to the Jews to inform the world about these atrocities?

Easy.

Because very few others, especially in the Christian world, cared to do so. After all, it didn't change the fact that the Jews killed Jesus – did it?

How is it that the children (Christians) of such distinguished parentage (Jews) can maintain such a ridiculously enduring hatred of them? A hatred which somehow overlooks it having been God's own plan that someone had to put Jesus on the cross – to pay for the sins of mankind. Theology can be entertaining, however frustratingly, if you are ready to have a good think about its messy contradictions. Not only, of course, in the Christian brand.

Anyway, to continue with examples of the terror experienced by those outside the cozy camps of the West.

More recently, the Sudan still smoulders with State sponsored terrorism even though the south has obtained its own statehood. Under the noses of everyone, China has completed its terrorist colonization of Tibet. Though more muted in recent times, Robert Mugabe remains in power and remains palatially unapologetic about his murderous and prolonged terror campaign in Zimbabwe – in which no intervention from anywhere was ever even contemplated. Black, poor and of little economic value to anyone. Without the prospect of serious economic gain or loss by the big players, morality just does not stack-up.

The UN completely failed to get the Russians to exercise any restraint whatsoever in its terrorist demolition of Chechnya. Muslim Chechnya that is. If there is anything worse than a communist, it's a Muslim, right? Ask the big guys at the Security Council.

The ongoing genocide of the Hmong in Cambodia and the terrorization of the Tamil speaking people (Hindu and Muslim alike) of Sri Lanka which claimed over 60,000 lives and which has left the government of Mahinda Rajapakse under UN investigation for war crimes and crimes against humanity, are other examples.

o O o

'A lot of illumination.'

Noam Chomsky

As the pawns which they have long been of those of the powerful nations who crave control of the Middle East, the nations of the region continue to hammer away at each other at greater and greater cost. The terrorization of their non-combatant populations and the spawning and nurturing of viciously fundamentalist entities and their outflow to other parts of the world continue apace. While in more recent times the resurgent cold war ambitions of Putin's Russia have diverted the focus of combat and big power political influence to Syria, it is Israel that will remain at the core of resentment, military ambition and terror in the region for a long time to come.

The blame for this is commonly assigned to the hardline leadership of figures such as Israel's Netanyahu, Palestine's Abbas, Syria's Assad, Iran's Ayatollahs and the ascendant terrorist militias. Which avoids having to acknowledge, let alone deal with, what is propping up this kind of leadership and what still incites these leaders to regard their key backers with such deep suspicion and mistrust.

Since the creation in 1947 of the sovereign state of Israel out of a huge slice of Palestine, in a wave of largely confected sympathy in the Christian West for what was done to the Jews by Hitler, both of the immediate sides to the ensuing conflict – the Israelis and the Palestinians – have time and time again had their claims and their aspirations betrayed in the interest of furthering, on the broader international stage, the power and influence of their backers. At stake was and still remains control of the hugely profitable oil rich Arab States – created as they had been by key Western colonial powers led by Britain.

Right from this beginning, the Israelis were confronted with an attempt by key elements of those nations backing the creation of their State to, at the least, seriously weaken Israel's viability. These elements managed to arm the new Israel's understandably angry Arab neighbours to the teeth while obstructing efforts to adequately protect the fledgling State. Though desperate for arms and effective political support, Israel's first Prime Minister, David Ben Gurion, found himself having to first assure the West that he was not about to accommodate communist Russia's willingness to fill these gaps. Ben Gurion would perhaps have regarded this bit of nonsense as just another inept mask for unabated anti-Jewish feeling throughout the Christian West.

Yes, this was a long time ago, but not so long in terms of what the Jews have endured, and survived, since the casting out of the Judaean Jews from the Land of Israel following their revolts, in CE 66–70 and CE 132–135, against the pagan rule of Imperial Rome, and the consequential destruction of their great Temple in Jerusalem. The very Temple which, adding further historical perspective, had been inspired by David, completed by his son Solomon in 827 BCE (both Jewish kings revered equally by Jews, Christians and Muslims – to the latter of whom they are Dawud and Suleiman), destroyed by the Babylonian's Nebuchadnezzar in 586 BCE and which, following further centuries of periodic persecution, was rebuilt by Herod the Great, Rome's vassal Hasmonean King of Judea, who was raised as a Jew, during his 37–4 BCE reign. Since the inception of the Church of Rome, and as long as it suits the fundamentals of Christian doctrine, the Jews will, for many, remain outcasts.

In the betrayal stakes, the Israelis and the Palestinians have a lot of unhappy history to brood over.

Such as, for the Israelis, a number of plausible versions of key moments in the 1973 Yom Kippur War. Including the one in which Richard Nixon's National Security Advisor, Henry Kissinger, while delaying the provision to Israel of vital intelligence about Egyptian led plans to invade them, was backing the provision to Egypt of equally vital intelligence regarding Israel's seriously unprepared military resources and deployments. A political play so fraught with competing consequences for good or bad timing that the remarkably well protected and well-resourced Egyptian plan actually had a chance of succeeding. At a desperate point in the war, while Nixon and Kissinger were fiddling and when Israel's Defense Minister, Moshe Dayan, may have been broaching with Prime Minister Golda Meir the unthinkable possibility of negotiating terms with the Arabs, Nixon's Chief of Staff, Alexander Haig, acting on his own – that is without the knowledge of Nixon, Kissinger or even Defense Secretary Schlesinger – authorized an emergency airlift to Israel of military materiel which included, remarkably, an ample supply of the US Army's newly developed top secret TOW (Tube-launched, Optically tracked, Wire-guided) missiles. The ensuing destruction of what had been Egypt's overwhelmingly superior tank force quickly turned the tide of the war in Israel's favor. Haig, so this version indicates, kept to himself what he had done (presumably in the President's name) until after it was accomplished. Leaving the notoriously anti-Semitic Nixon and his abjectly sycophantic Kissinger hardly able to condemn it – at least not publicly. The Israelis prevailed, but only just, and the clear potential for a catastrophic bloodbath within their borders was averted.

Among rewarding exchanges with him about this book, the eminent American academic, dissident, philosopher and author, Noam Chomsky, though hardly a darling of the American right, preferred a view more favorable to Kissinger. He wrote: *'In '73, Israel intelligence had all of the relevant information and chose to disregard it in that period of euphoria. Kissinger backed Israel all the way, from its rejection of Sadat's peace offers from February '71 to authorizing Israel to violate the '73 ceasefire so as to surround the Egyptian third army … He shared Israel's convictions about Arab incompetence, and bore considerable responsibility for the war by rejecting Sadat's peace initiatives and dismissing his repeated assertion that if the US-Israel continued to reject peace and to carry out the huge settlement programs in the Sinai, he would go to war.'*

Whatever the truth is about the Yom Kippur War, this and further DNA searing examples of perceived betrayals will continue to produce and support hardline leadership in Israel and to reinforce an enduring belief that anti-Jewish feeling around the world remains as strong as ever. Not, perhaps, quite so openly proclaimed as it once was, but still just as mindlessly out there.

At the time of the creation of the State of Israel, Palestinian outrage and aspiration were buried by the assumption of those who until then had been the imperial masters of the Middle-East – foremost among whom were the British, the French and the Americans – that Arabia, however newly upstart, would just have to wear the theft of Palestinian land. The remnants of their territory achieved neither statehood nor a pathway to achieving it. This was not, however, alleviated by their backers throughout the Muslim Middle East having preferred to institutionalize Palestinians as refugees in order to harness desperate Palestinian youth to what morphed into an Islamic war against Israel and its principal backers in the West. With the emergence of successively better equipped and trained fighters, and careless Western leadership – especially in the USA and Britain – this achieved results beyond their wildest dreams. Results which led directly to the serially stupid USA led invasions of Iraq and Afghanistan, the collapse into dreadful disarray of Tunisia and Libya, and the ensuing flashpoints between Russia and the West, and now Turkey: Syria. In which the Americans – as the professed leaders of the free world – yet again proved to be catastrophically inept.

All of which has greatly increased hostility and diminished moderation in the region, and contributed directly to the emergence, in 2017, of the most immoderate, divisive and willfully ignorant presidency – Trump's – ever seen in the USA.

Understanding as they do these root causes of the ever growing conflict in the region, the Netanyahus and Abbas's of today and tomorrow have very little cause to let their guards down. Little cause, that is, to do anything other than hold on until, say, the Old World values of the

Muslim dominated Middle-East, and the New World values of the Christian dominated West have reached some kind of accommodation.

This could be very long in coming, given that the hatreds arising from all of this are based on fundamentalist religious beliefs wherein, on the one hand – the Middle East – the Word of the Prophet has not yet been separated from the Will of the People and, on the other – the West – the separation between Church and State (the People) has had several centuries to mature. Even more so given that the big players in the Middle-East have not yet been able to get past a belief, steeped as it so damnably is in the newly dusted-off chimera of the 'Warrior', that ultimate victory of one over the other can still, somehow, be achieved by force.

There was a time of hope, during the Obama years of informed diplomacy, reason and restraint, that this could be changed. But it would have only been possible had there been at the same time a Gorbachev in Russia and matching moderates of good will throughout the Middle East, Iran and Turkey. Instead, we have the likes of Trump, Putin, Erdogan, Rouhani, the Al-Saud dynasty and the ever shrinking violets of Europe.

o O o

In Cuba, Fidel Castro was reviled by the Americans from the very beginning for rescuing his people, in the late 1950s, from the profoundly corrupt and decadent rule of Fulgencio Batista and his American mafia and big business cronies. How was it, they fumed and fumed, that a movement like his could have succeeded without their say-so and their support. It was just so inexplicably and outrageously beyond the imaginings of Washington. Perhaps not so inexplicably given that even the young Senator John Kennedy was said to have happily indulged in the decadence of Batista's Christian Cuba and to have shared the girlfriend of one of America's top Mafiosi with strong Batista connections. And why not for Christ's sake? Wasn't everyone else in on the fun?! They had their chances in the early Castro years but, blinded by their holy war against communism, and not about to support a revolution not of their own making, they blew it. Just as badly as, a bit later on, they conceived of and blew the Bay of Pigs invasion. How thoroughly Castro rubbed their noses in it and how well they deserved it. And how hard they tried to have him rubbed out – with one of the options having been to co-opt mafia goons for the purpose. Amazing stuff, but very typical of the Americans at that time.

In a chapter entitled 'Reflections on 9–11' which was reproduced in *The Essential Chomsky* edited by Anthony Arnov (published by Palgrave Macmillan, 2007), Noam Chomsky notes:

> … forty years have passed since President Kennedy ordered that 'the terrors of the earth' must be visited upon Cuba until their leadership is eliminated, having violated good form by successful resistance to U.S. run invasion. The terrors were extremely serious, continuing into the 1990s. Twenty years have passed since President Reagan launched a terrorist war against Nicaragua, conducted with barbaric atrocities and vast destruction, leaving tens of thousands dead and the country ruined perhaps beyond recovery – and also leading to condemnation of the U.S. for international terrorism by the World Court and the UN Security Council (in a resolution the U.S. vetoed). But no one believed that Cuba or Nicaragua had the right to set off bombs in Washington or New York, or to assassinate U.S. political leaders. And it is all too easy to add many far more severe cases, up to the present.

o O o

Retribution from the masters of the colonies? What retribution?

By the time change came, one of the oldest races in the world, living as they had been from way back in the dream time and more or less in unchanging harmony with nature, Australia's aborigines had been decimated to the tip of extinction – surviving as outcasts in pitiful little shanties on the fringes of the white communities.

Australia's aborigines know a great deal more about terror than the victims of 9/11. It's seared into their DNA.

Not forgetting too a principal origin of the clusters of those of Pacific Islands origin which sprung up in Australia's north east in the late 1800s.

But hadn't they simply paddled their way over our way looking for adventure and opportunity?

Yes, there may have been a few such, but the truth unknown to most Australians is that tens of thousands were stolen from their island homes by a process which at its euphemistic best was known as 'blackbirding'. Requiring cheap labour on the sugar and cotton plantations and other farms that were springing up in Queensland, men from these islands were simply rounded up from the shore, shipped off and dumped in these plantations and farms to work as, in effect, slaves. Known as 'Kanaks', differences of opinion over the circumstances of this trade and how these men were treated is most tellingly settled in the definition of choice for that word – animal men.

In the killing and the terrorizing of our aborigines and of neighboring islanders, our forebears no doubt had in their bannered onward Christian marches taken heart from examples such as the one where their fledgling American brothers had sung hallelujahs to their God's 'gift' of smallpox – against which, as an outcome of earlier epidemics, most Europeans had acquired immunity. For the purpose of stealing the productive farmlands of settled and mostly hospitable Indian farming communities, these colonial brothers had passed on this gift in the form of deliberately infected blankets which, to their abiding joy, decimated Indian communities along their eastern seaboard. A decimation which turned out to be but a preliminary to white America's appallingly drawn out slaughter, dispossession, degradation and transportation of their once fabulously diverse and advanced Indian Nations.

And how on earth can America's sustained terrorization of its African American communities be explained? How could these stolen people, brought to America in chains, flogged, furiously degraded and terrorized for generations, have been so demonized? How could the twisted theology of the southern Christian crazies have prevailed for so long? How on earth could white, Christian, America have been so surprised and so outraged about the vigour and the courage of the entirely consequential black identity and black power movements? About Malcolm X, Martin Luther King, Bobby Seale, Angela Davis, Eldridge Cleaver, Muhammed Ali and many others. And about their equally consequential appeal to formerly devout, though widely excluded, black Christian communities of other religions – yes, including Islam?

o O o

Much of the conquest and the slaughter and the genocide and the pillage and the repression of pre 9/11 has been haughtily consigned by the perpetrators to the basket of Lessons Learned. New and ongoing crises that do not threaten Western interests are either left to the collection box or to await some sort of attention by the languid UN. Left, still, to a hugely discredited organization whose most abiding talent has been to support its weak and indulgent leadership and privileged lifestyle.

Among the defeated and the terrorized peoples of pre and post 9/11, confusion and resentment smoulder and now, with more deadly regularity, flare.

Confusion and resentment which are fed, in the age of instant information, by a growing comprehension of the roots of their disempowerment and the effects of their continuing inability to compete with power and wealth.

Power and wealth which are either in the hands of the West or the hands of those who are sponsored or tolerated by the West, or of those who posture on the world stage at either the expense of dealing with the needs of their people or in order to mask how much they are lining their own pockets – or both.

Resentment which will continue to smoulder and erupt long after the last troops of the Coalition of the Willing have left Iraq and Afghanistan. Long after the George Ws, however moderated by the occasional Obamas, move on and as the despotic and hugely wealthy leaders of many of these places, such as Saudi Arabia, continue to laugh up their sleeves about the West's naïve and toothless insistence on western-style freedom and democracy for all.

Who knows where the new Egypt and the new Libya and whatever rises out of the ashes of Syria and Iraq will fit into this – but it will most likely not be in the form of something which suits Western taste, however much new money is poured in and however many devious deals are stitched up.

o O o

There is much huffing and puffing among the more or less allied nations of the Western world about the Third World War being underway – the war against terrorism. Well, if it is and if this ridiculous sort of feeling has come about because of the shock of a mere three thousand lives lost in the attacks of 9/11, the West, still so smug in its bastions of wealth and power, must face up to the fact that, in so many ways and in so many places – at least in more contemporary times – they started it. That the invariably imperious, self-satisfied, often resentful, acts of departure from their pillaged colonies and crony states did not only not finish it, but helped spawn what is, in turn, being aimed at it today.

These are the roots of today's terrorist activities against the West and lopping off the odd branch of a Saddam Hussein or an Osama bin Laden or a Bashar al Assad, or pulling the plug on old servants like Hosni Mubarak or latterly converted fools like Muammar Gadaffi, or pointing the finger at Islam, will not stop it. The posturing of resources rich Iran, which endured America's despotic and vicious Shah for so long, should not be so surprising.

o O o

So what will be 9/11s place in history? How will it be regarded in twenty or fifty or a hundred years?

Who knows? But we can hope that it might have become part of a critical turning point towards an era in which the rich and the powerful nations had stopped simply hoping that the poor and the poorly led nations would just adopt the model of the West or work out something that would not be too much of a nuisance or which could be fixed by the occasional mighty whack – until the next one was needed. That it might have become part of a realisation that the puppets and the bribes and the whacks and lies of the Western exceptionalists did more to foster hatred and terrorism than stop it.

Towards an era in which religion, race, color, venture capital and all of their abundantly associated prejudices and greed had been kept out of it.

Whose worthy God or Allah, or whose other worthy Deities, or whose humanity would have had us do otherwise?

Footfalls echo in the memory
Down the passage which we did not take
Towards the door we never opened
Into the rose garden.

– T.S. Eliot
'Burnt Norton', from *Four Quartets*

Album

India 1966. With two little orphans at the Cheshire Ryder Home in Dehra Dun. My regular food orders from Austalia included as much as I could carry in the car for the orphanage part of the Home. Here they are eating fat Australian sausagees which I had cooked and brought up in an esky.

Kashmir, India. 1977

Clockwise from top:

Our little Andrew just before sliding off this rock into this icy, fast flowing headwater of the Jhelum River.

Joosik drying him off after his frantic rescue by Howard.

Followed, very soon afer, by breakfasing on our trout catch with our cook and assorted guides.

Belgrade 1979. The Annual 'Dexburger Tennnis Cup'. American Embassy team (three) on the left, US Ambassador, Larry Eagleburger (later, for a time, Acting US Secretary of State) with his hand on John Murphy's head, me (bending) and the much admired Australian Ambassador, Barrie Dexter, holding the cup.

Trincomalee, Sri Lanka 1993.
With Janaka Perera, right, then Commander 6 Brigade (Welioya). Perera rose to military, diplomatic and political prominence. Following appointments as High Commissioner to Australia and then Ambassador to Indonesia, he retired with his family in Canberra, Australia, where we became friends. In 2008, against my strongest possible personal advice, he returned to Sri Lanka to enter the political fray in opposition to Mahinda Rajapaksa's corrupt predsidency. He and his wife, Vajira, were killed in a suicide bombing at Anuradhapura on 6 October 2008.

Sri Lanka, 1993. Happy days. Our Andrew with the tea ladies near Nuwara Eliya.

Sri Lanka, 1993. Happy days. Our Jamie at an Elephant Orphanage.

The Sunchang Cho Clan – 1999. Front Row: the sisters – 4th and 5th from the left, Joohee and Jooningee; centre, mother Changwoo; 3rd from right, Joosik. Back row: the brothers 2nd from the left (hands on hips), eldest brother, Chanjoo; 4th and 5th from the left, Younjoo and Kwangjoo. Brother, Changjoo, died at age 46 in 1988. Father, Youngsik, died at age 80 in 1994. Mother, Changwoo, died at 93 in 2007.

Mungangmyon, Korea 1999.
Joosik's eldest brother, Chanjoo, planting rice

15 October, 2000. Joosik with the towering Tom Dolan, son of our neighbours in Arlington, VA. Tom won gold at the 1996 Atlanta Olympic Games, men's 400 metre individual medley (swimming) – and he successfully defended this with a world record time at the Sydney Olympic Games in 2000.

Joosik, (far right) with, from left, brothers-in-law Taesok and Taedok, and sisters Joohee and Jooningee, on top of the World Trade Centre, New York, on 26 June 2001 – shortly before its destruction.

'One day, I thought, one day.'

At Everest, 2009.

2017 – Howard and Joosik at the Taj Mahal, Agra.

Afterword

Those Ambassadors and High Commissioners who had the greatest influence on me, both professionally and personally, during my formative years overseas in the Foreign Service included Sir Arthur Tange for his relentless setting of and insistence on high standards, Alan Loomes for his trust and unruffled support in a moment of great uncertainty for me when I was just setting out, Peter Curtis for the calm good humor of his leadership and Barry Dexter for his clarity and human touch.

Those colleagues who over the years helped me in various ways to build and apply sound professional values were legion. The positive ones far outweighed the negative. They included K Krishnamoorthy (Mr KM) way back on my first posting in New Delhi, Ray Percival and Okada san on my first posting in Tokyo, Toni Blicblau in Tel Aviv, Joe Procida and Connie Izzie in Rome, Mira Orlovic in Belgrade, Alan Moore and too many of the Thai staff in Bangkok to single out, Romanie Thambayah in Colombo and, finally, the dauntless John Stokes and the ever good-humored Jack Mossop in Washington DC.

At several important times from its beginning to its end, Frank Murray's intersections with my career infused into me at least some of his energy and boldness. Closer to the end of my career, Ashton Calvert, the personification of intellect and wit, had faith in me and applied it.

The values derived from these relationships were strengthened by the bad behavior of some – all Australians. But these can be left to their deserved anonymity. By the time I came across the worst of them, inevitably at the highest levels of the department, the available manner of dealing with them and redressing their effect on me and on others was no longer mysterious.

About the Cover Painting

My specification for the artist.

In the foreground, though not especially dominant, is the image of a youth, standing at an elevated vantage point overlooking the sweep of a river expanding beyond into a broad bend. He is in a contemplative stance.

He is seen from the rear, silhouetted against moonlight shimmering off the water and the moon in a suitable place, relative to the shimmer, but about true to life.

There is a small boat, mainsail up, leaning into the bend of the river. About to find whatever it will find. Overall, the image is to convey a wistful dream of what might be waiting 'round the bend.

Ken Strong's sketch.

Painting by Ken Strong for the book.

Title – *Waiting 'round the Bend*

Oil paint on board.

870 mm x 910 mm

For the 3rd edition, coloration of the original painting has been partly manipulated in order to accentuate the *Moon River* theme.

www.ingramcontent.com/pod-product-compliance
Lightning Source LLC
Chambersburg PA
CBHW021212090426
42740CB00006B/187

* 9 7 8 1 9 2 2 6 0 3 3 7 1 *

Praise for *Waiting 'round the Bend.*

Noam Chomsky – eminent US academic, dissident, philosopher and author

About 9/11 and beyond... 'Compelling.'

'The major publishers are not much interested in the kinds of 'awful truths' that we are writing about.'

Gareth Evans – former Australian Attorney-General and Foreign Minister

'... he has an engaging style and a real flair for storytelling.'

Russell Lansbury – Emeritus Professor, University of Sydney

'... a gripping assessment of ... 9/11 and its truer place in history.'

Phillip Adams – broadcaster, writer and public intellectual

He has '... a gift for narrative ... that's a pleasure to read.'

Sydney Morning Herald

'... tales of a life less ordinary carry the reader along.'